COOKIES
UNLIMITED

OKIES

UNLIMITED

NICK MALGIERI

PHOTOGRAPHS BY
TOM ECKERLE

HarperCollinsPublishers

Grateful acknowledgment is made to reprint
Maida Heatter's Skinny Peanut Wafers, pages 51- 52,
from *Maida Heatter's Brand-New Book of Great Cookies*
by Maida Heatter. Copyright © 1995 by Maida Heatter
Reprinted by permission of Random House, Inc.

DESIGNED BY JOEL AVIROM AND JASON SNYDER

DESIGN ASSISTANT: MEGHAN DAY HEALEY

ILLUSTRATIONS BY LAURA HARTMAN MAESTRO

LINE DRAWINGS BY JASON SNYDER

FOOD STYLING BY ANDREA TUTUNJIAN,

BARBARA BRIA PUGLIESE, AND CARA TANNENBAUM

HarperCollins books may be purchased for educational, business,
or sales promotional use. For information please write: Special Markets
Department, HarperCollins Publishers Inc., 10 East 53rd Street,
New York, NY 10022.

FIRST EDITION

Printed on acid-free paper

Library of Congress Cataloging-in-Publication Data

Malgieri, Nick.
    Cookies unlimited / Nick Malgieri.—1st ed.
        p. cm.
    Includes bibliographical references and index.
    ISBN 0-06-019285-2
        1. Cookies.

TX772 .M27 2000
641.8'654—dc21

                                        99-087185

00 01 02 03 04 RRD 10 9 8 7 6 5 4 3 2 1

For my mother,
Antoinette Malgieri,
whose childhood
nickname was
biscottini e taralluzzi

CONTENTS

INTRODUCTION

I WAS GENETICALLY PROGRAMMED WITH A PASSION FOR COOKIES. WHEN MY mother was a little girl in Italy, she loved all types of little sweets so she got the nickname *biscottini e taralluzzi* (*biscottini* are little biscotti, or cookies in general; *taralli* are ring cookies that are usually salty, but diminutive ones, *taralluzzi*, are usually sweet). I never had a chance. I have always loved cookies, though I don't eat nearly as many as I would like to. I can never resist them. Whether they are offered at the end of a cocktail party as a signal it's time to leave, or at the end of a meal in a fancy restaurant, no matter how sated I am, I always have room for a cookie or two.

When I was a child, my maternal grandmother, who loved to bake, lived with us. Her repertoire was limited to the southern Italian recipes she had grown up with but she made biscotti and her other specialties often. Though I never got a recipe from my grandmother, I'm sure her influence was what led me to dedicate my life to baking.

The other great cookie and baking influence in my early life was my father's sister, whose given name was Rachel, but who was always called Katy or Kitty. She was the American baker in our family. The first chocolate chip cookies I tasted were from her oven as were almond crescents, love knots, and many of her other specialties.

Of course, growing up in the 1950s, it was impossible not to see (and taste) the increasing number of industrially made cookies then coming on the market. My parents were never afraid to try something new and though we made occasional forays to bakeries and the cookie aisle of the supermarket, we preferred our homemade baked goods.

My first real exposure to European cookies came when I was an apprentice in Switzerland. As the Christmas holidays approached, the pastry shop of the hotel where I was working was filled with the scent of chocolate, nuts, and spices. The pastry chef and his assistants were busy preparing traditional Swiss *Weinachtsguetzli* (literally, Christmas goodies)—various cookies with many shapes, textures, and flavors. There were *Spitzbueben*, *Anisbroetli*, and *Basler Leckerli*, all traditional *Guetzli*, and you'll find recipes for them in this book. Swiss baking reaches its apogee with small things such as cookies; and you can see the perfect uniformity when they are lined up on trays in pastry shop showcases and windows. The beautiful precision the Swiss bring to baked goods in general had a lasting influence on both my taste and my vision of how desserts should be presented.

I didn't discover the delicate little cookies known as petits fours until I had left Switzerland and gone to Monaco to work at the Sporting Club in Monte Carlo. In fact a large part of my job as a *commis patissier* (pastry chef's assistant) during the first season I worked there was to arrange platters of dainty petits fours served in the restaurant after dessert. On gala evenings, when we had as many as a thousand guests for a set menu, every table received such a platter. One of the great rewards of working there was seeing and then learning the elaborate presentations made when Prince Rainier and Princess Grace attended a soiree at the Sporting Club. The pastry chef and his staff would spend the better part of a week getting ready and much of that time was spent preparing the great platter of petits fours presented after dessert. The recipes in this book for champagne fingers and tuiles date from those days.

I began collecting Italian cookie and biscotti recipes around the same time, because from Monaco I often had the chance to visit Italy. Later, when I was doing research for my Italian dessert book, I spent several months in Italy, looking around for interesting recipes, buying cookbooks (I came home with 200), and tasting

lots of cookies. Many of those recipes are in that book, but some others are here.

I started teaching in 1979 and the most popular classes of the year have remained those about holiday baking, especially holiday cookies. People love cookies because the recipes are usually simple, they don't require a lot of time to make, and, let's face it—hardly anyone ever refuses a cookie.

There are lots of those simple straightforward recipes in this book but there is also the occasional challenging one that will require a bit more from the baker than dropping dough onto a pan from a teaspoon. And for those of you who enjoy decorating projects, there is a chapter of cookie houses and centerpieces. You'll see, they can be fun to do if you approach them patiently with a relaxed attitude.

I love collecting recipes and then fine-tuning them to my taste and style. The recipes that follow are the result of a lifetime spent collecting from family, friends, colleagues, and anywhere cookie recipes are found—they are like cookies themselves, diverse, sweet, and fun and I hope you enjoy them.

New York City
June 1999

A SHORT HISTORY
OF COOKIES

WE KNOW THAT SMALL CAKES HAVE BEEN SERVED SINCE BAKING AS WE KNOW it began. The Romans celebrated important events such as weddings and fertility rites with cakes made with honey and rye flour and studded with nuts and dried fruit. These were the ancestors of fruitcake, *panforte* (an Italian fruit and nut cake), certain kinds of cookies such as *mostaccioli* in Italy and *Lebkuchen* in German-speaking countries, and many of the baked goods we still make today.

The Greeks also produced small cookie-like cakes made from flour and honey. These were called *boen* and that's how we got the word "bun."

The word "cookie" first appeared in an English dictionary in the eighteenth century, in a reference to the Dutch word *koekje*, which means "little cake." The word became common in America where Dutch settlers baked *koekjes* in indoor and outdoor ovens or on a griddle set over hot coals. This may also be one of the origins of the cookie sheet.

French petits fours (meaning "little ovens") are small fancy cookies also originating some time in the eighteenth century. These elegant cookies, small sweet items, were baked at a lower oven temperature and placed in the oven after the larger ones had been removed.

By the end of the nineteenth century, wood- and coal-burning iron stoves had made cookie baking more accessible for home cooks. Cookies rapidly became a standard snack and lunch box item.

Soon to follow was commercial cookie production, and within the first 15 years of the twentieth century, several industrial cookie companies had introduced a wide variety of packaged cookies.

Brownies, which are a close relation of the cookie, first emerged before 1910. Although the term "brownie" had been seen in print prior to this, there is no documentation on who actually invented it. It may have even been a mistake when a chocolate cake accidentally collapsed.

By the middle of the twentieth century, cookies were a staple in every household kitchen. The chocolate chip cookie was first introduced by Ruth Wakefield at her Toll House Inn in the 1930s. Chocolate chip cookies still have the lead among cookie popularity, and over 90 million bags of chocolate chips are sold annually.

Though commercially and industrially made cookies are finding wider and wider audiences, there is still no replacement for a home-made cookie, fresh from the oven and made with care in a small quantity.

MAKING COOKIES

THE COOKIE PANTRY

THOUGH COOKIE INGREDIENTS ARE NOT really different from the ingredients needed for any kind of baking, the following is a list of items you need to have on hand for the recipes in this book.

BUTTER: The first and foremost ingredient in cookie recipes. It's true that not every cookie recipe contains butter, but most do and it's important not to skimp. Use good, fresh unsalted butter; it provides a fragility, a depth of flavor, and a delicacy that no other fat can duplicate. By the way, there are a few recipes that call for oil—for those use a mild, bland oil, such as canola, peanut, or corn oil.

MILK is whole milk in all the recipes that call for it.

CREAM is heavy whipping cream.

BUTTERMILK is the cultured low-fat variety easily found in the supermarket.

EGGS: Whenever eggs are called for they should be graded large.

FLOUR: The recipes here call for either all-purpose or cake flour. Use either bleached or unbleached all-purpose flour—it will make no difference in these recipes. Cake flour should be plain cake flour, not the self-rising type. To substitute all-purpose flour for cake flour, subtract 2 tablespoons from each cup of cake flour called for. Remember to measure all flour with nested, graduated-size dry-measure cups, not the clear glass or plastic cups meant for measuring liquids. And even more important, gently scoop or spoon the flour into the dry-measure cup, then level it off with the straight side of a metal or rubber spatula or the back of a knife. Don't dip and sweep.

CORNSTARCH: In certain very tender cookie recipes cornstarch is used in combination with flour. This is done to lower the flour's protein content, so the dough will have a weaker gluten formation, and consequently the cookies will be more tender.

BREAD CRUMBS: Make your own by pulverizing day-old French or Italian bread in the food processor. If you buy commercial bread crumbs in the supermarket, be sure to get the unflavored variety.

SUGAR: Plain granulated sugar is called for in most of the recipes in this book.

COARSE OR SANDING SUGAR: This is a coarser-textured white sugar for decorating or coating some cookies before baking. Coarse sugar is not readily available in the supermarket, but is easy to get from mail-order sources (see page 333).

BROWN SUGAR: Remember that the difference between light and dark brown sugar is only the amount of molasses added to the sugar. There is more in dark brown than in light. Granulated light brown sugar may be substituted for moist light brown.

CONFECTIONERS' SUGAR: This very finely ground sugar with some cornstarch added so it doesn't clump is used to sprinkle on cookies or to make glazes. Confectioners' sugar may also be an ingredient in some very delicate doughs used for making tender, fragile cookies. Before sprinkling confectioners' sugar on cookies, make sure they have cooled thoroughly or the sugar will melt. Also, be sure to sprinkle the sugar lightly—too heavy a coating is cloyingly sweet and messy to boot.

MOLASSES: Molasses comes in mild (unsulphured) and robust flavors. I don't find a great deal of difference between the two and use them interchangeably.

CORN SYRUP: Corn syrup, either light or dark, figures mostly in recipes for fillings and glazes rather than in cookie recipes. In certain British and Australian recipes, I have used corn syrup rather than golden syrup with very good results. Golden syrup is a very thick sugar syrup, originally developed as a honey substitute. You can also use honey.

HONEY: Be sure to use a dark, robust-flavored honey.

DECORATIVE COLORED SUGARS AND NONPAREILS: The former are coarse sugar crystals like sanding sugar but they come in a variety of different colors and mixed multicolored assortments. They are sometimes available in the supermarket, but if you have difficulty finding them, see Sources at the end of the book. Nonpareils are tiny spheres of opaque sugar that come in white or multicolored assortments. The same type of sugar used to make nonpareils is used to make little colored season-specific decorations such as green Christmas trees or orange pumpkins. All these decorations should be used sparingly on cookies to avoid an unappetizing and overburdened look.

LEAVENERS: I always use double-acting baking powder. Several nonaluminum-based brands on the market give results as good as the standard types. Baking soda, called for in a few recipes, is used if the recipe contains an acid ingredient, such as honey, cocoa, molasses, brown sugar, citrus, or a cultured dairy product. The acidity reacts with the alkalinity of the baking soda to make carbon dioxide form and foam up and leaven the dough or batter. Bicarbonate of ammonia is an unusual leavener. It not only causes rising during baking but also promotes the complete desiccation of the dough or batter to which it is added, making very dry and crisp cookies. It is called for in only a few recipes here, and regular baking powder may always be substituted.

SALT: Fine sea salt has been used to test all these recipes. Never substitute kosher or other coarse salt. The crystals of these salts are larger, so measurements will not be accurate.

NUTS: Nuts provide flavor, tenderness, and textural variety in many cookie recipes. Try to purchase nuts in vacuum cans or in a store where you can taste them to be sure they are fresh and sweet-tasting, not rancid. Nuts should be stored in a plastic bag in the freezer. For best results, bring the nutmeats to room temperature before grinding them.

To blanch almonds or pistachios, bring them to a boil in a pan of water and drain. Rub the nuts in a coarse-textured towel to loosen the skins, then go over each one to separate the nuts from the skins. Place blanched nuts on a jelly roll pan and dry them out in a 300 degree oven for about 5 to 10 minutes (don't let them color) and cool before using.

To blanch hazelnuts, toast them at 350 degrees on a jelly roll pan until the skins have loosened, then proceed with the towel as for almonds. It is not necessary to dry out hazelnuts.

To chop nuts, pulse them briefly in the food processor, or to get uniformly larger pieces, chop by hand using a large chopping knife on a cutting board. To grind nuts, pulse them repeatedly in the food processor until they are ground very fine. Stop the machine occasionally and scrape down the inside bottom of the bowl where the finest particles may accumulate.

CANDIED FRUIT: Best quality candied fruit is usually only found in import and specialty stores. The type available in the supermarket at holiday time for typical fruitcake baking is usually bitter and undercandied, resulting in an inexpensive product which lacks flavor and sweetness. If you don't plan ahead and order fine quality candied fruit from one of the mail-order sources at the end of the book, wait until you can, rather than use the supermarket type.

GINGER IN SYRUP: A type of candied ginger suspended in a thick syrup, usually sold in jars. Crystallized ginger is not a substitute.

CRYSTALLIZED GINGER: Candied ginger dried and rolled in granulated sugar. Taste it first to see if it is tender, sweet, and peppery, not dry and tough.

CHOCOLATE: Unsweetened, semisweet, or bittersweet, milk and white chocolates are used in recipes in this book. Make sure any chocolate you use tastes good on its own, because the chocolate is what gives the cookies their taste. I use a serrated knife to chop chocolate into ¼-inch pieces before using it in a recipe or melting it.

To melt chocolate, place pieces in a heatproof bowl, then bring a saucepan half filled with water to a boil. Turn off the heat and put the bowl over the pan of hot water. Stir occasionally with a spoon or spatula until the chocolate is melted. Remove the bowl from the pan and cool the chocolate slightly before using. Or place the chocolate in a microwave-safe bowl and microwave, on half-power if possible, for about 20 to 30 seconds at a time, removing the bowl and stirring the chocolate occasionally, until it is melted.

COCOA: Both nonalkalized and alkalized cocoa are called for in my cookie recipes. The difference between the two is that alkalized (Dutch process) cocoa has been treated with alkali to make it darker and slightly less bitter. In these recipes, they may be used interchangeably.

FLAVORINGS: Always purchase pure flavoring extracts, not artificial ones. Nowadays, unfortunately, there are mixtures of the two. I like to purchase vanilla extract at a cooking specialty store—it may be a little more expensive, but premium brands of vanilla have the strongest flavor. If you use vanilla beans, make sure they are plump and moist. I like Madagascar Bourbon vanilla extract and beans the best. Other extracts called for in the recipes are almond, anise, lemon, and orange.

FLAVORING OILS: There are excellent ones available. Follow the manufacturer's guidelines about substituting for extracts. Generally, use half as much oil as extract.

SPICES AND HERBS: Make sure spices are strong and fragrant when you purchase them. I have listed a couple of very good mail-order sources at the end of the book. Remember to keep spices in a cool, dark place and discard them after a year or so when their aroma begins to weaken.

EQUIPMENT

MIXER: I love my Kitchen-Aid mixer and wouldn't know what to do without it. When you use a heavy-duty stand mixer, remember that the paddle attachment is for all general mixing purposes, such as beating butter—always softened to room temperature—or incorporating flour into a dough. The wire whisk is used only to incorporate air into whipped cream or whipped eggs or egg whites.

FOOD PROCESSOR: This propeller-bladed mixing and chopping machine was first introduced here in the early seventies and has since become standard home kitchen equipment. It is essential for chopping and grinding nuts, and also great for mixing pastry doughs and other preparations that don't need to be aerated.

ROLLING PIN: I prefer a straight wooden rolling pin about 24 inches long with no handles. My friend Dorie Greenspan recently gave me a new French pin that is made from hard white nylon (it looks just like plastic) and it works very well because it has such a smooth surface. Whatever type of rolling pin you use, make sure to scrape off any little pieces of dough stuck to it and wipe it with a damp cloth after each use. Never wash a rolling pin by immersing it in water.

BRUSHES: I like natural bristle brushes and am particularly fond of black-bristled ones because the stray hairs are easy to spot if the brush begins to shed.

GRATERS: A standard box grater works well. Just be sure to look for one that has diagonally placed holes—citrus zest will not stick as it does in the standard round nail holes. There is a relatively new grater on the market that looks like a carpenter's rasp, which works really well for citrus zest. See Sources at the end of the book for purchasing it.

CUTTERS: I have a collection of cookie cutters going back to my childhood, but I keep using the same ones over and over. My favorites are the sets of round plain and crinkled cutters that come in several increasing diameters. These are also now available in hard plastic. Of course, there are hundreds of specialty shapes available from most kitchenware and hardware stores. See Sources at the end of the book.

ICE CREAM SCOOPS: These can be very handy for forming cookies. Look for these in a serious kitchenware store or restaurant supply store for the best quality and the largest selection of sizes; 1-tablespoon and ½-tablespoon sizes are practical for most of the cookies here.

MOLDS: Cookie molds are used to make shortbread; anise cookies, such as Swiss *Anisbroetli* or German Springerle; or spicy Dutch speculaas. If you don't find these in a specialty cookware store, see Sources. By the way, I think individual Springerle molds, like little tiles, do a better job of marking the dough than the Springerle rolling pins.

PANS: Because I visit cooking schools to teach all over North America, I have used and continue to use all types of pans for baking cookies. I don't think it matters whether the pan has sides or not: A classic cookie sheet of 12 × 15 inches usually only has one raised side, and jelly roll pans, available in sizes between 10 × 15 inches to 12 × 18 inches, usually have four sides and are about an inch deep. Remember that shiny pans promote light baking and dark pans encourage cookies to bake darker, especially on the bottom.

The bar cookies are baked in 9 × 13 × 2-inch or 10 × 15 × 1-inch pans. The ones I use are aluminum and are standard home-style ones you can buy in any kitchen or hardware store. If your pans of this type are particularly thin, place them on a cookie sheet or jelly roll pan or double them. This will prevent the bottoms of cookies from burning. I almost always bake cookies on pans lined with parchment or foil—it makes both removing or unmolding cookies or bars and cleanup so easy. The only other pans I use are a pair of heavy steel nonstick-coated 9 × 14-inch French pans, with slightly raised sides. These are great for tuiles or any other cookies that need to spread and become very thin during baking. Though I don't own any, I have used insulated cookie sheets often at the many cooking schools I visit. These pans are wonderful because they prevent the bottoms of cookies from burning. This is exactly the same result you get by stacking two cookie sheets or jelly roll pans together.

SILICON MATS: These are all the rage in professional baking circles. They are thin mats of pure silicon that are placed on a baking pan (they come in the sizes that commercial pans measure, 12 × 18 inches being the smallest) to provide a perfectly nonstick surface for baking. Fairly expensive, they may be used thousands of times and only need to be wiped clean after each use. If you like to collect every new kitchenware item that emerges, then by all means get some, though I don't find that they are so useful for home baking.

RACKS: I like sturdy stainless steel racks the same size as the pans I use. I usually slide the paper or foil that the cookies have been baked on directly off the sheet and onto the rack to cool. If you have baked bars, just place the whole pan on the rack until completely cooled.

When you need to cool cookies over a cylindrical form to curve them, steady a rolling pin on a jelly roll pan by bunching a kitchen towel underneath it. If you are going to make a lot of curved cookies, save the cardboard cores from inside rolls of paper towels, foil, plastic wrap, or wax paper, cover them with foil, and use these to curve cookies.

KNIVES: My favorite knife is the offset serrated knife. It makes cutting bars and chopping chocolate a real breeze. See Sources for purchasing one. In general I use stainless steel knives when I'm baking cookies.

SPATULAS: Large and small offset spatulas are the best for spreading batter in pans, or spreading thin disks of batter on sheets for tuiles or tulipes.

TECHNIQUES

BAKING COOKIES After mixing up excellent ingredients to make a batch of cookies, you certainly don't want to burn them while they are baking. Follow these simple rules to avoid burning cookies.

Use an oven thermometer to make sure your oven is actually running at the temperature it's set for. Bake cookies in the middle level of the oven for even coloring and best results. As the cookies are baking reverse the position of the pan from front to back once or twice. If you are

baking more than one pan of cookies at a time, place racks so they divide the oven into thirds. Double the pan or use an insulated cookie sheet on the lower rack. About a third of the way during the baking time, switch the pan from the bottom of the oven to the top and vice versa (remember the pan on the bottom of the oven should be doubled when you switch racks). Also rotate the pans back to front for even coloring. Work quickly so the oven doesn't lose too much heat while you are switching the pans around.

COOLING COOKIES See "Racks" opposite.

COOKIE STORAGE Keep cookies in a tin or plastic container with a tight-fitting cover. If you must stack cookies on top of each other, put sheets of wax paper or parchment between the layers—this will keep filled, sandwich, or iced cookies from sticking together. Use the same method for freezing cookies (though, if I am going to freeze cookies, I prefer to sandwich or ice them before serving for neatest results).

FREEZING COOKIES Everyone likes to get ahead and get a few batches of cookies into the freezer before the year-end holidays or another big event. Whether the cookies survive freezing depends more on your own freezer than anything else. If the freezer is very clean, not too crowded, and you don't open it often, your cookies will come through the freezing process relatively unscathed. Crisp cookies may become somewhat limp upon defrosting—if possible, preheat the oven to 300 degrees and reheat them on a cookie sheet for less than 10 minutes, then let them cool before serving.

Perhaps the best choices for freezing are bar and refrigerator cookies. For bars, bake and cool the large cake without cutting it. Wrap and freeze, then cut into individual cookies according to the recipe after you have defrosted the cake. Rolls of refrigerator cookie dough that have been frozen only need to come up a little in temperature before being sliced and baked—a great way to utilize the freezer and get freshly baked cook-

What to Do If You Have Only Two Cookie Sheets

Many of the recipes here call for making several dozen cookies. If you don't have a lot of cookie sheets, here's a simple solution: Cut parchment or foil sheets the same size as your pans. Line the pans and bake the first batch of cookies. While they are baking, form more cookies on the precut sheets. When the first cookies are baked, slide the papers off the pans, cool the pans until they are no longer hot, then slide the papers with more cookies onto the pans to bake. Also remember that cookie sheets and jelly roll pans are relatively inexpensive and that with two cookie sheets and two each jelly roll pans of two different sizes you can tackle almost any recipe here and not have to wait for pans to cool between baking batches of cookies.

ies at the same time. In any case, if you want to prepare a large assortment of cookies, choose some bar and refrigerator cookies that may be frozen, but don't confine the whole list to frozen cookies.

SHIPPING COOKIES There are two keys to shipping cookies successfully: Wrap them loosely and individually in plastic wrap and use small containers. If you want to ship a lot of cookies, get a lot of small containers and nestle them in Styrofoam (or real) popcorn in a large box. This has recently become easier and less expensive with the availability of the multiple-use disposable plastic containers.

BAR COOKIES

Mother B's

Orange Shortbread Squares

Bittersweet Chocolate
Shortbread Squares

Cinnamon Diamonds

Elegant Almond Bars

Chewy Almond Bars

Chocolate-Iced Peanut Squares

Basler Leckerli (Basel "Lickers")

Pecan-Studded Apricot Bars

Banana Walnut Squares

Currant Squares

Date and Walnut Bars

Fruitcake Bars

Doreen's Ginger Squares

Ultimate Lemon Squares

Cheesecake Squares

Viennese Linzer Squares

Honey Pecan Squares

Osgood Squares

Hungarian Apricot Bars

Lekvar Squares

BROWNIES

Cheesecake Brownies

Espresso Brownies

Pecan Brownies

White Chocolate Chunk
Brownies

West Tenth Street Brownies

PERPAHS THE EASIEST OF ALL COOKIES TO PREPARE, BAR COOKIES ARE REALLY A large cake, divided. The dough or batter is poured into a large pan (all the bar cookie recipes here use a 13 × 9 × 2-inch or a 10 × 15 × 1-inch pan), then spread flat. The baked cake is then cut into bars or squares. Some recipes call for dough used as a base for a topping, yet others have fillings like large rectangular pies or tarts cut into squares.

Perhaps the richest and most elegant bar cookies are brownies, and they are in a special section at the end of this chapter.

HINTS FOR BAR COOKIES

1 Prepare the pan carefully to ensure that the baked cake will be easy to unmold. I like to butter the pan, then line it completely, bottom and sides, with a large piece of parchment paper or foil. The butter on the pan holds the paper in place. I also butter the paper, just to be extra careful. **2** On a rack, cool the baked cake in the pan for 10 minutes. Then remove it from the rack. Using the paper lining, lift it from the pan, and transfer back to the rack to cool completely. **3** After the cake has cooled, lift it, again by the paper lining, to a board to cut it. If necessary, slide a knife or spatula between the cake and the paper to loosen, then slide the cake from the paper to the board. **4** I usually trim away the edges before cutting bar cookies so that the cookies will be more uniform. **5** Neatness counts! Use a ruler to mark the cake into 2-inch squares (or any other size squares or rectangles you wish) before you cut. **6** Use a sharp knife and wipe it frequently with a damp cloth for neatest cutting. **7** Finally, to prevent the bars from drying, store them between layers of wax paper or parchment in a tin or plastic container with a tight-fitting cover. **8** For longer storage, wrap individually in cellophane or plastic wrap and freeze.

Quantity Baking Hint: A double recipe calling for a 9 × 13 × 2-inch pan will fit perfectly in a 12 × 18 × 1-inch half sheet pan as will 1½ times a recipe for a 10 × 15 × 1-inch pan.

Mother B's

This nutmeg-scented bar cookie comes from my old friend Stephanie Weaver. They are named for her suburban Detroit childhood neighbor, Mrs. Barnes, who gave the recipe to Stephanie's mother in the 1960s. A variation of an old-fashioned Southern cookie called a pound cake cookie, these will quickly become favorites.

Makes one 9 × 13 × 2-inch pan,
about twenty-four 2-inch squares

1¾ cups all-purpose flour

1½ teaspoons freshly grated nutmeg

½ teaspoon baking soda

¼ teaspoon salt

8 tablespoons (1 stick) unsalted butter, softened

1 cup sugar

1 large egg

½ cup buttermilk or sour milk

One 9 × 13 × 2-inch pan, buttered
and lined with buttered parchment or foil

1 Set a rack in the middle level of the oven and preheat to 350 degrees. 2 Measure the flour, nutmeg, baking soda, and salt into a mixing bowl and stir well to combine. 3 In the bowl of an electric mixer, beat the butter and sugar together, using the paddle attachment on medium speed. Beat in the egg and continue beating until the mixture is smooth. 4 Lower the mixer speed and beat in half the dry ingredients. When this is incorporated, slowly add the buttermilk and beat until smooth. Then beat in the rest of the dry ingredients. 5 Remove the bowl from the mixer and stir the batter well with a rubber spatula. Scrape the batter into the prepared pan and smooth the top evenly. 6 Bake the cake about 25 to 30 minutes, until well risen and a light golden color, and a toothpick or small knife inserted in the center emerges clean. Remove from the oven and cool on a rack for 10 minutes, then, using the paper, lift the cake from the pan onto a rack and let cool completely.
7 To cut the bars, use the paper to transfer the cake onto a cutting board. Slide a long knife or spatula under it to loosen the paper or foil, then pull it away. Use a ruler to mark, then cut the cake into 2-inch squares. 8 The squares will keep between sheets of parchment or wax paper in a tin or plastic container with a tight-fitting cover for several days. Freeze for longer storage.

ORANGE SHORTBREAD SQUARES

CRUMBLY SHORTBREAD IS ONE OF THE best and most buttery of all cookies. Baking them as a bar cookie makes them really easy to prepare.

Makes one 10 × 15 × 1-inch pan,
or about thirty-five 2-inch squares

20 tablespoons (2½ sticks) unsalted butter, softened

½ cup sugar

1 teaspoon orange extract

2 teaspoons finely grated orange zest

¼ teaspoon salt

3 cups all-purpose flour

One 10 × 15 × 1-inch pan, buttered
and lined with buttered parchment or foil

1 Set a rack in the middle level of the oven and preheat to 325 degrees. **2** In the bowl of an electric mixer fitted with the paddle attachment, combine the butter, sugar, extract, zest, and salt. Beat on medium speed until very light colored and fluffy, about 10 minutes. Add the flour and mix in on lowest speed. **3** Remove the bowl from the mixer and use a large rubber spatula to finish mixing the dough. **4** Scrape the dough into the prepared pan and with the lightly floured palm of your hand press into all the corners. Use the back of a spoon to smooth the top of the dough evenly if necessary. With the tines of a fork pierce the dough all over at ½-inch intervals. **5** Bake the shortbread about 25 to 30 minutes, until it is slightly puffed and firm. **6** Remove the pan to a rack to cool until the shortbread is lukewarm—not completely cooled. **7** Invert the shortbread from the pan onto a cutting board, and remove the paper. Use a ruler to mark, then cut the shortbread into 2-inch squares. **8** For up to several days the squares can be stored between sheets of parchment or wax paper in a tin or plastic container with a tight-fitting cover. Freeze for longer storage.

NOTE Lemon would work as well as orange if you want to vary this: Just use the same amounts of lemon extract and zest for the orange in the recipe above.

BITTERSWEET CHOCOLATE SHORTBREAD SQUARES

I LOVE SHORTBREAD AND I CERTAINLY love chocolate, so I decided to combine the two in this really chocolaty cookie. I had to resist gilding the lily by adding a filling—but I can report that these are particularly good with ice cream. This is another variation of a shortbread baked in one piece, then cut into squares like Orange Shortbread Squares (page 5).

Makes one 10 × 15 × 1-inch pan,
or about thirty-five 2-inch squares

24 tablespoons (3 sticks) unsalted butter, softened

⅔ cup sugar

¼ teaspoon salt

4 ounces bittersweet chocolate, melted and cooled

3 cups all-purpose flour

**One 10 × 15 × 1-inch pan, buttered
and lined with buttered parchment or foil**

1 Set a rack in the middle level of the oven and preheat to 325 degrees. **2** In the bowl of an electric mixer fitted with the paddle attachment, combine the butter, sugar, and salt. Beat on medium speed until very light colored and fluffy, about 10 minutes. Stop the mixer and scrape in the chocolate with a rubber spatula. Continue to beat until the chocolate is incorporated and the mixture is smooth. Add the flour and beat in on lowest speed. **3** Remove the bowl from the mixer and use a large rubber spatula to finish mixing the dough. **4** Scrape the dough into the prepared pan and with the lightly floured palm of your hand press the dough into all the corners. Use the back of a spoon to smooth the top of the dough evenly if necessary. With the tines of a fork, pierce the dough all over at ½-inch intervals. **5** Bake the shortbread about 30 to 35 minutes, until it is slightly puffed and firm. **6** Remove the pan to a rack to cool until the shortbread is lukewarm—not completely cooled. **7** Invert the shortbread from the pan onto a cutting board and remove the paper. Use a ruler to mark, then cut the shortbread into 2-inch squares. **8** For up to several days store the squares between sheets of parchment or wax paper in a tin or plastic container with a tight-fitting cover. Freeze for longer storage.

CINNAMON DIAMONDS

THIS INTRIGUING RECIPE WAS GIVEN TO me by Phil Krampetz, co-owner with Kyle Stewart of the Cultured Cup in Dallas. Once sampled, these easy-to-prepare cookies are destined to become a holiday tradition in many families.

Makes one 10 × 15 × 1-inch pan,
or about thirty-five 2-inch diamonds or squares

2 cups all-purpose flour

1 cup light brown sugar, firmly packed

1½ teaspoons ground cinnamon

¼ teaspoon freshly grated nutmeg

¼ teaspoon salt

16 tablespoons (2 sticks) cold unsalted butter, cut into 16 pieces

1 large egg, separated

1 cup walnut pieces, chopped into ¼-inch pieces

One 10 × 15 × 1-inch pan, buttered and lined with buttered parchment or foil

1 Set a rack in the middle level of the oven and preheat to 350 degrees. **2** In the work bowl of a food processor fitted with the steel blade, combine the flour, brown sugar, spices, and salt. Pulse repeatedly to mix thoroughly. Add the butter and continue to pulse until the mixture resembles a coarse cornmeal. Pour the mixture from the work bowl into a large mixing bowl. Make a well in the center and add the egg yolk. Beat the yolk with a fork, then gradually use the fork to draw in the crumbly flour mixture. As you do so, keep stirring and tossing the mixture with the fork to distribute the egg yolk evenly throughout. The mixture will remain fairly crumbly, though it will be somewhat moister than before the yolk was added. **3** Scrape the crumbly mixture into the prepared pan and with the flat floured palm of one hand, press it into all the corners of the pan. Use the back of a spoon to smooth the top of the dough evenly if necessary. **4** With a small whisk or a fork whip the egg white in a small bowl, just until it is liquid. Use a pastry brush to paint the egg white on the dough, then scatter the walnuts evenly over the egg white, and press them in gently with the palm of your hand. **5** Bake the pastry about 20 to 25 minutes, until it is light golden and firm. **6** Remove the pan to a rack until the pastry is lukewarm. **7** To cut the diamonds, use the paper to transfer the whole pastry from the pan to a cutting board. Slide a long knife or spatula under the pastry to loosen the paper or foil, then pull it away. Mark with a ruler, then cut the pastry into 1½-inch strips, then across into diamonds. Or cut the pastry into 2-inch squares. **8** For up to several days store the squares between sheets of parchment or wax paper in a tin or plastic container with a tight-fitting cover. Freeze for longer storage.

ELEGANT ALMOND BARS

THIS IS A DECIDEDLY FANCY COOKIE, great with ice cream or sherbet as the dessert for an elaborate or plain meal. The recipe comes from my friend Gary Peese of Austin, Texas, who is always sending me wonderful recipes— even when I forget they were from him.

Makes one 10 × 15 × 1-inch pan,
or about thirty-five 2-inch squares

1 cup all-purpose flour

¼ teaspoon salt

1 teaspoon baking powder

One 8-ounce can almond paste,
cut into ½-inch pieces

1 cup sugar

6 large eggs

16 tablespoons (2 sticks) unsalted butter, softened

1 teaspoon finely grated lemon zest

1 teaspoon vanilla extract

4 ounces (about 1 cup) blanched sliced almonds

Confectioners' sugar for finishing

One 10 × 15 × 1-inch pan, buttered
and lined with buttered parchment or foil

1 Set a rack in the middle level of the oven and preheat to 350 degrees. **2** Combine the flour, salt, and baking powder in a bowl and stir well to combine. **3** In the bowl of an electric mixer fitted with the paddle attachment, beat together on low speed, until smooth, the almond paste, sugar, and one of the eggs, about 2 minutes. **4** Add the butter, lemon zest, and vanilla and continue beating on medium speed for about another 5 minutes, until the mixture is very smooth and light. Add the remaining eggs, one at a time, scraping the bowl and beater after each addition. Remove the bowl from the mixer and use a large rubber spatula to stir in the flour mixture by hand. **5** Scrape the batter into the prepared pan and spread it evenly with an large offset spatula. Scatter the sliced almonds uniformly over the batter. **6** Bake the cake for about 30 to 40 minutes, until well risen, and a toothpick or small knife inserted in the middle emerges clean. **7** Cool on a rack for 10 minutes, then remove the pan from the rack. Use the paper to transfer the cake from the pan back onto the rack to cool completely. **8** Use the paper to move the cake onto a cutting board. Slide a long knife or spatula under it to loosen the paper or foil and pull it away. Use a ruler to mark, then cut the cake into 2-inch squares. **9** For up to several days, store the squares between sheets of parchment or wax paper in a tin or plastic container with a tight-fitting cover. Freeze for longer storage. Dust with confectioners' sugar before serving.

CHEWY ALMOND BARS

THIS IS A GREAT RECIPE FOR USING leftover nuts. It's great with one type of nut, but it's just as good with a mixed bag of chopped nuts. This recipe comes from Patsye Hardin of Dallas, Texas.

One 9 × 13 × 2-inch pan,
about twenty-four 2-inch squares

3 tablespoons unsalted butter

3 large eggs

2 teaspoons vanilla extract

1½ cups dark brown sugar

½ cup all-purpose flour

¾ teaspoon baking soda

1½ cups slivered almonds or other nuts, cut into ¼-inch pieces

Confectioners' sugar for finishing

One 9 × 13 × 2-inch pan

1 Set a rack in the middle level of the oven and preheat to 350 degrees. **2** Melt the butter in a small pan over low heat and pour it into the baking pan. Tilt the pan so the butter coats the sides, too. Set aside. **3** In a large bowl whisk together the eggs and vanilla just until whites and yolks are combined. Combine the brown sugar, flour, baking soda, and nuts, then fold into the egg mixture. Scrape the batter into the prepared pan. Don't stir the batter and butter together. **4** Bake about 30 to 35 minutes, until firm and golden. Cover a rack with aluminum foil and invert the baked bar onto it. Lift off the pan and allow to cool completely. **5** Transfer the cake onto a cutting board and slide away the foil. Using a ruler as a guide, cut into 2-inch squares. Just before serving, dust lightly with confectioners' sugar. **6** For up to several days, store the squares between sheets of parchment or wax paper in a tin or plastic container with a tight-fitting cover. Freeze for longer storage.

Elegant Almond Bar (LEFT)
and Chewy Almond Bar

CHOCOLATE-ICED PEANUT SQUARES

I LOVE PEANUT BUTTER COOKIES OF all kinds—especially when they have chocolate icing on them. Sometimes I vary these by using chunky peanut butter, or by adding a handful of chopped honey-roasted peanuts to the dough. They are great unfrosted, but adding the chocolate icing and the chopped peanuts really makes them extraordinary.

One 9 × 13 × 2-inch pan,
about twenty-four 2-inch squares

PEANUT BUTTER DOUGH

12 tablespoons (1½ sticks) unsalted butter, softened

⅓ cup peanut butter

⅔ cup light brown sugar

½ cup granulated sugar

1 large egg

1 large egg yolk

1½ teaspoons vanilla extract

2½ cups all-purpose flour

TOPPING

4 tablespoons (½ stick) unsalted butter, softened

6 ounces semisweet or bittersweet chocolate, melted and cooled

½ cup coarsely chopped honey-roasted peanuts

One 9 × 13 × 2-inch pan, buttered and lined with buttered parchment or foil

1 Set a rack in the middle level of the oven and preheat to 350 degrees. **2** In the bowl of an electric mixer fitted with the paddle attachment, beat the butter and peanut butter about half a minute on medium speed until well mixed. Beat in both sugars and continue beating until the ingredients are combined, about another half a minute. Beat in the egg, yolk, and vanilla extract. **3** Remove the bowl from the mixer and stir in the flour with a wooden spoon. Scrape the dough into the prepared pan and use your floured palms to press it evenly into the pan. **4** Bake the cake about 20 to 25 minutes, or until firm and lightly brown. Cool in the pan on a rack. **5** To make the topping, stir the soft butter into the melted chocolate with a small rubber spatula. **6** Use the paper to transfer the cake to a cutting board. Slide a long knife or spatula under the cake to loosen the paper, then pull it away. With a small offset spatula spread the icing evenly over the top. Sprinkle immediately with the chopped peanuts. **7** Let the cake stand at room temperature for several hours to set the glaze, or place briefly in the freezer or refrigerator to hasten the process. **8** Using a ruler as a guide, cut into 2-inch squares. **9** For up to several days, store the squares between sheets of parchment or wax paper in a tin or plastic container with a tight-fitting cover. Freeze for longer storage.

BASLER LECKERLI
Basel "Lickers"

THIS CLASSIC SWISS COOKIE GETS ITS name from the way kids often suck on them— the way they do a lollipop. They're great as Christmas cookies, but also good any time.

Makes one 10 × 15 × 1-inch pan,
about fifty 1½ × 2-inch rectangles

LECKERLI DOUGH

3 cups all-purpose flour

1½ teaspoons ground cinnamon

½ teaspoon ground cloves

½ teaspoon freshly grated nutmeg

1 teaspoon baking powder

½ teaspoon baking soda

1 cup dark honey

¾ cup granulated sugar

3 tablespoons kirsch

⅔ cup finely chopped candied orange peel

8 ounces (about 2 cups) whole unblanched almonds, chopped into ¼-inch pieces

SUGAR GLAZE

2 tablespoons water

⅓ cup granulated sugar

2 tablespoons confectioners' sugar

One 10 × 15 × 1-inch pan, buttered and lined with buttered parchment or foil

1 Set a rack in the middle of the oven and pre-heat to 325 degrees. **2** Measure the flour into a large mixing bowl and add the spices, baking powder, and baking soda. Stir well to combine.

3 Mix the honey and the ¾ cup granulated sugar in a 1½-quart saucepan. Bring to a simmer over medium heat, stirring occasionally. Remove from heat and stir in the kirsch, candied orange peel, and almonds. Stir the honey mixture into the flour and spices using a rubber spatula.

4 Scrape the dough into the prepared pan and use the floured palms of both hands to fill the pan. Use the back of a spoon to smooth the top.

5 Bake 25 to 30 minutes, until puffed and firm, but not dry. Remove the pan from the oven and immediately use the paper to lift out the baked Leckerli and place it on a rack to cool.

6 Prepare the glaze: Combine the water and the ⅓ cup granulated sugar in a small saucepan and bring to a boil over low heat, stirring often to dis-solve the sugar. After the syrup comes to a boil, let it boil for 10 or 15 seconds so it reduces slightly. Remove the pan from the heat and immediately sift over and stir in the confectioners' sugar. Quickly brush the glaze over the cooled Leckerli and allow the glaze to dry for 10 minutes.

7 When the glaze has dried, transfer the Leck-erli to a cutting board. Using a sharp, serrated knife, cut it into 1½ × 2-inch rectangles. **8** Store between sheets of parchment or wax paper in a tin or plastic container with a tight-fitting cover.

PECAN-STUDDED APRICOT BARS

DRIED APRICOTS AND PECANS ARE A great combination, though you may substitute raisins, currants, or chopped prunes for the apricots or use other nuts with equal success. Thanks to Jayne Sutton for sharing this recipe.

Makes one 9 × 13 × 2-inch pan,
about twenty-four 2-inch squares

1¾ cups all-purpose flour

2 teaspoons baking powder

½ teaspoon salt

8 tablespoons (1 stick) unsalted butter, softened

2 cups light brown sugar, firmly packed

1½ teaspoons vanilla extract

2 large eggs

⅔ cup dried apricots, snipped into ¼-inch pieces

3 ounces (about ⅔ cup) coarsely chopped pecan pieces

One 9 × 13 × 2-inch pan, buttered
and lined with buttered parchment or foil

1 Set a rack in the middle level of the oven and preheat to 350 degrees. **2** Place the flour, baking powder, and salt into a mixing bowl and stir well to mix. **3** In the bowl of an electric mixer fitted with the paddle attachment, beat the butter and brown sugar about a minute on medium speed until well mixed. Beat in the vanilla extract, then the eggs, one at a time. On low speed, beat in the flour mixture. **4** Remove the bowl from the mixer and use a large rubber spatula to give the batter a final stir. Fold in the apricots and pecans. **5** Scrape the batter into the prepared pan and smooth the top. Bake about 25 to 35 minutes, until the cake is well risen and a deep golden color and a toothpick or a small knife inserted into the center emerges clean. Cool on a rack for 10 minutes. Use the paper to transfer the cake from the pan to the rack to cool completely. **6** Use the paper to move the cake to a cutting board. Slide a long knife or spatula under it to loosen the paper or foil, then pull it away. Use a ruler to mark, then cut the cake into 2-inch squares. **7** For up to several days, store the squares between sheets of parchment or wax paper in a tin or plastic container with a tight-fitting cover. Freeze for longer storage.

BANANA WALNUT SQUARES

THIS IS ONE OF MY FAVORITE COMBINA-
tions of fruit and nuts—they seem perfect
together. For the best banana flavor make sure
you use really ripe bananas—ones whose skins
are flecked with brown. If you substitute
peanuts for the walnuts you'll echo the flavors
of Elvis Presley's favorite sandwich.

Makes one 9 × 13 × 2-inch pan,
about twenty-four 2-inch squares

1½ cups all-purpose flour

1 teaspoon baking powder

¼ teaspoon salt

½ teaspoon ground cinnamon

6 tablespoons (¾ stick) unsalted butter, softened

¾ cup dark brown sugar, firmly packed

1 teaspoon vanilla extract

2 large eggs

¾ cup finely mashed bananas (about 2 medium)

⅓ cup strained apricot preserves (See Note)

1 teaspoon lemon juice

1 cup coarsely chopped walnut pieces

One 9 × 13 × 2-inch pan, buttered
and lined with buttered parchment or foil

1 Set a rack in the middle level of the oven and
preheat to 350 degrees. **2** Measure the flour,
baking powder, salt, and cinnamon into a mixing
bowl and stir well to combine. **3** In the bowl of
an electric mixer fitted with the paddle attachment, beat the butter and brown sugar about a
minute on medium speed until well mixed. Beat
in the vanilla extract, then the eggs, one at a
time, beating until smooth after each addition.
4 Beat in the mashed bananas, preserves, and
lemon juice. **5** Remove the bowl from the
mixer and with a large rubber spatula stir in the
dry ingredients, then ½ cup of the walnuts.
6 Scrape the batter into the prepared pan and
smooth the top with an offset spatula. Scatter the
remaining walnuts over the batter. **7** Bake the
cake for about 30 to 35 minutes, or until it is well
risen, well colored, and a toothpick or a small
knife inserted into the center emerges clean.
Cool on a rack for 10 minutes, then remove the
pan from the rack. Use the paper to transfer the
cake from the pan to the rack and cool completely. **8** Use the paper to help move the cake
onto a cutting board. Slide a long knife or spatula under it to loosen the paper or foil and pull it
away. Use a ruler to mark, then cut the cake into
2-inch squares. **9** For up to several days, store
the squares between sheets of parchment or wax
paper in a tin or plastic container with a tight-
fitting cover. Freeze for longer storage.

NOTE If the preserves are very chunky, puree
them in the food processor rather than strain
them.

CURRANT SQUARES

NOTHING IS HOMIER OR MORE COM-forting than these old-fashioned moist squares loaded with currants. Of course, you may substitute dark or golden raisins or a combination, if you choose.

By the way, the standard supermarket currants called for here are really very tiny raisins, not dried, tart red, black, or white currants, which are related to gooseberries. The French name for the tiny raisins used here is *raisins de Corinthe,* or Corinthian raisins, and the English word "currant" is a corruption of "Corinth."

Makes one 9 × 13 × 2-inch pan,
about twenty-four 2-inch squares

⅔ cup water

1½ cups currants

1 teaspoon baking soda

2 cups all-purpose flour

1½ teaspoons baking powder

½ teaspoon freshly grated nutmeg

12 tablespoons (1½ sticks) unsalted butter, softened

1 cup sugar

1 teaspoon vanilla extract

2 large eggs

One 9 × 13 × 2-inch pan, buttered and lined with buttered parchment or foil

1 Combine the water and currants in a medium saucepan. Bring to a full boil over medium heat. Remove from the heat, stir in the baking soda, and set aside to cool completely. **2** Set a rack in the middle level of the oven and preheat to 350 degrees. **3** Place the flour, baking powder, and nutmeg into a bowl. Stir well to mix. **4** In the bowl of an electric mixer fitted with the paddle attachment, beat the butter and sugar on medium speed until well mixed, about a minute. Beat in the vanilla extract, then the eggs, one at a time, beating until smooth after each addition. **5** Remove the bowl from the mixer and with a large rubber spatula stir in the currants and water. Then stir in the flour mixture. **6** Scrape the batter into the prepared pan and smooth the top with an offset spatula. **7** Bake the cake for about 30 to 40 minutes, or until it is well risen, well colored, and a toothpick or a small knife inserted in the center emerges clean. Cool on a rack for 10 minutes, then remove the pan from the rack. Use the paper to transfer the cake from the pan to the rack to cool completely. **8** Place the cake on a cutting board and slide a long knife or spatula under it to loosen the paper or foil and remove it. Use a ruler to mark, then cut the cake into 2-inch squares. **9** For up to several days, store the squares between sheets of parchment or wax paper in a tin or plastic container with a tight-fitting cover. Freeze for longer storage.

DATE AND WALNUT BARS

THIS RECIPE CHUGGED IN THROUGH my fax machine one day from Tina Korting at the Western Reserve Cooking School in Hudson, Ohio. Tina wrote that this cookie was a holiday tradition in her family and that her grandmother wrapped the bars in colored cellophane to give as gifts. I've been to Hudson to teach dozens of times, first at my friend Zona Spray's cooking school, then later when Zona sold the school to Carol Ferguson.

Makes one 9 × 13 × 2-inch pan,
about twenty-four 2-inch squares

1 cup all-purpose flour

1 teaspoon baking powder

2 large eggs

1½ cups sugar

16 tablespoons (2 sticks) unsalted butter, melted and cooled

1 cup chopped pitted dates

1 cup coarsely chopped walnut pieces

One 9 × 13 × 2-inch pan, buttered and lined with buttered parchment or foil

1 Set a rack in the middle level of the oven and preheat to 350 degrees. **2** Measure the flour and baking powder into a mixing bowl and stir well to mix. **3** In a mixing bowl, whisk the eggs until whites and yolks are combined. Whisk in the sugar in a stream and continue whisking for a few seconds, so that the mixture is well blended. Fold in one third of the flour mixture, then half the butter. Add half the remaining flour and all the remaining butter. Finally fold in the last of the flour. **4** Fold in the dates and walnuts and scrape the batter into the prepared pan. **5** Bake about 30 to 35 minutes, until the cake is well risen and a light golden color and until a toothpick or a small knife inserted in the center emerges clean. Cool on a rack for 10 minutes, then remove the pan from the rack. Use the paper to transfer the cake to the rack to cool completely. **6** To cut the bars, use the paper to place the cake on a cutting board and slide a long knife or spatula under it to loosen the paper or foil and then pull it away. Use a ruler to mark, then cut the cake into 2-inch squares. **7** For up to several days, store the squares between sheets of parchment or wax paper in a tin or plastic container with a tight-fitting cover. Freeze for longer storage.

Fruitcake Bars

This is the best way I know to convert people to fruitcake. A small square of moist, fragrant cake covered with sweet, aromatic marzipan never fails to seduce even the most confirmed fruitcake hater. The secret is to bake the cake as a thin slab—it bakes quickly so it never becomes bitter and the result tastes like a really good cake, not the butt of Christmas jokes. You may bake and age the fruitcake for several months before finishing it with the marzipan.

The total amount of dried and candied fruit and nuts is 2 pounds. Feel free to use more of the ones you like and less or none of the ones you don't. Just make sure you have the full weight of fruit and nuts.

Makes one 9 × 13 × 2-inch pan,
about twenty-four 2-inch squares

FRUITCAKE BATTER

4 ounces each pitted dates, dried figs, candied orange peel, candied pineapple, golden raisins, currants, walnut halves, and whole almonds

¼ cup dark rum, plus extra for moistening the cake after it is baked

1¼ cups all-purpose flour

1 teaspoon ground cinnamon

½ teaspoon freshly grated nutmeg

¼ teaspoon ground cloves

½ teaspoon salt

½ teaspoon baking powder

¼ teaspoon baking soda

8 tablespoons (1 stick) unsalted butter, softened

½ cup firmly packed dark brown sugar

2 large eggs

MARZIPAN TOPPING

One 8-ounce can almond paste

2 cups confectioners' sugar, plus more for rolling out the marzipan

½ cup light corn syrup

One 9 × 13 × 2-inch pan, buttered and lined with buttered parchment or foil

1 Check the dates for pits, then cut the fruit into ½-inch pieces. Stem the figs and cut the same size. Rinse the orange peel and pineapple and cut into ¼- to ½-inch pieces. Place the cut fruit in a large bowl and add the other fruits and nuts. Stir in ¼ cup rum. Cover the bowl and let the fruit macerate with the rum for a few hours, or up to several days. **2** When you are ready to bake the fruitcake bars, set a rack in the middle level of the oven and preheat to 300 degrees. **3** Measure the flour into a bowl and stir in the spices, salt, baking powder, and baking soda. **4** In the bowl of an electric mixer fitted with the paddle attachment, combine the butter and brown sugar and beat 2 or 3 minutes on medium speed until light. Beat in the eggs, one at a time, beating smooth after each addition. Lower the speed and beat in the dry ingredients. **5** Scrape out the batter over the fruit and nuts and fold them together with a large rubber spatula. At first it will seem as though there is not enough batter, but eventually all the fruit and nuts will be lightly bound with the batter. **6** Scrape into the prepared pan and press and spread with the same rubber spatula until the surface is even. Make sure the batter goes into all the corners of the pan and is straight and even on the top. Press a piece of buttered parchment or foil against the top of the cake to keep the top from coloring too deeply during baking. **7** Bake the fruitcake for about an hour, or until it is firm and slightly risen. **8** Use the lining paper to lift the fruitcake onto a rack to cool. After the cake has cooled, sprinkle with more rum and double wrap it in plastic wrap. You may leave the cake this way in a cool dark place for several weeks before proceeding, or finish and serve the cake on the same day, as you wish. **9** To finish the cake, unwrap it and place it on a cutting board. **10** To make the marzipan, cut the almond paste into ½-inch pieces. In the work bowl of a food processor fitted with the steel blade, combine the marzipan, confectioners' sugar, and half the corn syrup. Pulse repeatedly to form a dough. If the mixture resists, add more corn syrup, a teaspoon at a time, until the marzipan forms a ball. Remove from the mixer and knead by hand until smooth. **11** Bring the remaining corn syrup to a boil and brush half of it over the fruitcake. On a clean surface dusted with more confectioners' sugar, roll out half the marzipan to the size of the fruitcake. Roll the marzipan up around the rolling pin and position it over the top of the fruitcake. Press to make it adhere. Invert the cake onto another board and repeat with the remaining corn syrup and marzipan. Double wrap in plastic wrap and store the marzipan-covered fruitcake in a cool, dark place until you intend to serve it. **12** Before serving the fruitcake, unwrap the cake, trim the edges, and cut it into 2-inch squares. If you intend to keep the fruitcake squares beyond the day you cut them, wrap them individually in cellophane and store them in a tin or plastic container with a tight-fitting cover.

DOREEN'S GINGER SQUARES

THIS RECIPE IS A WONDERFUL SOUTH African import from my friend Kyra Effren in Dallas. Doreen was Kyra's mother's best friend, who died unexpectedly soon after passing the recipe on to Kyra. So thanks to Kyra, the recipe wasn't lost.

You'll need some ginger preserved in syrup to make this recipe. See Sources for mail-order suppliers if you can't find it locally.

Makes one 10 × 15 × 1-inch pan,
or about thirty-five 2-inch squares

GINGER SQUARES

2½ cups all-purpose flour

1 cup sugar

2 tablespoons ground ginger

2 teaspoons baking powder

16 tablespoons (2 sticks) unsalted butter

1 large egg

¼ cup drained preserved ginger, finely chopped (reserve the drained syrup)

¼ cup finely chopped candied cherries

2 tablespoons reserved ginger syrup

LEMON GLAZE

2 cups confectioners' sugar

3 tablespoons strained lemon juice

One 10 × 15 × 1-inch pan, buttered and lined with buttered parchment or foil

1 Set a rack in the middle level of the oven and preheat to 375 degrees. **2** Combine the flour, sugar, ground ginger, and baking powder in a bowl and stir well to combine. **3** Melt the butter in a 2-quart saucepan over low to medium heat. Off the heat stir in the flour and sugar mixture. **4** Beat the egg, preserved ginger, cherries, and ginger syrup into the dough, beating with a wooden spoon. **5** Scrape the dough onto the prepared pan and use the floured palm of your hand to press the dough evenly into all corners of the pan. Use the back of a spoon to smooth the top of the dough if necessary. **6** Bake the cake about 20 to 30 minutes, or until lightly browned and firm to the touch. **7** Place the cake on a rack and immediately mix the confectioners' sugar and lemon juice for the glaze. Add water, a teaspoon at a time, if the icing is too thick to spread. Brush the glaze over the hot ginger cake so the glaze will set as the cake cools. Allow to cool completely. **8** To cut the ginger squares, slide the whole cake on the paper to a cutting board. Slide a long knife or spatula under the cake to loosen the paper or foil, then pull it away. Use a ruler to mark, then cut the cake into 2-inch squares. **9** For up to several days, store the squares between sheets of parchment or wax paper in a tin or plastic container with a tight-fitting cover. Freeze for longer storage.

ULTIMATE LEMON SQUARES

THIS GREAT VERSION OF A CLASSIC comes from my friend and former student, Cara Tannenbaum. Cara now works with us at Peter Kump's New York Cooking School and is one of our star baking teachers.

Makes one 9 × 13 × 2-inch pan, about twenty-four 2-inch squares

COOKIE BASE

16 tablespoons (2 sticks) unsalted butter, softened

½ cup confectioners' sugar

1 teaspoon vanilla extract

2 cups all-purpose flour

LEMON TOPPING

4 large eggs

2 cups sugar

6 tablespoons strained lemon juice

1 tablespoon finely grated lemon zest

Confectioners' sugar for finishing

One 9 × 13 × 2-inch pan, buttered and lined with buttered parchment or foil

1 Set a rack in the middle level of the oven and preheat to 350 degrees. **2** For the base, in a standing mixer fitted with the paddle attachment, beat the butter on medium speed. Beat in the confectioners' sugar and vanilla and continue beating a minute or two, until light. Lower the speed and beat in the flour. **3** Spread the dough over the bottom of the prepared pan, using a small offset spatula or the back of a spoon to smooth it. Bake the base about 20 to 25 minutes, until golden and baked through. **4** While the base is baking prepare the topping. Be careful not to overmix the topping, or it will have a coarse-textured foam on the top when baked. In a large mixing bowl, whisk the eggs just to break them up. Whisk in the sugar, then the lemon juice and zest. **5** As soon as the base is baked, remove it from the oven and pour on the topping. Immediately return the pan to the oven and continue baking the squares another 25 to 30 minutes, or until the topping is set and firm. **6** Cool on a rack until completely cooled. **7** To cut the cake, use the paper to transfer it to a cutting board and slide a long knife or spatula under it to loosen the paper or foil, then pull it away. Trim the edges, use a ruler to mark, then cut the cake into 2-inch squares. **8** Dust with confectioners' sugar before serving. For up to several days, store the squares in a tin or plastic container with a tight-fitting cover.

CHEESECAKE SQUARES

What a great way to take some of the guilt out of eating cheesecake: Streamline it into a bar cookie. This is a great recipe that may be varied in many ways according to season and mood. Sometimes I like to scatter the baked crust with fresh raspberries before pouring on the cheesecake batter. Apple slices (about two apples' worth) cooked with some butter, sugar, and cinnamon also make a good surprise filling between the cheesecake mixture and the crust. Or if you want something really simple to dress this up, spread the baked dough with strained raspberry or apricot preserves.

Makes one 9 × 13 × 2-inch pan,
about twenty-four 2-inch squares

COOKIE BASE

16 tablespoons (2 sticks) unsalted butter, softened

½ cup confectioners' sugar

1 teaspoon vanilla extract

2 cups all-purpose flour

CHEESECAKE BATTER

16 ounces cream cheese, at room temperature

½ cup granulated sugar

1 tablespoon lemon juice

1 teaspoon vanilla extract

2 large eggs

**One 9 × 13 × 2-inch pan, buttered
and lined with buttered parchment or foil**

1 Set a rack in the middle level of the oven and preheat to 350 degrees. **2** For the base, in a standing mixer with the paddle attachment, beat the butter at medium speed. Beat in the confectioners' sugar and vanilla and continue beating a minute or two, until light. Lower the speed and beat in the flour. **3** Spread the dough evenly over the bottom of the prepared pan; use a small offset spatula or the back of a spoon to smooth it. Bake 25 to 30 minutes, until golden and baked through. **4** While the base is baking, prepare the cheesecake batter. In the bowl of an electric mixer fitted with the paddle attachment, beat the cream cheese, granulated sugar, lemon juice, and vanilla on medium speed for about a minute, or until smooth. Scrape the bowl and beater well, then beat in one of the eggs. Scrape again and beat in the remaining egg, until just incorporated. **5** As soon as the base is baked, remove it from the oven and pour on the cheesecake batter. Continue baking another 25 to 30 minutes, or until the cheesecake batter is set and firm. **6** Place on a rack until completely cooled. **7** To cut the cake, use the paper to transfer it to a cutting board and slide a long knife or spatula under it to loosen the paper or foil, then pull it away. Trim the edges, use a ruler to mark, then cut the cake into 2-inch squares. **8** Store the squares for up to 3 days covered with plastic wrap and in the refrigerator. Bring to room temperature for an hour before serving.

VIENNESE LINZER SQUARES

THE COMBINATION OF RICH, SPICY dough is excellent with the slight sharpness of the raspberry preserves. This is an adaptation of an authentic Viennese recipe so the result is a cakey-textured torte. Really, the only difference between this and a typical Linzertorte is the shape.

I adapted this from the bible of Viennese baking, *Wiener Süss-speisen* ("*Viennese Sweets*") (Trauner Verlag, Linz, Austria, 1968) by Eduard Mayer.

Makes one 9 × 13 × 2-inch pan, about twenty-four 2-inch squares

2½ cups all-purpose flour

6 ounces (about 1½ cups) whole unblanched hazelnuts, finely ground in the food processor

1 cup granulated sugar

1½ teaspoons ground cinnamon

½ teaspoon ground cloves

1½ teaspoons baking powder

16 tablespoons (2 sticks) cold unsalted butter, cut into 16 pieces

2 large eggs

1 cup seedless raspberry preserves or jam

1 ounce (about ¼ cup) sliced almonds

Confectioners' sugar for finishing

One 9 × 13 × 2-inch pan, buttered and lined with buttered parchment or foil

1 Set a rack in the middle level of the oven and preheat to 350 degrees. **2** Combine the flour, ground hazelnuts, granulated sugar, spices, and baking powder in the work bowl of a food processor and pulse to mix. Add the butter and pulse again until the butter is finely incorporated, but stop before the mixture becomes pasty. Add the eggs and pulse until a soft dough forms. **3** Use an offset spatula to spread half of the dough evenly over the bottom of the pan. **4** Leaving a ½-inch margin all around spread the preserves on top of the dough. **5** Place half the remaining dough in a pastry bag fitted with a ½-inch plain tube (Ateco #806) and pipe five equidistant lines of the dough along the length of the pan. Use the remaining dough to pipe six or seven lines diagonally across the first ones. **6** Scatter and press the sliced almonds on top of the lattice. Bake the cake for about 40 minutes, or until it is well risen, well colored, and firm to the touch. Cool the cake in the pan on a rack for 10 minutes. Use the paper to transfer the cake from the pan to the rack and let it cool completely. **7** To cut the cake, place it on a cutting board and slide a long knife or spatula under it to loosen the paper or foil, then pull it away. Use a ruler to mark, then cut the cake into 2-inch squares. Dust lightly with confectioners' sugar immediately before serving. **8** For up to several days, store the squares between sheets of parchment or wax paper in a tin or plastic container with a tight-fitting cover. Freeze for longer storage.

HONEY PECAN SQUARES

THIS IS A RICH AND EASY RECIPE GIVEN to me by Jayne Sutton of Darien, Connecticut. I'm proud to say that Jayne has been coming to my classes for more than 20 years, recently bringing her daughter Leslie, too.

*Makes one 9 × 13 × 2-inch pan,
about twenty-four 2-inch squares*

COOKIE DOUGH

2 cups all-purpose flour

⅓ cup granulated sugar

¼ teaspoon salt

1 teaspoon baking powder

8 tablespoons (1 stick) cold unsalted butter

2 large eggs

FILLING

12 tablespoons (1½ sticks) unsalted butter

¾ cup light brown sugar, firmly packed

3 tablespoons dark honey

Pinch salt

2 tablespoons heavy whipping cream

**3 cups pecan halves or a mixture
of halves and pieces**

**One 9 × 13 × 2-inch pan, buttered
and lined with buttered parchment or foil**

1 For the dough, combine the flour, granulated sugar, salt, and baking powder in the bowl of a food processor and pulse several times to mix. Cut the butter into about sixteen pieces and add to the work bowl. Continue pulsing until the butter is finely worked into the dough and the mixture is a fine powder again. Add the eggs; continue pulsing until the dough forms a ball. **2** Place the dough on a floured surface. Roll into a roughly 9 × 13-inch rectangle. Fold the dough in half (to make it easier to handle) and transfer it to the prepared pan. Unfold the dough and press it out evenly over the bottom of the pan. Use the back of a spoon to smooth it if necessary. With your fingertips, press the dough about an inch up the sides of the pan all the way around. Chill the dough while you prepare the filling. **3** Set a rack in the middle level of the oven and preheat to 350 degrees. **4** For the filling, combine the butter, brown sugar, honey, and salt in a medium saucepan and bring to a simmer, stirring occasionally with a metal spoon. Pour in the cream and allow the mixture to boil up once. Remove from the heat and stir in the pecans. Let cool for about 15 minutes, then pour over the chilled crust. With the point of a spoon, spread the pecans evenly over the dough. Bake for about 25 to 30 minutes, or until the pastry is baked through and the filling is bubbling. **5** Place on a rack until completely cooled. **6** Transfer the pastry to a cutting board and slide a long knife or spatula under it to loosen the paper or foil, then pull it away. Trim the edges, use a ruler to mark, then cut the pas-try into 2-inch squares. **7** For up to several days, store the squares in a tin or plastic container with a tight-fitting cover. Freeze for longer storage.

OSGOOD SQUARES

THIS IS AN ADAPTATION OF A RECIPE for Osgood pie, recently shared by Bennie Sue Dupy, originally from Mart, Texas, near Waco. These rich raisin and pecan squares are like a combination of pecan pie and a rich butter raisin custard.

Makes one 9 × 13 × 2-inch pan,
about twenty-four 2-inch squares

COOKIE DOUGH

2 cups all-purpose flour

¼ teaspoon salt

1 teaspoon baking powder

⅓ cup sugar

8 tablespoons (1 stick) cold unsalted butter

2 large eggs

FILLING

8 tablespoons (1 stick) unsalted butter, softened

1 cup sugar

4 large eggs, separated

4 ounces (about 1 cup) coarsely chopped pecan pieces

1 cup dark raisins

Pinch salt

One 9 × 13 × 2-inch pan, buttered and lined with buttered parchment or foil

1 Set a rack in the middle level of the oven and preheat to 350 degrees. **2** For the dough, combine the flour, salt, baking powder, and sugar in the bowl of a food processor and pulse several times to mix. Cut the butter into about sixteen pieces and add to the work bowl. Continue pulsing until the mixture is a fine powder again. Add the eggs and pulse repeatedly. Continue pulsing until the dough forms a ball. **3** On a floured surface, roll the dough into a roughly 9 × 13-inch rectangle. Fold the dough in half for easier handling and transfer it to the prepared pan. Unfold the dough into the pan and press it evenly against the bottom of the pan. Use the back of a spoon to smooth the surface if necessary. Using your fingertips, press the dough about an inch up the sides of the pan. Chill the dough while preparing the filling. **4** For the filling, in the bowl of a standing electric mixer fitted with the paddle attachment, combine the butter and sugar. Beat several minutes on medium speed until light. Beat in the egg yolks, one at a time, and continue to beat until the mixture is smooth. Remove from the mixer and stir in the pecans and raisins. **5** In a mixer fitted with the whisk attachment, in a clean, dry mixer bowl, whip the egg whites with the salt on medium speed until they are white, opaque, and beginning to hold their shape. Continue whipping the egg whites until they hold a soft peak. With a rubber spatula, fold the egg whites into the pecan and raisin mixture, until no streaks of white remain. Scrape the filling into the chilled pan and bake for about 35 to 40 minutes, or until the pastry is baked through and the filling is set and a deep gold. **6** Cool completely on a rack. **7** Place the pastry on a cutting board and slide a long knife or spatula under it to loosen the paper or foil, then pull it away. Trim the edges, use a ruler to mark, then cut the pastry into 2-inch squares. **8** For up to several days, store the squares in a tin or plastic container with a tight-fitting cover. Freeze for longer storage.

HUNGARIAN APRICOT BARS

THIS WONDERFUL RECIPE FOR A TRIPLE decker bar was shared by an old friend, Nancy Berzinec, who lives out in Pennsylvania Dutch country. I met Nancy in 1985 when she was the cooking school director at Sue and Lynn Hoffman's Kitchen Shoppe in Carlisle, Pennsylvania, where I taught. Nancy says that this is a favorite Christmas cookie in her family.

Makes one 10 × 15 × 1-inch pan,
about thirty-five 2-inch squares

APRICOT FILLING

12 ounces dried apricots, coarsely chopped

1½ cups water to cover apricots

½ cup sugar

COOKIE BASE

1 cup all-purpose flour

Pinch salt

½ teaspoon baking powder

8 tablespoons (1 stick) unsalted butter, softened

½ cup sugar

1 teaspoon finely grated lemon zest

2 large egg yolks (you'll be using the whites for the topping)

NUT MERINGUE TOPPING

2 large egg whites

Pinch salt

¼ cup sugar

4 ounces (about 1 cup) finely chopped blanched almonds

One 10 × 15 × 1-inch pan, buttered and lined with buttered parchment or foil

1 Combine the apricots, water, and sugar in a 1½-quart saucepan. Bring to a simmer, cooking over medium heat, for about 25 to 30 minutes, or until the apricots are soft and somewhat thickened. Use a small whisk to break up the cooked apricots further. Pour the filling into a bowl to cool. (You may cover and refrigerate the filling for several days before proceeding.) **2** When you are ready to bake the bars, set a rack in the middle level of the oven and preheat to 350 degrees. **3** For the base, mix together the flour with the salt and baking powder. In a standing mixer fitted with the paddle attachment, beat the butter on medium speed. Beat in the sugar and lemon zest and continue beating a minute or two, until light. Beat in the egg yolks, then lower the speed and beat in the flour mixture. **4** Spread the dough over the bottom of the prepared pan. Use a small offset spatula or the back of a spoon to smooth it. **5** Spread the cooled apricot filling evenly over the base and set aside while preparing the topping. **6** In the bowl of an electric mixer fitted with the whisk attachment, whip the egg whites and salt on medium speed. Continue whipping until the egg whites are very white and opaque and beginning to hold their shape. Increase the speed to the maximum and add the sugar in a steady stream. Continue whipping until the egg whites hold a firm peak. Remove from the mixer and gently fold in the almonds. **7** Spread the almond meringue over the filling. Bake the pastry for about 45 minutes, or until it is baked through and the almond meringue is a deep golden color. **8** Place on a rack until completely cool. **9** To cut the pastry, transfer it to a cutting board and slide a long knife or spatula under it to loosen the paper or foil, then pull it away. Trim the edges, use a ruler to mark, then cut the pastry into 2-inch squares. (Use a very sharp knife—the topping is sticky.) **10** For up to several days, store the squares in a tin or plastic container with a tight-fitting cover.

Hungarian Apricot Bars (LEFT) *and Cheesecake Brownies, page 30*

LEKVAR SQUARES

THIS IS ANOTHER OLD-FASHIONED Hungarian favorite shared by my friend Nancy Berzinec. Lekvar is prune butter and if it is available in a supermarket where you live it might be under that name. This is a cookie for die-hard prune lovers—like me. If you're not sure where you stand on prunes try these cookies and I'll bet you become a convert. If you don't like prunes at all, you may substitute apricot lekvar with equally good results.

By the way, the best lekvar I know is available at Russ and Daughters on East Houston Street in Manhattan—see Sources for mail-order information.

Makes one 10 × 15 × 1-inch pan,
about thirty-five 2-inch squares

DOUGH

3 cups all-purpose flour

½ cup sugar

½ teaspoon salt

1 teaspoon baking powder

12 tablespoons (1½ sticks) cold unsalted butter

3 eggs

FILLING

2 cups prune lekvar (see Note)

½ cup finely chopped walnuts

Confectioners' sugar for finishing

One 10 × 15 × 1-inch pan, buttered and lined with buttered parchment or foil

1 Set a rack in the middle level of the oven and preheat to 400 degrees. 2 For the dough, combine the flour, sugar, salt, and baking powder in the bowl of a food processor and pulse several times to mix. Cut the butter into about twelve pieces and add to the work bowl. Continue pulsing until the mixture is a fine powder again. In a medium bowl, whisk the eggs together. With a rubber spatula, scrape all the mixture into the work bowl. Pulse to mix in the liquid and continue pulsing until the dough forms a ball.

3 Remove the dough to a floured surface and divide it in half. Roll half the dough into a roughly 10 × 15-inch rectangle. Fold the dough in half for easier handling and transfer it to the prepared pan. Unfold the dough in the pan and press it evenly against the bottom of the pan. Use the back of a spoon to smooth the top if necessary. 4 Use an offset spatula to spread the lekvar evenly over the dough. Scatter the chopped walnuts over the lekvar. 5 On a floured surface, roll out the remaining dough to a 15-inch square. With a serrated cutting wheel, cut the dough into fifteen 1-inch strips. Place six of the strips on the filling going the length of the pan. Place the remaining strips diagonally across the first ones, spacing them about an inch from each other. Trim the excess dough from the second set of strips so they are even with the sides of the pan. You don't want the lekvar to come to a boil in the oven, so chill the pan for an hour before you bake it to lessen the possibility. 6 About 20 minutes before you are ready to bake the pastry, set a rack in the middle level of the oven and preheat to 400 degrees. Bake about 25 minutes, or until the pastry is deep gold. 7 Cool completely on a rack. 8 Transfer the pastry to a cutting board and slide a long knife or spatula under it to loosen the paper or foil, then pull it away. Trim the edges, use a ruler to mark, then cut the pastry into 2-inch squares. 9 Dust very lightly with confectioners' sugar before serving. 10 For up to several days, store the squares in a tin or plastic container with a tight-fitting cover.

NOTE To make your own prune butter, take one pound of pitted prunes, ½ cup water, ⅓ cup sugar, and 1 teaspoon grated lemon zest and cook in a medium saucepan over medium heat until thickened. Puree the mixture in a food processor.

BROWNIES

LOTS OF STORIES EXIST TRYING TO EXPLAIN THE ORIGIN OF THE BROWNIE.
One even states that they were invented in upstate New York by a college student whose
nickname was Brownie. Whatever their origin, they are certainly the most popular of all
bar cookies. Although for my other books I've written numerous recipes for brownies,
I still have a few unusual ones for this volume.

Though many bar cookies are just thinner versions
of cakes, brownies are in a special category. They are richer
and chewier than any cake would ever be. I don't think I
would like a wedge of a round brownie covered with a
rich frosting and eaten with a fork like a cake—brownies
are casual and meant to be eaten out of hand. And
besides, they are easier to make than almost any cake.

Pecan Brownie, page 33

CHEESECAKE BROWNIES

THOUGH THESE ARE OVER-THE-TOP
rich, if you're going to splurge, why not do it
by combining two of the richest desserts,
brownies and cheesecake, in one spectacular
treat. Be careful not to overbake these or both
the cheese and the chocolate parts will become
dry and uninteresting.

*Makes one 9 × 13 × 2-inch pan,
about twenty-four 2-inch brownies*

BROWNIE BATTER

8 tablespoons (1 stick) unsalted butter

6 ounces bittersweet chocolate

3 large eggs

½ teaspoon salt

1 teaspoon vanilla extract

1½ cups sugar

1 cup all-purpose flour

CHEESECAKE BATTER

16 ounces cream cheese, at room temperature

⅔ cup sugar

1 teaspoon vanilla extract

2 large eggs

**One 9 × 13 × 2-inch pan, buttered
and lined with buttered parchment or foil**

1 Set a rack in the middle level of the oven and preheat to 350 degrees. **2** For the brownie batter, melt the butter in a saucepan over medium heat. Off the heat add the chocolate. Let stand 2 minutes, then whisk smooth. If all the chocolate has not melted, return the pan to very low heat and stir constantly to melt the chocolate. **3** In a large bowl, whisk the eggs, salt, and vanilla, just until mixed. Whisk in the sugar in a stream, then whisk in the chocolate and butter mixture. Switch to a rubber spatula and fold in the flour. **4** To make the cheese-cake batter, in the bowl of a standing electric mixer fitted with the paddle attachment, beat the cream cheese and sugar on medium speed for about a minute, or until smooth. Add the vanilla. Scrape the bowl and beater well, then beat in one of the eggs. Scrape again and add the remaining egg. Beat only until incorporated. **5** Scrape the brownie batter into the prepared pan and smooth the top with an offset spatula. Drop tablespoons of the cheesecake batter over the brownie batter to cover it completely. **6** Bake the cake for about 45 to 50 minutes, or until a toothpick or a small knife inserted into the center emerges clean. Cool completely on a rack. **7** Wrap and refrigerate the pan so that the cake solidifies completely—at least 4 hours; overnight is best. This also makes the cake easier to cut. **8** Transfer the whole cake to a cutting board and slide a long knife or spatula under it to loosen the paper or foil, then pull it away. Use a ruler to mark, then cut the cake into 2-inch squares. **9** For up to several days, store the brownies between sheets of parchment or wax paper in a tin or plastic container with a tight-fitting cover in the refrigerator. Freeze for longer storage. If you plan to keep the brownies for any length of time, it is better to wrap them individually in cellophane.

ESPRESSO BROWNIES

THESE BROWNIES, MOIST WITH JUST A hint of dark espresso flavor, are a perfect ending to a light meal. Of course they are also good between meals and any other time you wish.

I prefer these without nuts, but if you insist on always having nuts in brownies, use about 1 cup coarsely chopped walnuts or hazelnuts; those flavors will be best with the coffee.

Makes one 9 × 13 × 2-inch pan,
about twenty-four 2-inch brownies

8 tablespoons (1 stick) unsalted butter

4 ounces unsweetened chocolate, cut into ¼-inch pieces

4 large eggs

2 tablespoons instant espresso powder (I use Medaglia d'Oro)

½ teaspoon salt

1 teaspoon vanilla extract

2 cups sugar

1 cup all-purpose flour

One 9 × 13 × 2-inch pan, buttered and lined with buttered parchment or foil

1 Set a rack in the middle level of the oven and preheat to 350 degrees. **2** Melt the butter in a saucepan over medium heat. Off the heat add the chocolate. Let stand 2 minutes, then whisk smooth. If all the chocolate has not melted, return the pan to low heat and stir constantly until the chocolate melts. **3** In a large bowl, whisk the eggs with the espresso powder, salt, and vanilla, just until mixed. Whisk in the sugar in a stream, then whisk in the chocolate and butter mixture. Switch to a rubber spatula and fold in the flour. **4** Scrape the batter into the prepared pan and smooth the top with an offset spatula. **5** Bake for about 30 to 35 minutes, or until a toothpick or a small knife inserted into the center emerges clean. Cool completely on a rack. **6** Wrap and refrigerate the pan so that the cake solidifies completely— at least 4 hours; overnight is best. This also makes the cake easier to cut. **7** Transfer the whole cake to a cutting board and slide a long knife or spatula under it to loosen the paper or foil, then pull it away. Use a ruler to mark, then cut the cake into 2-inch squares. **8** For up to several days, store the brownies between sheets of parchment or wax paper in a tin or plastic container with a tight-fitting cover. Freeze for longer storage. If you plan to keep the brownies for any length of time, it is better to wrap them individually in cellophane.

PECAN BROWNIES

THESE ARE A VARIATION OF ONE OF MY favorite recipes: Supernatural Brownies in my chocolate book. I could eat a pan of these every week, but so that I don't, mostly I make them to bring to parties or to put in Christmas cookie baskets.

Makes one 9 × 13 × 2-inch pan,
about twenty-four 2-inch brownies

16 tablespoons (2 sticks) unsalted butter

8 ounces bittersweet chocolate, cut into ¼-inch pieces

4 large eggs

1 cup dark brown sugar, firmly packed

1 cup granulated sugar

2 teaspoons vanilla extract

½ teaspoon salt

1 cup all-purpose flour

10 ounces (about 2½ cups) coarsely chopped pecan pieces

One 9 × 13 × 2-inch pan, buttered and lined with buttered parchment or foil

1 Set a rack in the middle level of the oven and preheat to 350 degrees. **2** Melt the butter in a saucepan over medium heat. Off the heat add the chocolate. Let stand 2 minutes, then whisk smooth. If all the chocolate has not melted, return the pan to very low heat and stir con-stantly until the chocolate melts. **3** In a large bowl, use a rubber spatula to stir one egg into the brown sugar. Make sure any lumps in the sugar are dissolved. Add the remaining eggs, one at a time, stirring each in with the rubber spatula in the same way. Stir in the granulated sugar, then the vanilla and salt. Stir in the chocolate mixture. **4** Finally, fold in the flour, then 2 cups of the pecans. **5** Scrape the batter into the prepared pan and smooth the top with an offset spatula. Scatter the remaining chopped pecans over the top of the batter and with your fingertips gently press them in. **6** Bake for about 30 to 35 min-utes, or until a toothpick or a small knife inserted into the center emerges clean. Cool completely on a rack. **7** Wrap and refrigerate the pan so that the cake solidifies completely—at least 4 hours; overnight is best. This also makes the cake easier to cut. **8** Transfer the whole cake to a cutting board and slide a long knife or spatula under it to loosen the paper or foil, then pull it away. Use a ruler to mark, then cut the cake into 2-inch squares. **9** For up to several days, store the brownies between sheets of parchment or wax paper in a tin or plastic container with a tight-fitting cover. Freeze for longer storage. If you plan to keep the brownies for any length of time, it is better to wrap them individually.

WHITE CHOCOLATE CHUNK BROWNIES

THIS IS A FUN RECIPE FROM MY friends Jeff Yoskowitz and Gregg Golden, proprietors of Maurice Pastry, a successful New York wholesale bakery. Every year when Bakers Dozen East, a group we belong to, holds its annual charity bake sale Jeff and Gregg bake these brownies and they are always sold in record time.

Makes one 9 × 13 × 2-inch pan,
about twenty-four 2-inch brownies

16 tablespoons (2 sticks) unsalted butter, softened

2 cups granulated sugar

1 cup unsweetened cocoa powder, sifted after measuring

1 cup light corn syrup

2 teaspoons vanilla extract

4 large eggs

2 cups all-purpose flour

8 ounces white chocolate, cut into ½-inch chunks

One 9 × 13 × 2-inch pan, buttered and lined with buttered parchment or foil

1 Set a rack in the middle level of the oven and preheat to 350 degrees. **2** In the bowl of a standing electric mixer fitted with the paddle attachment, beat together the butter and sugar on medium speed. When they are combined, lower speed as far as you can and add the cocoa, corn syrup, and vanilla extract. Increase speed to medium again and beat until the mixture is lightened, about 3 minutes. Add the eggs one at a time, beating smooth after each addition. Lower the speed again and beat in flour. **3** Remove the bowl from the mixer and mix for a moment with a large rubber spatula. Fold in a little more than half the white chocolate pieces. **4** Scrape the batter into the prepared pan and smooth the top with an offset spatula. **5** Bake the cake for about 40 to 50 minutes, or until a toothpick or a small knife inserted into the center emerges clean. Remove the pan from the oven and immediately scatter the remaining white chocolate pieces over the top of the cake. Return the pan to the oven for 1 to 3 minutes so that the white chocolate melts and crusts slightly. Cool completely on a rack. **6** Wrap and refrigerate the pan so that the cake solidifies completely— at least 4 hours; overnight is best. This also makes the cake easier to cut. **7** Transfer the whole cake to a cutting board and slide a long knife or spatula under it to loosen the paper or foil, then pull it away. Use a ruler to mark, then cut the cake into 2-inch squares. **8** For up to several days, store the brownies between sheets of parchment or wax paper in a tin or plastic container with a tight-fitting cover. Freeze for longer storage. If you plan to keep the brownies for any length of time, it is better to wrap them individually in cellophane.

WEST TENTH STREET BROWNIES

THE NAME OF THIS RECIPE IS THE result of my finding it in Greenwich Village a few blocks from where I live. As I walked east on Tenth Street, I saw a yellowed index card lying on the sidewalk. When I picked it up I saw written in a spidery hand in blue fountain pen ink a recipe for "The Best Brownie's [sic] in the World." Well, I put it aside in a miscellaneous recipe file, and a few months later tried it. They turned out to be sensational and certainly a contender for the title. If you like very sweet brownies, these will be your favorites.

Makes one 9 × 13 × 2-inch pan,
about twenty-four 2-inch brownies

16 tablespoons (2 sticks) unsalted butter

3 ounces unsweetened chocolate,
cut into ¼-inch pieces

4 large eggs

½ teaspoon salt

1 teaspoon vanilla extract

2 cups sugar

1 cup all-purpose flour

1 cup (a 6-ounce bag) semisweet chocolate chips

4 ounces (about 1 cup) coarsely chopped
pecan or walnut pieces

One 9 × 13 × 2-inch pan, buttered and lined
with buttered parchment or foil

1 Set a rack in the middle level of the oven and preheat to 350 degrees. **2** In a medium saucepan, melt the butter over medium heat. Off the heat add the chocolate. Let stand 2 minutes, then whisk until smooth. If all the chocolate has not melted, return the pan to low heat and stir constantly until the chocolate melts. **3** In a large bowl, whisk the eggs with the salt and vanilla, just until mixed. Whisk in the sugar in a stream, then whisk in the chocolate and butter mixture. Switch to a rubber spatula and fold in the flour. **4** Set the batter aside until it has cooled to room temperature (test it with your fingertip). Fold in the chocolate chips and nuts. **5** Scrape the batter into the prepared pan and smooth the top with an offset spatula. **6** Bake the cake for about 30 to 35 minutes, or until a toothpick or a small knife inserted in the center emerges clean. Cool completely on a rack. **7** Wrap and refrigerate the pan so that the cake solidifies—at least 4 hours; overnight is best. This also makes the cake easier to cut. **8** Transfer the whole cake to a cutting board and slide a long knife or spatula under it to loosen the paper or foil, then pull it away. Use a ruler to mark, then cut the cake into 2-inch squares. **9** For up to several days, store the brownies between sheets of parchment or wax paper in a tin or plastic container with a tight-fitting cover. Freeze for longer storage. If you plan to keep the brownies for any length of time, it is better to wrap them individually in cellophane.

DROP COOKIES

Pennsylvania Dutch
Soft Sugar Cookies

Ricotta Drops

Sour Cream Cinnamon Drops

Lemonade Cookies

Fancy Jumbles

Hermits

Pennsylvania Dutch
Soft Molasses Cookies

ANZAC Biscuits

Spicy Oatmeal Walnut Cookies

Chewy Oatmeal Raisin Cookies

Aunt Ida's Poppy Seed Cookies

Maida Heatter's
Skinny Peanut Wafers

Pecan Wafers

Easy Coconut Drops

Sesame Seed Wafers

Loaded with Chips
Chocolate Chip Cookies

Glazed Chocolate Chocolate
Chip Cookies

Sour Cream Fudge Cookies

Cinnamon Pecan Meringues

Chocolate Meringue Rocks

TUILES

Traditional French Tuiles

Orange-Scented Almond Tuiles

Hazelnut Tuiles

Coconut Tuiles

Pierre Hermé's Orange Tuiles

Caramel Pecan Cookies

Almond Lace Cookies

I'VE INCLUDED TWO TYPES OF DROP COOKIES HERE. THE FIRST ARE THE SIMPLEST— you merely drop the batter from a spoon onto a pan and the cookies are ready as soon as they are baked.

Some drop cookies, however, need to be shaped after they are baked—these are the whole family of tuile- (French curved roofing tile) type cookies. They are really just drop cookies, and in most cases you could leave them flat as they emerge from the oven, but traditionally the warm cookies are draped over a rolling pin or some other cylindrical form to make them curve.

HINTS FOR DROP COOKIES

1 Don't overmix the dough or batter, especially if the recipe begins by mixing butter and sugar. Overmixing drop cookie batters can overaerate them. If that happens the cookies puff up too much in the oven then fall miserably into flat, greasy pancakes. Your objective is gently risen, light cookies. **2** Make sure you drop only as much dough or batter as the recipe tells you. Otherwise your cookies could become gigantic. Space the cookies far enough apart on the baking sheets so there is room for them to spread. Most drop cookies spread quite a bit while they are baking. **3** If you drop too much batter on the pan too close together, all the cookies may run together into one vast rectangular cookie—maybe that's how some bar cookies were invented! **4** Review the rules for baking in "Baking Cookies" (page xviii)—most drop cookies are delicate and need to be handled carefully and the pans moved around often for even baking. **5** Drop cookies will keep at room temperature for up to a week or so. Freeze for longer storage. It is not recommended to freeze delicate drop cookies such as tuiles or they will soften.

Pennsylvania Dutch Soft Sugar Cookies

THIS DELICIOUS, HOMEY RECIPE COMES from veteran baker and recipe collector Nancy Berzinec. Though buttermilk works well in the recipe, in the past these were probably a vehicle for using up milk that had soured.

Makes about 60 cookies

4 cups all-purpose flour

2 teaspoons baking powder

1 teaspoon baking soda

Pinch salt

16 tablespoons (2 sticks) unsalted butter, softened

2 cups sugar

3 teaspoons vanilla extract

3 large eggs

1 cup buttermilk or sour milk (see Note)

3 or 4 cookie sheets or jelly roll pans covered with parchment or foil

1 Set the racks in the upper and lower thirds of the oven and preheat to 375 degrees. **2** In a bowl, combine the flour, baking powder, baking soda, and salt; stir well to mix. **3** In the bowl of a standing electric mixer fitted with the paddle attachment, beat together the butter and the sugar until combined, then beat in the vanilla. Add the eggs, one at a time, beating smooth after each addition. Lower the speed and beat in a third of the flour mixture, then half the buttermilk, and another third of the flour mixture. Scrape the bowl and beater often. Beat in the remaining buttermilk, then the remaining flour mixture. **4** Scrape the bowl and beater, then remove the bowl from the mixer, and give the dough one final mixing with a large rubber spatula. **5** Drop tablespoons of the dough 3 or 4 inches apart onto the prepared pans. **6** Bake the cookies for about 15 minutes, or until they spread and rise—they should be lightly golden. **7** Slide the papers off the pans onto racks. **8** After the cookies have cooled, detach them from the paper and store them between layers of parchment or wax paper in a tin or plastic container with a tight-fitting cover.

NOTE To make a cup of fresh milk sour add a teaspoon of some acidic liquid such as vinegar or lemon juice.

RICOTTA DROPS

THIS WAS SENT TO ME BY A READER whose name got separated from the recipe, but I tried the cookies, and they were terrific! They have an old-fashioned tender texture and stay quite moist if you keep them airtight. Thank you, whoever you are.

As a variation, you might want to finish these with confectioners' sugar icing (see page 205).

Makes about 75 cookies

2½ cups all-purpose flour

¼ teaspoon salt

½ teaspoon baking soda

8 tablespoons (1 stick) unsalted butter, softened

1 cup sugar

1½ teaspoons vanilla extract

Finely grated zest of 1 lemon

Finely grated zest of 1 orange

1 cup whole-milk ricotta (about half of one 15-ounce container)

1 large egg

2 egg yolks

Confectioners' sugar for finishing

2 or 3 cookie sheets or jelly roll pans covered with parchment or foil

1 Set the racks in the upper and lower thirds of the oven and preheat to 325 degrees. 2 In a bowl, combine the flour, salt, and baking soda; stir well to mix. 3 In the bowl of a standing electric mixer fitted with the paddle attachment, beat the butter and the sugar together until combined, then beat in the vanilla, lemon zest, and orange zest. 4 Beat in the ricotta and continue beating until the mixture is smooth. Beat in the egg, then the yolks, one at a time, beating smooth after each addition. 5 Remove the bowl from the mixer and, with a large rubber spatula, stir in the dry ingredients. 6 Drop teaspoonfuls of the dough 2 or 3 inches apart on the prepared pans. 7 Bake for 12 to 15 minutes, or until the cookies spread and become firm. They should remain very pale and only color a little on the bottom. 8 Slide the papers off the pans onto racks. 9 After the cookies have cooled, detach them from the paper and store them between layers of parchment or wax paper in a tin or plastic container with a tight-fitting cover. 10 Just before serving, dust lightly with confectioners' sugar.

SOUR CREAM CINNAMON DROPS

THIS SIMPLE COOKIE DESERVES TO BE better known—it's easy to prepare and has the soft, tender texture of the great homey cookies.

Makes about 48 cookies

COOKIE BATTER

2 cups all-purpose flour

¼ teaspoon salt

½ teaspoon baking soda

4 tablespoons (½ stick) unsalted butter, softened

1 cup sugar

1 large egg

1 cup sour cream

CINNAMON SUGAR

1 teaspoon ground cinnamon

3 tablespoons sugar

2 or 3 cookie sheets or jelly roll pans covered with parchment or foil

1 Set the racks in the upper and lower thirds of the oven and preheat to 375 degrees. 2 In a bowl, combine the flour, salt, and baking soda; stir well to mix. 3 In the bowl of a standing electric mixer fitted with the paddle attachment, beat together the butter and the sugar until combined. Beat in the egg and continue beating until smooth. 4 Lower the speed and beat in half the flour mixture. Add the sour cream. Scrape the bowl and beater and beat the batter smooth. Beat in the remaining flour mixture. Remove the bowl from the mixer and give the dough a final mixing with a large rubber spatula. 5 Drop heaping tea-spoonfuls of the dough 2 or 3 inches apart on the prepared pans. Mix the cinnamon and sugar together and sprinkle some on each cookie before putting the cookies in the oven. 6 Bake the cookies for 12 to 15 minutes, or until they spread and become firm. They should remain fairly pale—not too dark. 7 Slide the papers off the pans onto racks. 8 After the cookies have cooled, detach them from the paper and store them between sheets of parchment or wax paper in a tin or plastic container with a tight-fitting cover.

LEMONADE COOKIES

THESE SOFT, CHEWY COOKIES PACK THE strongest lemon flavor I have ever experienced in a cookie—they are definitely not for anyone who doesn't like really big flavors. This is based on a recipe given to me by Amber Sunday.

Makes about 70 cookies

LEMON MIXTURE

¾ **cup strained lemon juice**

¾ **cup sugar**

2 tablespoons light corn syrup

1 tablespoon finely grated lemon zest

COOKIE BATTER

3 cups all-purpose flour

1 teaspoon baking soda

¼ **teaspoon salt**

16 tablespoons (2 sticks) unsalted butter, softened

1 cup sugar

2 large eggs

⅓ **cup reserved lemon mixture (see above) for finishing the cookies**

Sugar for sprinkling

3 or 4 cookie sheets or jelly roll pans covered with parchment or foil

1 For the lemon mixture, combine the juice, sugar, and corn syrup in a medium nonreactive saucepan and bring to a simmer over medium heat, stirring occasionally. When all the sugar is dissolved, remove the pan from the heat and cool the mixture to room temperature. Stir in the grated zest. This may be prepared 1 day before using, but no longer. The zest will make the mixture bitter if it stays in it too long. Set aside ⅓ cup lemon mixture for finishing the cookies. **2** When you are ready to bake the cookies, set the racks in the upper and lower thirds of the oven and preheat to 400 degrees. **3** In a bowl, combine the flour, baking soda, and salt; stir well to mix. **4** In the bowl of a standing electric mixer fitted with the paddle attachment, beat together the butter and the sugar until combined. Beat in the eggs, one at a time, beating smooth after each addition. Lower the speed and beat in half the flour mixture, then the lemon mixture (don't add the reserved ⅓ cup at this point), and the remaining flour mixture. **5** Remove the bowl from the mixer and give the batter one final mixing with a large rubber spatula. **6** Drop rounded teaspoonfuls of the batter 3 or 4 inches apart on the prepared pans. **7** Bake the cookies for about 8 to 10 minutes, or until they have spread and risen—they should be lightly golden. **8** Slide the papers off the pans onto racks and immediately brush the cookies with the reserved lemon mixture. Sprinkle the outsides of the cookies with granulated sugar after they have cooled. **9** Detach the cookies from the paper and store them between sheets of parchment or wax paper in a tin or plastic container with a tight-fitting cover.

FANCY JUMBLES

JUMBLES ARE A KIND OF SOFT COOKIE made with sour cream or buttermilk and there are hundreds of recipes for them. The name is undoubtedly a corruption of the Italian *ciambelle,* which means "ring cookies," and some American versions are actually made in that shape. They are a homey, old-fashioned cookie, even in this spiced-up version with currants and nuts in it.

Makes about 35 cookies

2½ cups all-purpose flour

1 teaspoon baking powder

½ teaspoon salt

½ teaspoon freshly grated nutmeg

8 tablespoons (1 stick) unsalted butter, softened

1 cup sugar (or half granulated sugar and half light brown sugar)

1 teaspoon vanilla extract

1 large egg

1 cup sour cream

⅔ cup currants

3 ounces (about ⅔ cup) coarsely chopped walnut pieces

3 or 4 cookie sheets or jelly roll pans covered with parchment or foil

1 Set the racks in the upper and lower thirds of the oven and preheat to 350 degrees. 2 In a bowl, combine the flour, baking powder, salt, and nutmeg; stir well to mix. 3 In the bowl of a standing electric mixer fitted with the paddle attachment, beat together the butter and the sugar until combined, then beat in the vanilla and finally the egg. 4 Beat in a third of the flour mixture, then half the sour cream. Scrape the bowl and beater with a rubber spatula and beat in another third of the flour. Scrape again, then beat in the remaining sour cream and then the rest of the flour. 5 Remove the bowl from the mixer and give the dough one final mixing with a large rubber spatula. Mix in the currants and nuts. 6 Drop rounded tablespoons of the dough 2 or 3 inches apart on the prepared pans. 7 Bake the cookies for about 15 to 20 minutes,

or until they spread and rise—they should be lightly golden. **8** Slide the papers off the pans onto racks. **9** After the cookies have cooled, detach them from the paper and store them between sheets of parchment or wax paper in a tin or plastic container with a tight-fitting cover.

VARIATIONS

PLAIN JUMBLES: Omit the currants and nuts.
LEMON JUMBLES: Omit the nutmeg and add the finely grated zest of 2 lemons and a teaspoon of lemon extract to the plain jumble.

HERMITS

DELIGHTFULLY OLD-FASHIONED COOKIES that deserve to be served more often, hermits may be made in a variety of ways. This version is made as a drop cookie, but others (don't miss Betty Shaw's Hermits in *How to Bake*) are made as bar cookies, and cut after they have baked.

Makes about 70 cookies

2 cups all-purpose flour

½ teaspoon baking soda

½ teaspoon salt

½ teaspoon freshly grated nutmeg

½ teaspoon ground cinnamon

8 tablespoons (1 stick) unsalted butter, softened

1 cup firmly packed dark brown sugar

1 large egg

¼ cup brewed coffee, cold, or milk

1¼ cups dark raisins

3 ounces (about ⅔ cup) coarsely chopped walnut pieces

3 or 4 cookie sheets or jelly roll pans covered with parchment or foil

1 In a large bowl, combine the flour, baking soda, salt, and spices; stir well to mix. **2** In the bowl of a standing electric mixer fitted with the paddle attachment, beat together the butter and brown sugar until combined. Beat in the egg until the mixture is smooth. **3** Lower the speed and beat in half the flour mixture, then all the cold coffee. Scrape the bowl and beaters well, then beat in the remaining flour mixture. Stir in the raisins and walnuts. Cover the bowl with plastic wrap and chill the dough for an hour. **4** About 20 minutes before you are ready to bake the cookies, set the racks in the upper and lower thirds of the oven and preheat to 400 degrees. **5** Drop teaspoonfuls of the dough 2 or 3 inches apart onto the prepared pans. **6** Bake the cookies for 10 to 12 minutes, or until they spread and become firm. **7** Slide the papers off the pans onto racks. **8** After the cookies have cooled, detach them from the paper and store them between sheets of parchment or wax paper in a tin or plastic container with a tight-fitting cover.

PENNSYLVANIA DUTCH
SOFT MOLASSES COOKIES

ANOTHER OLD-FASHIONED NINETEENTH-century recipe, straight from the middle of Pennsylvania Dutch country, Carlisle, Pennsylvania. It comes from Esther Hoffman, mother of my friend Lynn Hoffman.

Makes about 40 cookies

3 cups all-purpose flour

1 teaspoon baking soda

½ teaspoon salt

½ teaspoon ground cinnamon

½ teaspoon ground ginger

8 tablespoons (1 stick) unsalted butter, softened

½ cup sugar

1 egg

¾ cup molasses

⅓ cup hot water

2 or 3 cookie sheets or jelly roll pans covered with parchment or foil

1 Set the racks in the upper and lower thirds of the oven and preheat to 350 degrees. **2** In a large bowl, combine the flour, baking soda, salt, and spices; stir well to mix. **3** In the bowl of a standing electric mixer fitted with the paddle attachment, beat together the butter and the sugar. Beat in the egg, then continue to beat until smooth. Beat in the molasses. **4** Lower the speed and beat in half the flour mixture, then all the hot water. Scrape the bowl and beater well, then beat in the remaining flour mixture. Remove the bowl from the mixer and give the dough a final mixing with a large rubber spatula. **5** Drop tablespoons of the dough 3 or 4 inches apart on the prepared pans. **6** Bake the cookies for 12 to 15 minutes, or until they rise and become firm. **7** Slide the papers off the pans onto racks. **8** After the cookies have cooled, detach them from the paper and store them between sheets of parchment or wax paper in a tin or plastic container with a tight-fitting cover.

ANZAC Biscuits

ANZAC IS AN ACRONYM FOR AUSTRALIA and New Zealand Army Corps and these cookies (or, as the British call them, "biscuits") were made during the Second World War by everyone Down Under to send to soldiers at the front. My friend Melbourne food stylist Maureen McKeon, who gave me the recipe, wrote that she remembers helping her Irish grandmother pack large tins of the cookies.

Makes about 45 cookies

1 cup rolled oats (regular oatmeal)

¾ cup firmly packed shredded sweetened coconut

1 cup all-purpose flour

8 tablespoons (1 stick) unsalted butter

1 cup sugar

2 tablespoons honey or Lyle's Golden Syrup

2 tablespoons hot water

1½ teaspoons baking soda

2 or 3 cookie sheets or jelly roll pans covered with parchment or foil

1 Set the racks in the upper and lower thirds of the oven and preheat to 325 degrees. **2** In a large bowl, combine the oatmeal, coconut, and flour; stir well to mix. **3** In a medium saucepan over low heat, melt the butter. Still over low heat, stir in the sugar and the honey. Cook until the mixture is beginning to simmer, stirring occasionally until the sugar melts. **4** Combine the water and baking soda in a little bowl, then off the heat stir into the simmered mixture—be careful, it will bubble up. Just keep on stirring and the foam will abate. **5** Stir the warm liquid into the oatmeal and flour mixture to make an evenly moistened batter. **6** Drop teaspoonfuls of the batter 2 or 3 inches apart on the prepared pans. **7** Bake the cookies for 12 to 15 minutes, or until they spread and color evenly. **8** Slide the papers off the pans onto racks. **9** After the cookies have cooled, detach them from the paper and store them between sheets of parchment or wax paper in a tin or plastic container with a tight-fitting cover.

SPICY OATMEAL WALNUT COOKIES

HERE IS ANTHER OATMEAL COOKIE variation, this one with walnuts, currants, and cinnamon. Thanks to David Grice of Dallas, who sent along his friends Phil Krampetz and Kyle Stewart to Kyra Effren's cookie party in December 1998 bearing this recipe.

Makes about 30 cookies

1¼ cups rolled oats (regular oatmeal)

¾ cup all-purpose flour

2 teaspoons ground cinnamon

½ teaspoon baking soda

8 tablespoons (1 stick) unsalted butter, softened

½ cup firmly packed dark brown sugar

¼ cup granulated sugar

1 large egg

1 tablespoon molasses

1 teaspoon vanilla extract

½ cup currants

8 ounces (about 2 cups) coarsely chopped walnut pieces

2 or 3 cookie sheets or jelly roll pans covered with parchment or foil

1 Set the racks in the upper and lower thirds of the oven and preheat to 350 degrees. 2 In a large bowl, combine the oatmeal, flour, cinnamon, and baking soda; stir well to mix. 3 In the bowl of a standing electric mixer fitted with the paddle attachment, beat together the butter, brown sugar, and granulated sugar until well mixed, about a minute. Beat in the egg, then beat in the molasses and vanilla. 4 Lower the mixer speed and beat in the flour and oatmeal mixture, then finally the currants and walnuts. 5 Drop tablespoons of the batter about 3 to 4 inches apart on the prepared pans. Flatten the mounds with the back of a fork. 6 Bake the cookies for 15 to 20 minutes, or until they spread and color evenly and become firm. 7 Slide the papers off the pans onto racks. 8 After the cookies have cooled, detach them from the paper and store them between sheets of parchment or wax paper in a tin or plastic container with a tight-fitting cover.

CHEWY OATMEAL RAISIN COOKIES

I KNEW I COULD COUNT ON MY FRIEND Sheri Portwood, Dallas caterer and all-around great baker, for a chewy, sweet, homey oatmeal cookie recipe. This recipe fulfills all the requirements you want in such a cookie—and is chock-full of raisins, nuts, and chocolate chips. If you want plainer cookies, make them just with raisins—or with any combination of the raisins, nuts, and chips. Just make sure to add a total of 3½ cups of whichever ingredient.

Makes about 60 cookies

2 cups all-purpose flour

1 teaspoon baking powder

1 teaspoon salt

2 cups rolled oats (regular oatmeal)

16 tablespoons (2 sticks) unsalted butter, softened

1 cup granulated sugar

1 cup firmly packed dark brown sugar

2 large eggs

1 teaspoon vanilla extract

1½ cups dark raisins

4 ounces (about 1 cup) coarsely chopped walnut or pecan pieces

1 cup (one 6-ounce bag) semisweet chocolate chips

3 or 4 cookie sheets or jelly roll pans covered with parchment or foil

1 Set the racks in the upper and lower thirds of the oven and preheat to 350 degrees. **2** In a large bowl, combine the flour, baking powder, salt, and oatmeal; stir well to mix. **3** In the bowl of a standing electric mixer fitted with the paddle attachment, beat together the butter, granulated sugar, and brown sugar until well mixed, about a minute. Beat in the eggs, one at a time, beating smooth after each addition, then beat in the vanilla. **4** Lower the mixer speed and beat in the flour and oatmeal mixture, then add the raisins, nuts, and chips. **5** Drop tablespoons of the batter about 3 to 4 inches apart on the prepared pans. Flatten the mounds with the back of a fork. **6** Bake the cookies for 15 to 20 minutes, or until they spread and color evenly and become firm. **7** Slide the papers off the pans onto racks. **8** After the cookies have cooled, detach them from the paper and store them between sheets of parchment or wax paper in a tin or plastic container with a tight-fitting cover.

Aunt Ida's Poppy Seed Cookies

THE AUNT IN THIS CASE IS NOT MINE. She belongs to those relentless cookbook, recipe, and kitchenware collectors, Marilynn and Sheila Brass of Cambridge, Massachusetts. My friend Sandy Leonard makes these and adds the grated zest of an orange. The Brass sisters prefer a pure old-fashioned Jewish cookie with lots of old-country poppy seed flavor without the orange zest—you can decide for yourself. Thanks also to my friend, cookbook dealer Bonnie Slotnick, who shared an almost identical recipe.

Makes about 60 cookies

3 cups all-purpose flour

2 teaspoons baking powder

Pinch salt

½ cup poppy seeds

3 large eggs

1 cup sugar

1 cup peanut or other mild oil

1 teaspoon vanilla extract

2 or 3 cookie sheets or jelly roll pans covered with parchment or foil

1 Set the racks in the upper and lower thirds of the oven and preheat to 325 degrees. **2** In a bowl, combine the flour, baking powder, and salt; stir well to mix. Stir in the poppy seeds. **3** In a large mixing bowl, whisk the eggs to break them up. Whisk in the sugar, then the oil and the vanilla extract. Use a rubber spatula to fold the dry ingredients in thoroughly. **4** Drop teaspoonfuls of the dough 2 or 3 inches apart on the prepared pans. Before you bake the cookies, flatten them slightly with the back of a fork or a small spatula. **5** Bake the cookies for 12 to 15 minutes, or until they spread, become firm, and are lightly colored around the edges. **6** Slide the papers off the pans onto racks. **7** After the cookies have cooled, detach them from the paper and store them between sheets of parchment or wax paper in a tin or plastic container with a tight-fitting cover.

Aunt Ida's Poppy Seed Cookie (LEFT) *and Pecan Wafer, page 52*

MAIDA HEATTER'S SKINNY PEANUT WAFERS

WHEN I WAS FINISHING THE MANUSCRIPT for this book, I was on the phone with Maida Heatter one morning and I asked her: "Maida, what's your favorite cookie?" Her answer was characteristic: "Well, my favorite cookie right now might not be my favorite cookie for later in the day or my favorite cookie after dinner." She said that she had been craving something spicy and crunchy and told me about some very spicy biscotti. No more than an hour later, Maida phoned me back to tell me that her all-time favorite cookies, bar none, are these peanut wafers, the recipe for which appears in *Maida Heatter's Brand-New Book of Great Cookies* (Random House, 1995).

Makes about 25 cookies

4 ounces (1 cup) honey-roasted peanuts, plus optional additional peanuts to use as a topping

1 cup sugar

2 tablespoons unsalted butter

1 cup sifted unbleached flour (sift before measuring, then spoon into a cup and level off with the back of a knife)

½ teaspoon baking soda

1 large egg

2 tablespoons milk

4 cookie sheets lined with aluminum foil, shiny side up

1 Set a rack in the center of the oven and preheat to 350 degrees. **2** In the work bowl of a food processor fitted with the steel blade, place 1 cup of peanuts. Add a few tablespoons of the sugar (reserve the remaining sugar). Briefly pulse the machine ten times to chop the nuts into coarse pieces; some will be powdery, some coarse, some still whole. Set aside. **3** Melt the butter in a small pan over moderate heat; set aside. **4** Sift together the flour and baking soda; set aside. **5** Place the egg, milk, melted butter, and the reserved sugar in the bowl of an electric mixer and beat until mixed. Add the sifted dry ingredients and the chopped peanuts and beat again until mixed. Transfer to a shallow bowl for ease of handling. **6** Rather generously spray a foil-lined sheet with Pam or some other nonstick spray. **7** Place the dough using slightly rounded tablespoonfuls (not heaping) on the prepared sheet, keeping the mounds 3 inches apart (I place six on a cookie sheet). Try to keep the shapes neat. Top each cookie with the optional peanuts—as many as you can fit on the top of each one. With your fingertips, press the tops to flatten the cookies a bit. **8** Bake one sheet at a time. After 5 minutes, reverse the sheet front to back. The cookies will rise up, spread out, and then flatten into very thin wafers with bumpy tops; they will spread out to 3½ to 4½ inches in diameter. Total baking time is 8 to

10 minutes. The cookies should bake until they are barely brown all over—but they will continue to brown a bit just from the heat of the sheet. 9 Remove from the oven. If the cookies have run into each other, cut them apart immediately, while very hot. Cool on the sheet for a minute or two. Then slide the foil off the sheet. Let the cookies stand until they are firm enough to be removed. Then it will be easy to peel the foil away from the backs. 10 As soon as they are cool, store in an airtight container with paper between the layers.

PECAN WAFERS

THESE ARE SUBLIME AS IS OR COUPLED around some melted milk chocolate. Either way, they are crisp, delicious, and easy to prepare.

Makes about 50 cookies,
half that many if sandwiched

8 tablespoons (1 stick) unsalted butter, softened

1 cup firmly packed light brown sugar

½ cup granulated sugar

1 large egg

1 teaspoon vanilla extract

1½ cups all-purpose flour

4 ounces (about 1 cup) pecan pieces, finely chopped but not ground

2 or 3 cookie sheets or jelly roll pans lined with parchment or foil

1 Set the racks in the upper and lower thirds of the oven and preheat to 375 degrees. 2 In the bowl of a standing electric mixer fitted with the paddle attachment, beat together the butter, brown sugar, and granulated sugar until combined, then beat in the egg and vanilla. Beat until smooth without overbeating. 3 Remove the bowl from the mixer and, with a large rubber spatula, stir in the flour and pecans. 4 Roll rounded teaspoonfuls of the dough into balls, then place them 2 or 3 inches apart on the prepared pans, and press them slightly to flatten. 5 Bake the cookies for 12 to 15 minutes, or until they have spread and are deep gold around the edges but still fairly pale on top. 6 Slide the papers off the pans onto racks. 7 After the cookies have cooled, detach them from the paper and store them between sheets of parchment or wax paper in a tin or plastic container with a tight-fitting cover.

VARIATION

For a change, substitute walnuts or macadamia nuts for the pecans.

EASY COCONUT DROPS

I CAN NEVER HAVE ENOUGH COCONUT, whether it's in cakes, cookies, or custards. This easy cookie with lots of coconut flavor and texture is my idea of perfection.

Makes about 40 cookies

One 7-ounce bag sweetened shredded coconut

1 cup all-purpose flour

1 teaspoon baking powder

¼ teaspoon salt

8 tablespoons (1 stick) unsalted butter, softened

¾ cup sugar

1 teaspoon vanilla extract

1 large egg

2 cookie sheets or jelly roll pans lined with parchment or foil

1 Set the racks in the upper and lower thirds of the oven and preheat to 375 degrees. **2** In the work bowl of a food processor fitted with the steel blade, place the coconut and pulse for 1-second intervals about a dozen times. Your object is to make the coconut smaller but not to grind it too fine. **3** In a bowl, mix the flour with the baking powder and salt. **4** Combine the butter and sugar in the bowl of an electric mixer fitted with the paddle. Beat on medium speed for about half a minute, then beat in the vanilla, then the egg. Beat until smooth again. **5** Lower the speed and beat in the flour mixture, then the coconut. **6** Remove the bowl from the mixer and complete the mixing with a large rubber spatula. **7** Drop teaspoonfuls of the batter on the prepared pans about 2 or 3 inches apart. Bake the cookies about 12 to 15 minutes, until they have spread and are golden around the edges. **8** Slide the papers from the pans onto racks. **9** After the cookies have cooled, detach them from the paper and store them between sheets of parchment or wax paper in a tin or plastic container with a tight-fitting cover.

SESAME SEED WAFERS

OFTEN CALLED BENNE WAFERS— *benne* is the Latin botanical name for sesame—these crisp cookies are reminiscent of all those caramel and sesame sweets from the Middle East and Sicily. This recipe is loosely based on recipes from two friends, Jayne Sutton and the late Richard Sax, who gave a recipe for toasted sesame cookies in his book *Classic Home Desserts* (Chapters, 1994).

Makes about 40 cookies

1¼ **cups sesame seeds (taste them when you buy them to make sure they are fresh, not rancid)**

¾ **cup all-purpose flour**

½ **teaspoon baking powder**

Pinch salt

8 **tablespoons (1 stick) unsalted butter, softened**

⅓ **cup firmly packed light brown sugar**

¼ **cup granulated sugar**

1 **teaspoon vanilla extract**

1 **large egg**

2 **or 3 cookie sheets or jelly roll pans covered with parchment or buttered foil**

1 Set the racks in the upper and lower thirds of the oven and preheat to 325 degrees. **2** Place the sesame seeds on a jelly roll or roasting pan and toast them, stirring occasionally, until they are golden, about 10 minutes. Pour the seeds onto a cold pan to cool. **3** In a bowl, combine the flour, baking powder, and salt; stir well to mix. Stir in the cooled sesame seeds. **4** In the bowl of a standing electric mixer fitted with the paddle attachment, beat the butter with both sugars on medium speed until well mixed, about 30 seconds. Beat in the vanilla, add the egg, and continue beating until smooth again. **5** Remove the bowl from the mixer and stir in the flour and sesame seed mixture with a large rubber spatula. **6** Drop teaspoonfuls of the dough 2 or 3 inches apart on the prepared pans. Before baking the cookies, flatten them slightly with the back of a fork or a small spatula. **7** Bake the cookies for 10 to 12 minutes, or until they spread, become firm, and are lightly colored. **8** Slide the papers off the pans onto racks. **9** After the cookies have cooled, detach them from the paper and store them between sheets of parchment or wax paper in a tin or plastic container with a tight-fitting cover.

LOADED WITH CHIPS CHOCOLATE CHIP COOKIES

I USED TO MAKE THESE SO OFTEN THAT now, when I taste chocolate chip cookies without double the amount of chips to the amount of batter, I'm disappointed. For a standard chocolate chip cookie, halve the weight of the chips.

Makes about 35 cookies

1¼ **cups all-purpose flour**

½ **teaspoon salt**

½ **teaspoon baking soda**

8 **tablespoons (1 stick) unsalted butter, softened**

½ **cup firmly packed light brown sugar**

¼ **cup granulated sugar**

1 **large egg**

1 **teaspoon vanilla extract**

2 **cups (one 12-ounce bag) semisweet chocolate chips**

3 **ounces (about ¾ cup) coarsely chopped walnut or pecan pieces, optional**

2 **or 3 cookie sheets or jelly roll pans covered with parchment or foil**

1 Set the racks in the upper and lower thirds of the oven and preheat to 375 degrees. **2** In a bowl, combine the flour, salt, and baking soda; stir well to mix. **3** In the bowl of a standing electric mixer fitted with the paddle attachment, beat together the butter, brown sugar, and granulated sugar until combined, then beat in the egg and vanilla, beating until smooth. Don't overbeat. **4** Remove the bowl from the mixer and with a large rubber spatula stir in the flour mixture. Stir in the chips and the optional nuts. **5** Drop teaspoonfuls of the dough 2 or 3 inches apart on the prepared pans. **6** Bake the cookies for 12 to 15 minutes, or until they are deep gold and firm. **7** Slide the papers off the pans onto racks. **8** After the cookies have cooled, detach them from the paper and store them between sheets of parchment or wax paper in a tin or plastic container with a tight-fitting cover.

VARIATION

CHOCOLATE CHUNK COOKIES: Instead of chocolate chips, use 12 ounces of dark, milk, or white chocolate, cut into ¼-inch pieces. Or try combining two kinds of chips or chunks in the same batch of cookies.

GLAZED CHOCOLATE CHOCOLATE CHIP COOKIES

THESE EASY COOKIES PACK A STRONG chocolate punch. An equally easy variation may be made using chunks or chips of white chocolate instead of the chocolate chips here.

Makes about 40 cookies

2 cups all-purpose flour

1 teaspoon baking powder

¼ teaspoon salt

8 tablespoons (1 stick) unsalted butter

**3 ounces unsweetened chocolate,
cut into ¼-inch pieces**

2 large eggs

½ cup light brown sugar

½ cup granulated sugar

1 teaspoon vanilla extract

½ cup sour cream

1 cup (one 6-ounce bag) semisweet chocolate chips

**1 batch Sugar-Based Chocolate Glaze for Cookies
(page 319)**

**2 or 3 cookie sheets or jelly roll pans
covered with parchment or foil**

1 Set the racks in the upper and lower thirds of the oven and preheat to 375 degrees. **2** In a bowl, combine the flour, baking powder, and salt; stir well to mix. **3** In a medium saucepan, melt the butter and let it heat for a few seconds. Remove from the heat, add the chocolate, and shake the pan to submerge the chocolate. Let the butter and chocolate stand for a minute. Whisk smooth and set aside. **4** Crack the eggs into a large mixing bowl and whisk them until the whites and yolks are combined. Whisk in first the brown sugar, then the granulated sugar and vanilla. Whisk smooth after each addition, then whisk in the chocolate mixture. **5** Use a large rubber spatula to fold in half the flour mixture, then all the sour cream, and finally fold in the remaining flour mixture. Fold in the chocolate chips. **6** Drop large teaspoonfuls of the dough 2 or 3 inches apart on the prepared pans. **7** Bake the cookies for 10 to 12 minutes, or until they rise and become firm. **8** Slide the papers off the pans onto racks. **9** Prepare the glaze. **10** Remove the cookies from the paper, hold them by one edge, and half-dip them in the glaze. Arrange them right side up on the paper they baked on. Or leave them on the paper and use a paper cone, squeeze bottle, or snipped non-pleated plastic bag to streak the cookies with the glaze. Let the glaze dry completely before you put the cookies away. **11** Store them between sheets of parchment or wax paper in a tin or plastic container with a tight-fitting cover.

SOUR CREAM FUDGE COOKIES

THESE MOIST COOKIES ARE LIKE INDI-
vidual tiny cakes. Try dressing them up a little
with an icing such as Sugar-Based Chocolate
Glaze for Cookies or Fluffy Egg White Icing.

Makes about 70 cookies

2 cups all-purpose flour

½ teaspoon baking soda

¼ teaspoon salt

8 tablespoons (1 stick) unsalted butter, softened

⅔ cup firmly packed dark brown sugar

⅓ cup granulated sugar

1 large egg

1½ teaspoons vanilla extract

2 ounces unsweetened chocolate, melted and cooled

¾ cup sour cream

¾ cup coarsely chopped pecan pieces

1 batch Sugar-Based Chocolate Glaze for Cookies (page 319), 1 batch Fluffy Egg White Icing (page 314), or confectioners' sugar for finishing

2 or 3 cookie sheets or jelly roll pans covered with parchment or foil

1 Set the racks in the upper and lower thirds of the oven and preheat to 350 degrees. **2** In a bowl, combine the flour, baking soda, and salt. **3** In the bowl of a standing electric mixer fitted with the paddle attachment, on medium speed, beat together the butter and both sugars until smooth, about 30 seconds. Beat in the egg and the vanilla, beating smooth after each addition. Scrape the bowl and beater and beat in the chocolate. **4** Lower the speed and beat in half the flour mixture. Then beat in the sour cream. Scrape the bowl and beater well and beat in the remaining flour mixture. **5** Remove the bowl from the mixer and give the dough a final mixing with a large rubber spatula. Stir in the pecans. **6** Drop teaspoonfuls of the dough 2 or 3 inches apart on the prepared pans. **7** Bake the cookies for 10 to 12 minutes, or until they rise and become firm. **8** Slide the papers off the pans onto racks. **9** Prepare the glaze. **10** Remove the cookies from the paper, hold them by one edge, and half-dip them in the glaze. Then arrange them right side up on the paper they baked on. Or leave them on the paper and use a paper cone, squeeze bottle, or snipped non-pleated plastic bag to streak the cookies with the glaze. Let the glaze dry completely before you put the cookies away. **11** Store them between sheets of parchment or wax paper in a tin or plastic container with a tight-fitting cover.

CINNAMON
PECAN MERINGUES

THESE EASY, CRUNCHY COOKIES ARE A breeze to prepare if you are careful about two things: First, make sure when you separate the eggs the yolks don't break, because a little speck of yolk will prevent the whites from beating up to a good volume. Second, make sure the egg whites are well beaten before you begin to add the sugar, or they will never have good volume.

See Macaroons, page 161, for other meringue cookies that are piped into fancy shapes before being baked.

Makes about 45 cookies

4 large egg whites (about ½ cup)

Pinch salt

1 cup sugar

4 ounces (about 1 cup) finely chopped (not ground) pecan pieces

1 teaspoon ground cinnamon

2 cookie sheets or jelly roll pans covered with parchment or foil

1 Set the racks in the upper and lower thirds of the oven and preheat to 250 degrees. **2** In the clean dry bowl of a standing electric mixer fitted with the whisk attachment, whip the whites and salt on medium speed until the egg whites are opaque and able to hold a very soft peak, about 2 or 3 minutes. Increase the speed to medium-high and while the mixer is running, slowly—a tablespoon at a time—add half the sugar. Continue whipping the egg whites and adding the sugar until the egg whites hold a stiff peak, but are not dry or grainy. **3** Remove the bowl from the mixer and fold in the remaining sugar, the pecans, and the cinnamon. **4** Use 2 teaspoons to drop the meringue onto the prepared pans: Pick up a heaping spoonful of the meringue with one spoon, then use the other spoon to scrape the meringue out of the first spoon. Let the meringue fall on the pan about 3 inches from the last spoonful. Don't try to make the meringues look too smooth or uniform—this type of cookie is always somewhat uneven looking. **5** Bake the cookies for about an hour, or until they are almost completely dry, but still white. Do not let them take on any color. **6** Cool the cookies on the pans, then remove them and store them between sheets of parchment or wax paper in a tin or plastic container with a tight-fitting cover.

VARIATIONS

Substitute other nuts for the pecans.

Omit the cinnamon for a plain nut meringue.

Add one 6-ounce bag (1 cup) chocolate chips to the meringue with the nuts.

CHOCOLATE MERINGUE ROCKS

THE CRAGGY APPEARANCE OF THIS cookie suggests a little stone, which is why they are called *rochers* (or "boulders") in French. These are a good way to use up left-over egg whites, though they are so good, you might want to make them when there are no egg whites to use up.

Makes about 36 cookies

3 large egg whites

Pinch salt

¾ cup sugar

4 ounces bittersweet chocolate, melted and cooled

4 ounces (about 1 cup) hazelnuts, lightly toasted, skins rubbed away, cooled and chopped

2 cookie sheets or jelly roll pans lined with parchment or foil

1 Set the racks in the upper and lower thirds of the oven and preheat to 300 degrees. **2** Half-fill a medium saucepan with water and bring it to a boil over medium heat. **3** Combine the egg whites, salt, and sugar in the bowl of a standing electric mixer but whisk them lightly together with a hand whisk. Place the bowl over the pan of simmering water and continue to whisk gently by hand until the egg whites are hot and the sugar is dissolved, about 2 or 3 minutes. **4** Fit the mixer with the whisk and whip the meringue on medium speed for about 5 minutes, or until it has cooled and is very stiff. **5** Fold in the chocolate, then the hazelnuts with a medium-sized rubber spatula. **6** Use 2 teaspoons to drop the meringue onto the prepared pans: Pick up a heaping spoonful of the meringue with one spoon, then use the other spoon to scrape the meringue out of the first spoon. Let the meringue fall on the pan about 3 inches from the last spoonful. Don't try to make the meringues look too smooth or uniform—this type of cookie is always somewhat uneven looking. **7** Bake the cookies for about 18 to 20 minutes, or until they are almost completely dry. **8** Cool the cookies on the pans, then remove them and store them between sheets of parchment or wax paper in a tin or plastic container with a tight-fitting cover.

VARIATIONS

Substitute other nuts for the hazelnuts.

Add one 6-ounce bag (1 cup) chocolate chips to the meringue with the nuts. If you choose to try this variation, make sure the meringue is completely cooled, or the chocolate chips will melt.

TUILES

I NEVER UNDERSTOOD WHY THESE CURVED COOKIES WERE CALLED TILES, because all the floor and wall tiles I had ever seen were square or rectangular and flat. It wasn't until I was working at the Sporting Club in Monte Carlo that I asked my chef, Alexandre Frolla, how the cookies got their name. My question was greeted with peals of laughter from all the Frenchmen who heard it. It seems that the French word *tuile* specifically means a curved clay roofing tile—very common on the Riviera, had I only looked up. A wall or floor tile would be called a *carreau*, or "square." I'm sure everyone was thinking: Americans!

Tuiles are among the most elegant and delicate of all cookies. A very thin drop cookie, a warm tuile is usually draped over a rolling pin or other cylindrical form to create the characteristic curve. This adds a lot of elegance to their appearance, but does nothing to alter the taste. So if you have to save time, leave them flat.

HINTS FOR PERFECT TUILES

1 Don't beat the batter a lot; aeration only makes the batter puff up. Tuile batters should just be stirred together. **2** When you are spooning the batter out onto the baking sheet, keep stirring up the batter as you spoon it out so the nuts stay in suspension. **3** Watch the cookies closely as they are baking—these are so thin that a minute can make the difference between perfect and burned. **4** Bake only one pan of tuiles at a time. You'll need time to curve the cookies and if you bake two pans simultaneously, one will either be burning or cooling to the point that the cookies will be too stiff to bend. **5** If you want to make lots of tuiles, enlist the help of a second person so that one can place the batter on the pan and the other can watch the oven. Both should do the curving: One person can remove the tuiles from the pans while the other places them on and removes them from the curved forms.

Traditional French Tuile (LEFT), *and Pierre Hermé's Orange Tuiles, page 68*

TRADITIONAL FRENCH TUILES

I HAVE USED THIS TUILE RECIPE SINCE my days in Monte Carlo in the early seventies. Michel Defino, the second-in-command pastry chef after M. Frolla, usually made these and I was always enlisted as the tuile-curving assistant.

Makes about 35 cookies

2 large eggs

Pinch salt

½ cup sugar

1 teaspoon vanilla extract

8 ounces (about 2 cups) blanched sliced almonds, slightly crushed

¼ cup all-purpose flour

2 or 3 cookie sheets or jelly roll pans, well buttered or covered with buttered foil

1 Set a rack in the middle level of the oven and preheat to 350 degrees. **2** In a medium bowl, use a small rubber spatula to stir together the eggs and salt until just amalgamated. Stir in the sugar, then the vanilla. Stir in the almonds, then the flour. Leave the rubber spatula in the bowl and keep stirring up the batter as you spoon it out. **3** Before you place a pan of cookies in the oven to bake, have a thin-bladed spatula, pancake turner, or thin, flexible plastic scraper ready to remove the cookies from the pan. Also, have several rolling pins or other rounded forms (see page xvi) ready to curve the cookies over, if you intend to do that. If not, have a couple of pans covered with foil to receive the baked cookies—they are much too fragile to cool on a rack. Finally, have a jelly roll pan ready for the cooled, curved cookies. If you intend to leave the cookies flat, tear off some sheets of wax paper or foil so you can stack the cookies on the pan. **4** Drop the batter by teaspoonfuls onto the prepared pans, leaving at least 3 inches between them. Use a fork or a spatula to flatten each mound of batter to evenly distribute the almonds before baking. **5** Place a single pan of cookies in the oven and bake for 5 to 7 minutes, until they start to bubble on the pan, spread and become thin, and take on a deep golden color. **6** Remove the pan from the oven and immediately replace with another prepared pan. Let the cookies you just removed firm up for a few seconds, then slide the spatula under each one and detach it. Move quickly. Either place on the rolling pin to curve or put them on one of the cooling pans. If the cookies become too cold and you can't remove them from the pan without shattering them, replace the pan in the oven for a few seconds to soften the cookies again. **7** Continue until all the cookies are baked. To reuse the pans, wipe them well, or line them with a fresh sheet of foil; just make sure the pans are cool before you spoon the batter onto them. **8** Store the flat cookies between sheets of parchment or wax paper in a tin or plastic container with a tight-fitting cover. I don't recommend trying to store curved ones more than a few hours before serving—they are too fragile.

Drop Cookies

THE NEXT TWO RECIPES COME FROM MY LATE FRIEND AND COOKING SCHOOL associate, Peter Kump. They used to be taught at the school before I revised all the pastry and baking classes in the mid-eighties. A few months before I started working on this book I was cleaning out some files and I came across the recipes and decided to try them. They are both exquisite. I don't know the origin of these recipes, but I'm sure Peter got them in France because they were written with metric weights.

ORANGE-SCENTED ALMOND TUILES

THESE ARE EQUALLY GOOD IF YOU substitute lemon zest for the orange zest.

Makes about 25 cookies

Grated zest of 1 large orange

1 egg

½ cup sugar

4 ounces (about 1 cup) sliced almonds

2 tablespoons all-purpose flour

3 tablespoons unsalted butter, melted

1 teaspoon orange liqueur

2 or 3 cookie sheets or jelly roll pans, well buttered or covered with buttered foil

1 Set the rack in the middle level of the oven and preheat to 350 degrees. **2** Combine the orange zest with the egg and sugar in a medium bowl. Use a small rubber spatula to stir in the almonds, then the flour. Fold in the butter, then the liqueur. **3** Before you place a pan of cookies in the oven to bake, have a thin-bladed spatula, pancake turner, or thin, flexible plastic scraper ready to remove the cookies from the pan. Also, have several rolling pins or other rounded forms (see page xvi) ready to curve the cookies over, if you intend to do that. If not, have a couple of pans covered with foil to receive the baked cookies—they are much too fragile to cool on a rack.

Finally, have a jelly roll pan ready for the cooled, curved cookies. If you intend to leave the cookies flat, tear off some sheets of wax paper or foil so you can stack the cookies on the pan. **4** Drop the batter by teaspoonfuls onto the prepared pans, leaving at least 3 inches between them. Use a fork or a spatula to flatten each mound of batter to evenly distribute the almonds before baking. **5** Place a single pan of cookies in the oven and bake for 5 to 7 minutes, until they start to bubble on the pan, spread and become thin, and take on a deep golden color. **6** Remove the pan from the oven and immediately replace with another prepared pan. Let the cookies you just removed firm up for a few seconds, then slide the spatula under each one and detach it. Move quickly. Either place on the rolling pin to curve or put them on one of the cooling pans. If the cookies become too cold and you can't remove them from the pan without shattering them, replace the pan in the oven for a few seconds to soften the cookies again. **7** Continue until all the cookies are baked. To reuse the pans, wipe them well, or line them with a fresh sheet of foil; just make sure the pans are cool before you spoon the batter onto them. **8** Store the flat cookies between sheets of parchment or wax paper in a tin or plastic container with a tight-fitting cover. I don't recommend trying to store curved ones more than a few hours before serving—they are so fragile they would turn into a tin of very delicious crumbs.

HAZELNUT TUILES

THESE ARE ATTRACTIVE AS WELL as delicious tuiles, especially if you use unblanched hazelnuts to make them—the little flecks of skin are so pretty in the cookies.

Makes about 30 cookies

1 large egg

1 large egg white

½ cup sugar

4 ounces (about 1 cup) ground raw hazelnuts

¼ cup all-purpose flour

1 teaspoon dark rum

2 or 3 cookie sheets or jelly roll pans, well buttered or covered with buttered foil

1 With a small rubber spatula, stir the egg and egg white together in a bowl to break them up. Stir in the sugar, then the hazelnuts, finally the flour. Be careful not to aerate the batter. Last, stir in the rum. **2** Before you place a pan of cookies in the oven to bake, have a thin-bladed spatula, pancake turner, or thin, flexible plastic scraper ready to remove the cookies from the pan. Also, have several rolling pins or other rounded forms (see page xvi) ready to curve the cookies over, if you intend to do that. If not, have a couple of pans covered with foil to receive the baked cookies—they are much too fragile to cool on a rack. Finally, have a jelly roll pan ready for the cooled, curved cookies. If you intend to leave the cookies flat, tear off some sheets of wax paper or foil so you can stack the cookies on the pan. **3** Drop the batter by teaspoonfuls onto the prepared pans, leaving at least 3 inches between them. Use a fork or a spatula to flatten each mound of batter to evenly distribute the hazelnuts before baking. **4** Place a single pan of cookies in the oven and bake for 5 to 7 minutes, until they start to bubble on the pan, spread and become thin, and take on a deep golden color. **5** Remove the pan from the oven and immediately replace with another prepared pan. Let the cookies you just removed firm up for a few seconds, then slide the spatula under each one and detach it. Move quickly. Either place on the rolling pin to curve or put them on one of the cooling pans. If the cookies become too cold and you can't remove them from the pan without shattering them, replace the pan in the oven for a few seconds to soften the cookies again. **6** Continue until all the cookies are baked. To reuse the pans, wipe them well, or line them with a fresh sheet of foil; just make sure the pans are cool before you spoon the batter onto them. **7** Store the flat cookies between sheets of parchment or wax paper in a tin or plastic container with a tight-fitting cover. I don't recommend trying to store curved ones more than a few hours before serving—they are so fragile they would turn into a tin of very delicious crumbs.

COCONUT TUILES

THESE CRISP, BUTTERY COOKIES ARE THE creation of Gramercy Tavern's brilliant pastry chef, Claudia Fleming. Claudia sandwiches sherbet or ice cream between them, but they are equally good on their own. This recipe, an excellent way to use leftover egg whites, makes a lot of cookies, but you can keep the batter in the refrigerator and use it over the course of several days. Though you may curve these after they are baked, Claudia leaves them flat and cools them on a rack. Remember to mix the batter the day before you intend to bake the cookies.

Makes about 50 cookies

2½ tablespoons unsalted butter, softened

1¼ cups sugar

7 large egg whites, at room temperature (warm the bowl of egg whites over a bowl of warm tap water if you have forgotten to bring them to room temperature)

2 cups unsweetened shredded coconut

¼ cup all-purpose flour

3 or 4 cookie sheets or jelly roll pans covered with buttered and floured foil

1 Combine the butter and sugar in the bowl of a standing electric mixer fitted with the paddle attachment. Beat on medium speed about 2 minutes, or until the mixture resembles wet sand. Gradually add the egg whites, making sure each addition of whites is absorbed before adding more. **2** On low speed beat in the coconut, then the flour. **3** Remove the bowl from the mixer and give the batter a good stir with a large rubber spatula. Cover the mixing bowl with plastic wrap and refrigerate the batter until the next day. **4** About 20 minutes before you intend to bake the cookies, set a rack in the middle level of the oven and preheat to 325 degrees. **5** Remove the batter from the refrigerator and stir it up again with a large rubber spatula. Drop heaping teaspoonfuls of the batter about 5 inches apart on the prepared pans, then use a small offset spatula or the back of a spoon to spread them to 4 inches in diameter. **6** Bake the cookies for about 15 minutes, or until they are a light golden color. **7** Remove the pan from the oven and immediately replace it with another. Leave the hot cookies to firm up for a few seconds, then quickly slide a spatula under each one to detach it. Place each cookie on a rack to cool, then quickly remove another. If the cookies cool too fast and harden, replace the pan in the oven for another minute to soften them again. **8** Continue until all the cookies are baked. To reuse the pans, just wipe them well, or line with a fresh sheet of foil. Make sure the pans are cool when you spoon the batter onto them. **9** Store the cookies between sheets of parchment or wax paper in a tin or plastic container with a tight-fitting cover.

PIERRE HERMÉ'S ORANGE TUILES

WHEN PIERRE HERMÉ CAME FROM PARIS to teach a class at Peter Kump's New York Cooking School in 1997, I assisted him. We had a crew of students, supervised by Andrea Tutunjian, doing all the prep, but before the class began he and I had to make about 75 of these extremely fragile cookies to decorate a delicate warm chocolate mousse cake we served with caramelized bananas. The recipe for the cake and accompanying bananas is in my book *Chocolate*.

These aren't difficult to make and they will turn a simple dessert of store-bought ice cream or sherbet into something memorable. But like all cookies this thin and delicate, they must be watched closely so they don't burn.

Makes about 20 cookies

2 teaspoons strained orange juice

¼ cup sugar

2 tablespoons flour

2 tablespoons unsalted butter, melted

Pinch salt

3 nonstick cookie sheets or jelly roll pans

1 Set a rack in the middle level of the oven and preheat to 325 degrees. **2** Combine the orange juice and sugar in a small bowl and use a small rubber spatula to mix well. Stir in the remaining ingredients in order. **3** Use a small offset spatula to spread ½ teaspoons of the batter paper-thin on the pans in streaks, about 1½ × 3¾ to 4 inches. Prepare all the pans at once, even though you will only be baking one at a time. **4** Bake one pan of cookies about 10 to 15 minutes, or until they are an even golden color. **5** Remove the pan from the oven and immediately replace with another. Let the cookies stand for a few seconds to cool slightly, then use a spatula or scraper to remove them from the pan to a rack to cool. **6** Keep the cookies between sheets of parchment or wax paper in a tin or plastic container with a tight-fitting cover. They keep for about a week.

CARAMEL PECAN COOKIES

THESE ARE ANOTHER COOKIE IN THE heavenly tuile family, and like the others, they taste just as good whether you curve them or not.

Many thanks to Jayne Sutton for sharing again from her endless recipe collection.

Makes about 30 cookies

4 tablespoons (½ stick) unsalted butter, softened

½ cup firmly packed dark brown sugar

1 large egg

½ teaspoon vanilla extract

⅛ teaspoon salt

3 tablespoons all-purpose flour

1 ounce (about ¼ cup) ground pecans

2 or 3 cookie sheets or jelly roll pans, well buttered or covered with buttered foil

1 Set a rack in the middle level of the oven and preheat to 350 degrees. **2** In a medium bowl, beat the butter with a wooden spoon or rubber spatula, then beat in the brown sugar. Add the egg and beat until smooth; beat in the vanilla and salt. Stir in the flour and ground nuts. **3** Drop the batter by small teaspoonfuls at least 3 inches apart on the prepared pans. Prepare all your pans even though you are only going to bake one at a time. **4** Have a thin-bladed spatula, pancake turner, or thin, flexible plastic scraper ready to remove the cookies from the pan, and several rolling pins or other forms (see page 66) to curve the cookies, if you intend to do that. If you want the cookies flat, have ready a couple of pans covered with foil to cool the baked cookies—they are much too fragile to put on a rack. Finally, have another jelly roll pan to receive the cooled, curved cookies. If you intend to leave the cookies flat, tear off some sheets of wax paper or foil to put between the layers of cookies on the pan. **5** Place a single pan in the oven and bake the cookies for 5 to 7 minutes, until they come to a simmer, spread and become thin, and take on a deep golden color. **6** Remove the pan from the oven and immediately replace it with another. Leave the cookies you just removed for a few seconds to firm up, then quickly slide the spatula under each one and detach it. Either place over the rolling pin to curve or put on one of the cooling pans. Move on to the next cookie immediately. If the cookies become too cold and hard to remove from the pan without shattering them, replace the pan in the oven to soften the cookies again. **7** Continue until all the cookies are baked. To reuse the pans, wipe them well, or line with a fresh sheet of foil. Make sure the pans are cool when you spoon the batter onto them. **8** Store the flat cookies between sheets of parchment or wax paper in a tin or plastic container with a tight-fitting cover. I don't recommend trying to store curved tuiles more than a few hours before serving—they are so fragile they would turn into a tin of very delicious crumbs.

(continued)

Drop Cookies

OTHER SHAPES: Curve the cookies around a cone-shaped metal form used to make cream horns (see Sources), a cannoli form for a cylinder, or the handle of a wooden spoon for a narrow cylinder. If you want to make these fancy shapes you must have another pair of hands to help with the shaping. Otherwise the cookies will cool and harden before you can get to them.

ALMOND LACE COOKIES

THIS EXQUISITELY DELICATE AND FRAGILE cookie is well worth the little trouble it takes to make. Usually with drop cookies, you can do other things while the cookies are baking, but with these, you must stand guard at the oven—a minute too long and they will burn. Also, if you wish to curve them, you have to time them carefully. Because they are so delicate they must be removed from the pan immediately after they are baked, so I recommend baking only one pan at a time.

By the way, it's no mistake that there is no flavoring in this recipe—the flavor comes from the delicate combination of the caramelized sugar blended with toasted almonds and butter.

Many thanks again to Jayne Sutton for another delicious recipe from her endless collection.

Makes about 30 cookies

8 tablespoons (1 stick) butter

½ cup sugar

2 tablespoons cream

3 ounces (about ¾ cup) finely ground blanched almonds

¼ cup flour

2 or 3 cookie sheets or jelly roll pans, well buttered or covered with foil

1 Set a rack in the middle level of the oven and preheat to 375 degrees. **2** Place the butter in a small saucepan and melt it over low heat. **3** Remove the pan from the heat, and stir in the sugar, cream, almonds, and flour. Return the pan to low heat and stir constantly with a wooden spoon, until the mixture thickens and bubbles. Remove the pan from the heat. **4** Drop the batter by small teaspoonfuls onto the prepared pans, leaving at least 3 inches between each cookie. Prepare all your pans even though you are only going to bake one at a time. 5 Have a thin-bladed spatula, pancake turner, or thin, flexible plastic scraper ready to remove the cookies from the pan, and several rolling pins or other forms (see page xvi) to curve the cookies over, if you intend to do that. If you want the cookies flat, have ready a couple of pans covered with foil to cool the baked cookies—they are much too fragile to put on a rack. Finally, have another jelly roll pan to receive the cooled, curved cookies. If you intend to leave the cookies flat, tear off some sheets of wax paper or foil to put between the layers of cookies on the pan. 6 Place a single pan in the oven and bake the cookies for 6 to 8 minutes, until they come to a simmer, spread and become thin, and take on a deep golden color. 7 Remove the pan from the oven and immedi-ately replace it with another. Leave the cookies you just removed for a few seconds to firm up, then quickly slide the spatula under each one and detach it. Either place over the rolling pin to curve or put on one of the cooling pans. Move on to the next cookie immediately. If the cookies become too cold and hard to remove from the pan without shattering them, replace the pan in the oven to soften the cookies again. 8 Continue until all the cookies are baked. To reuse the pans, wipe them well, or line with a fresh sheet of foil. Just make sure the pans are cool when you spoon the batter onto them. 9 Store the flat cookies between sheets of parchment or wax paper in a tin or plastic container with a tight-fitting cover. I don't recommend trying to store curved tuiles more than a few hours before serving—they are so fragile they would turn into a tin of very delicious crumbs.

REFRIGERATOR COOKIES

French Vanilla Sablés

Almond Cream Wafers

Palm Beach Lemon Cookies

Tennessee Icebox Cookies

Pistachio Thins

"Truffled" Breton Shortbreads

Chocolate Chip
Refrigerator Cookies

Dutch Almond Cookies

Old-fashioned
Molasses Slices

Orange Spice
Refrigerator Wafers

Zaleti Bolognesi

Dark Chocolate Sablés

Chocolate Mint Wafers

Chocolate Walnut Slices

Checkerboard Cookies

Sicilian Fig Pinwheels

Linzer Roll

Lemon Fruit Swirls

Two-Tone Peanut Butter Thins

WHEN I WAS A CHILD IN THE FIFTIES, THESE COOKIES WERE STILL KNOWN AS icebox cookies—and there were even a few actual iceboxes still in use. This type of cookie is made from a dough shaped into a cylinder or rectangle—or other compact form—then chilled. Right before baking, the dough is cut into thick or thin slices and placed on the pans. These cookies are the original convenience foods. You can mix up the dough today and slice and bake cookies tomorrow—or even next week or next month if you freeze the dough.

HINTS FOR REFRIGERATOR COOKIES

1 Make the shaped log of dough uniform so the cookies will be all the same size when they are sliced. Use a ruler to verify the size of the log given in the recipes. **2** Make sure the shaped dough is thoroughly chilled before attempting to cut it. Otherwise the dough will compress and lose its shape and the resulting cookies will not look neat. **3** Slice the cookies to the thickness specified in the recipe. If necessary, use a ruler and mark the piece of dough before you cut. **4** As you slice, rotate or turn the piece of dough so you aren't starting to cut at the same place every time—this is to keep the dough from getting squashed down and distorted. **5** If the dough softens while you are cutting it, replace it in the refrigerator until it becomes firm again before continuing.

HOW TO FORM REFRIGERATOR COOKIES

Each individual recipe has specific instructions for forming the dough. What follows is a general procedure for most recipes.

1 Scrape the dough from the mixer bowl onto a lightly floured work surface and shape and squeeze into a rough cylinder, about 10 inches long and 2 inches in diameter (individual recipes may specify different lengths or more than one roll). **2** Wrap a piece of parchment or wax paper around the dough and use the side of a cookie sheet or a piece of stiff cardboard to press the paper tight around it, as in the illustration (following page). Chill the dough until firm. **3** If you want square or rectangular cookies, press the dough into a plastic or foil-lined 8- or 9-inch square pan, then chill. Unmold the dough,

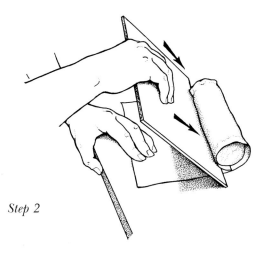

Step 2

cut it into 1½- to 2-inch wide lengths—depending on the depth of the dough in the pan—and slice across the rectangular bars to make individual cookies. **4** Another shape variation that makes good-looking refrigerator cookies is a finger (as in a lady finger). Form the dough into cylinders, and press down on the length of the cylinder so that when viewed from one of the narrow ends the dough appears to be a narrow oval. Chill, and cut finger-shaped cookies.

FRENCH VANILLA SABLÉS

THESE ARE EASY-TO-MAKE AND elegant cookies. *Sablé* means "sandy" in French and refers to the crumbly texture of this cookie. They may be varied infinitely by adding solid elements, such as nuts, chocolate chips, or diced dried or candied fruit to the dough. Or you could roll the formed dough in cinnamon sugar or chopped nuts to encrust the outside—use your imagination.

Makes about 40 cookies

12 tablespoons (1½ sticks) unsalted butter, softened

⅓ cup sugar

1 teaspoon vanilla extract

1 egg yolk

1½ cups all-purpose flour

2 cookie sheets or jelly roll pans lined with parchment or foil

1 In the bowl of a standing electric mixer fitted with the paddle attachment, beat the butter and sugar on medium speed until well mixed, light colored, and fluffy, about 4 or 5 minutes, then beat in the vanilla and egg yolk. Continue beating until very smooth, about 2 more minutes. **2** Scrape the bowl and beater well and beat in the flour. **3** Scrape the dough from the mixer bowl onto a lightly floured work surface and shape and squeeze it into a rough cylinder, about 10 inches long and 2 inches in diameter. **4** Roll a piece of parchment or wax paper around the dough. Tighten the paper around by pressing in with the side of a cookie sheet or a piece of stiff cardboard, as in the illustration opposite. Chill the dough until firm. Or, at this stage, it can be double-wrapped in plastic, frozen, and kept for up to several weeks. **5** When you are ready to bake the cookies, set the racks in the upper and lower thirds of the oven and preheat to 350 degrees. Slice the cookies ¼ inch thick, rotating the roll of dough often so it won't become squashed and mis-shapen from the weight of the knife. **6** Arrange the cookies on the prepared pans with about an inch between them in all directions. Bake for about 12 to 15 minutes, until the cookies have puffed somewhat and become dull and are firm to the touch. Slide the papers from the pans onto racks. **7** After the cookies have cooled, store them between sheets of parchment or wax paper in a tin or plastic container with a tight-fitting cover.

ALMOND CREAM WAFERS

THESE DELICATE COOKIES ARE STUDDED
with tiny pieces of sliced almond—just enough
to provide a little contrast of texture in an
exquisitely pure and simple cookie. These
are perfect cookies for tea or with ice creams
and sherbets.

Makes about 48 cookies

2½ cups all-purpose flour

1 cup sugar

¼ teaspoon salt

**16 tablespoons (2 sticks) cold unsalted butter,
cut into 16 pieces**

4 ounces (about 1 cup) blanched sliced almonds

½ cup heavy whipping cream

1 teaspoon vanilla extract

**3 cookie sheets or jelly roll pans covered
with parchment or foil**

1 In the work bowl of a food processor fitted
with the steel blade, combine the flour, sugar,
and salt. Pulse several times to mix. **2** Add the
butter and pulse until the butter is uniformly
mixed. Add the sliced almonds and pulse again
once or twice. **3** Add the cream and vanilla and
pulse until a sticky dough forms. **4** Scrape
the dough onto a lightly floured work surface
and shape and squeeze it into a rough cylinder,
about 12 inches long and 2 inches in diameter.
5 Roll a piece of parchment or wax paper
around the dough, then tighten the paper by
pressing it in with the side of a cookie sheet or a
piece of stiff cardboard, as in the illustration on
page 76. Chill the dough about 1 hour, or until
firm. Or, at this stage, it can be double-wrapped
in plastic, frozen, and kept for up to several
weeks. **6** When you are ready to bake the cookies, set the racks in the upper and lower thirds of
the oven and preheat to 350 degrees. Slice the
cookies ¼ inch thick. Rotate the roll of dough
often as you slice so it won't become squashed
from the weight of the knife. **7** Arrange the
cookies on the prepared pans about an inch
apart in all directions and bake them for about
15 to 18 minutes, until they have puffed somewhat and become dull; they should be firm to the
touch. Slide the papers from the pans onto racks.
8 After the cookies have cooled, store them
between sheets of parchment or wax paper in a
tin or plastic container with a tight-fitting cover.

PALM BEACH LEMON COOKIES

THIS ZINGY COOKIE COMES FROM MY old friend, veteran cooking teacher and renowned hostess Myrtle Singer, of Palm Beach, Florida.

Makes about 100 small thin cookies

3 cups all-purpose flour

½ teaspoon baking powder

½ teaspoon baking soda

¼ teaspoon salt

10 tablespoons (1¼ sticks) unsalted butter, softened

1 cup sugar, plus more for sprinkling the cookies before baking

Finely grated zest of 1 large lemon

3 large eggs, separated

4 tablespoons strained lemon juice

3 or 4 cookie sheets or jelly roll pans lined with parchment or foil (you will need to cool and reuse them)

1 In a bowl, combine the flour, baking powder, baking soda, and salt; stir well to mix. **2** In the bowl of a standing electric mixer fitted with the paddle attachment, beat the butter and sugar together on medium speed until well mixed, about a minute, then beat in the lemon zest. **3** Beat in the egg yolks, one at a time, beating until smooth after each addition. Lower the mixer speed and beat in half the flour mixture, then all the lemon juice. Scrape the bowl and beater well;

beat in the remaining flour mixture. **4** Scrape the dough onto a lightly floured work surface and shape and squeeze it into two rough cylinders, each about 8 inches long and 2 inches in diameter. **5** Roll a piece of parchment or wax paper around each piece of dough and tighten the paper by pressing it in with the side of a cookie sheet or a piece of stiff cardboard, as in the illustration on page 76. Chill the dough until firm. Or, at this stage, it can be double-wrapped in plastic, frozen, and kept for up to several weeks. **6** When you are ready to bake the cookies, set the racks in the upper and lower thirds of the oven and preheat to 350 degrees. **7** In a small bowl, beat the egg whites with a fork, just until mixed. Cut each log into approximately 48 cookies (six slices per inch). Make sure to rotate the roll of dough often so it doesn't become squashed from the weight of the knife. **8** Arrange the cookies on the prepared pans about an inch apart in all directions. Brush the surface of each cookie with the egg white, then sprinkle each cookie with a pinch of sugar. Bake the cookies for about 10 to 12 minutes, until they have spread slightly and are a very pale golden color. Slide the papers from the pans onto racks. **9** After the cookies have cooled, store them between sheets of parchment or wax paper in a tin or plastic container with a tight-fitting cover.

TENNESSEE ICEBOX COOKIES

WHEN I WAS ON TOUR PROMOTING MY book *Chocolate,* I made a stop in Nashville and was invited to be on the radio with Mindy Merrell, whom I've known for many years in her capacity as publicist for the Jack Daniel's distillery. Mindy's other guest that day was Tammy Algood from the University of Tennessee's Agricultural Extension Service and Tammy had brought a basket of treats to the studio. One of them was this cookie, which was so good I immediately begged for the recipe. It comes from her grandmother Betsey McPherson and the cookies are heavenly.

Makes about 80 cookies

3 cups all-purpose flour

1 teaspoon baking soda

¼ teaspoon salt

16 tablespoons (2 sticks) unsalted butter, softened

2½ cups firmly packed light brown sugar

1 tablespoon vanilla extract

2 large eggs

4 ounces (about 1 cup) coarsely chopped slivered almonds

3 or 4 cookie sheets or jelly roll pans lined with parchment or foil (you will need to cool and reuse them)

1 In a bowl, combine the flour, baking soda, and salt; stir well to mix. **2** In the bowl of a standing electric mixer fitted with the paddle attachment, beat the butter and brown sugar together on medium speed until well mixed, about a minute, then beat in the vanilla. **3** Beat in the eggs, one at a time, beating smooth after each addition. Scrape the bowl and beater well and beat in the flour mixture followed immediately by the almonds. **4** Scrape the dough onto a lightly floured work surface and shape and squeeze it into two rough cylinders, each about 10 inches long and 2 inches in diameter. **5** Roll a piece of parchment or wax paper around each piece of dough and tighten by pressing it in with the side of a cookie sheet or a piece of stiff cardboard, as in the illustration on page 76. Chill the dough until firm. Or, at this stage, it can be double-wrapped in plastic, frozen, and kept for up to several weeks. **6** When you are ready to bake the cookies, set the racks in the upper and lower thirds of the oven and preheat to 350 degrees. Slice the cookies ¼ inch thick, rotating the roll of dough often as you slice so it doesn't become squashed from the weight of the knife. **7** Arrange the cookies on the prepared pans about an inch apart in all directions and bake them for about 12 to 15 minutes, until they have puffed somewhat and have become dull and are firm to the touch. Slide the papers from the pans onto racks. **8** After the cookies have cooled, store them between sheets of parchment or wax paper in a tin or plastic container with a tight-fitting cover.

PISTACHIO THINS

ANY RECIPE IS ALWAYS DRESSED UP BY the aromatic flavor and striking appearance of pistachios. Here, the nuts are in a meltingly tender dough and create a delicious cookie. Make sure when you bake the cookies to leave them pale, or the color of the pistachios will be obscured.

Makes about 40 cookies

1¼ cups all-purpose flour

½ cup cornstarch

¼ teaspoon salt

12 tablespoons (1½ sticks) unsalted butter, softened

⅔ cup confectioners' sugar

1 large egg, separated

1 teaspoon finely grated lemon zest

6 ounces (about 1½ cups) finely chopped unsalted pistachios, divided

2 or 3 cookie sheets or jelly roll pans lined with parchment or foil

1 In a bowl, combine the flour, cornstarch, and salt; stir well to mix. **2** In the bowl of a standing electric mixer fitted with the paddle attachment, beat together the butter and confectioners' sugar at medium speed until well mixed, about a minute. **3** Beat in the egg yolk and lemon zest until they are well incorporated and the mixture is smooth. Scrape the bowl and beater well and beat in the flour mixture. Finally, beat in 1 cup of the chopped pistachios. **4** Scrape the dough onto a lightly floured work surface and shape and squeeze it into a rough cylinder, about 10 inches long and 2 inches in diameter. **5** Roll a piece of parchment or wax paper around the dough and tighten it by pressing in with the side of a cookie sheet or a piece of stiff cardboard, as in the illustration on page 76. Quickly unwrap the dough and roll it out onto the work surface. Paint the dough all around with the reserved egg white and roll it in the remaining ½ cup pistachios. The outside of the dough should be completely covered. Rewrap the dough in parchment or wax paper and repeat the tightening if the shape has become distorted. Chill the dough until firm. Or, at this stage, it can be double-wrapped in plastic, frozen, and kept for up to several weeks. **6** When you are ready to bake the cookies, set the racks in the upper and lower thirds of the oven and preheat to 350 degrees. Slice the cookies ¼ inch thick, rotating the roll often so it doesn't become squashed from the weight of the knife. **7** Arrange the cookies on the prepared pans about an inch apart in all directions and bake them for about 10 to 12 minutes, until they have puffed somewhat and become dull and feel firm to the touch. Slide the papers from the pans onto racks. **8** After the cookies have cooled, store them between sheets of parchment or wax paper in a tin or plastic container with a tight-fitting cover.

"TRUFFLED" BRETON SHORTBREADS

BRETON SHORTBREADS OR SABLÉS ARE very popular in France, and this amusing variation with chunks of milk chocolate was created by one of France's best-known pastry chefs, Frederic Bau. "Truffled" in recipes usually refers to foods studded with black Périgord truffles, an aromatic fungus, sort of a subterranean mushroom. The chopped chocolate throughout the cylinder of cookie dough makes the roll of dough resemble a sweet trompe l'oeil version of a rich sausage. This recipe is loosely adapted from *Caprices de Chocolat ("Chocolate Fantasies")* (Editions Albin Michel, 1998) by Bau.

Makes about 48 cookies

"Truffled" Breton Shortbread (LEFT) *and Tennessee Icebox Cookie, page 80*

2 cups all-purpose flour

½ teaspoon baking powder

¼ teaspoon salt

10 tablespoons (1¼ sticks) unsalted butter, softened

¾ cup sugar

4 egg yolks

4 ounces milk chocolate cut into ¼-inch pieces, sifted after chopping to remove all the tiny particles

2 cookie sheets or jelly roll pans lined with parchment or foil

1 In a bowl, combine the flour, baking powder, and salt; stir well to mix. **2** In the bowl of a standing electric mixer fitted with the paddle attachment, beat together the butter and sugar on medium speed until well mixed and fluffy, about 4 or 5 minutes, then beat in the egg yolks, one at a time, beating smooth after each addition. **3** Scrape the bowl and beater well and beat in the flour mixture. Then, using a large rubber spatula, mix in the chocolate. **4** Scrape the dough onto a lightly floured work surface and shape and squeeze it into a rough cylinder, about 12 inches long and 2 inches in diameter. **5** Roll a piece of parchment or wax paper around the dough and tighten the paper by pressing it in with the side of a cookie sheet or a piece of stiff cardboard, as in the illustration on page 76. Chill the dough until firm. Or, at this stage, it can be double-wrapped in plastic, frozen, and kept for up to several weeks. **6** When you are ready to bake the cookies, set the racks in the upper and lower thirds of the oven and preheat to 350 degrees. Slice the cookies ¼ inch thick, rotating the roll often so it doesn't become squashed from the weight of the knife. **7** Arrange the cookies on the prepared pans about an inch apart in all directions and bake them for about 12 to 15 minutes, until they have puffed somewhat and become dull and feel firm to the touch. Slide the papers from the pans to racks to cool. **8** After the cookies have cooled, store them between sheets of parchment or wax paper in a tin or plastic container with a tight-fitting cover.

CHOCOLATE CHIP REFRIGERATOR COOKIES

THINK OF THIS AS MAKING YOUR VERY own brand of "slice and bake" cookies, but with better ingredients than you find in the prepared supermarket dough. Of course all refrigerator cookies are slice and bake but, for some reason, it's always more reassuring to have almost-instant chocolate chip cookies.

Makes about 60 cookies

2½ cups all-purpose flour

¼ teaspoon baking soda

¼ teaspoon salt

16 tablespoons (2 sticks) unsalted butter, softened

½ cup granulated sugar

½ cup firmly packed light brown sugar

1 teaspoon vanilla extract

2 large eggs

One 12-ounce bag semisweet chocolate chips

3 or 4 cookie sheets or jelly roll pans lined with parchment or foil (you will need to cool and reuse them)

(continued)

1 In a bowl, combine the flour, baking soda, and salt; stir well to mix. **2** In the bowl of a standing electric mixer fitted with the paddle attachment, beat together the butter and sugars on medium speed until well mixed, about a minute, then beat in the vanilla. **3** Beat in the eggs, one at a time, beating smooth after each addition. Lower the mixer speed and beat in the flour mixture, then the chocolate chips. **4** Scrape the dough onto a lightly floured work surface and shape and squeeze it into two rough cylinders, each about 8 inches long and 2 inches in diameter. **5** Roll a piece of parchment or wax paper around each piece and tighten it by pressing it in with the side of a cookie sheet or a piece of stiff cardboard, as in the illustration on page 76. Chill the dough until firm. Or, at this stage, it can be double-wrapped in plastic, frozen, and kept for up to several weeks. **6** When you are ready to bake the cookies, set the racks in the upper and lower thirds of the oven and preheat to 350 degrees. Slice the cookies ¼ inch thick, rotating the roll often so it doesn't become squashed from the weight of the knife. **7** Arrange the cookies on the prepared pans about an inch apart in all directions. Bake the cookies for about 12 to 15 minutes, until they have spread slightly and are a very pale golden color. Slide the papers from the pans onto racks. **8** After the cookies have cooled, store them between sheets of parchment or wax paper in a tin or plastic container with a tight-fitting cover.

DUTCH ALMOND COOKIES

THIS IS A VERSION OF THE POPULAR Dutch cookie called Janhagel—one of these arrives on the saucer when you order a cup of coffee in Holland. This easy-to-prepare recipe makes a lot of cookies, but they may be baked over several days.

Makes about 90 cookies

3 cups all-purpose flour

1 teaspoon baking soda

1 teaspoon ground cinnamon

12 tablespoons (1½ sticks) unsalted butter, cut into 12 pieces

1 cup firmly packed light brown sugar

1 cup granulated sugar

6 tablespoons water

2 cups whole blanched almonds

TOPPING

½ cup granulated sugar

1 teaspoon ground cinnamon

One 8-inch square pan, buttered and lined with plastic wrap or foil, for chilling the dough

2 or 3 cookie sheets or jelly roll pans covered with parchment or foil (you will need to cool and reuse them)

1 In a bowl, combine the flour, baking soda, and cinnamon; stir well to mix. **2** Melt the butter in a large saucepan over medium heat. Remove from the heat and stir in the brown sugar, granulated sugar, and water. Return to the heat and bring to a boil, stirring occasionally, until the sugar has melted. Remove from the heat and stir in the almonds. **3** Pour the sugar and almond mixture into a large bowl and stir in the dry ingredients. Press the dough into the prepared square pan, cover with plastic wrap, and chill overnight or until firm. **4** About 20 minutes before you are ready to bake the cookies, set the racks in the upper and lower thirds of the oven and preheat to 350 degrees. **5** To make the topping, combine the sugar and cinnamon thoroughly in a small bowl. **6** Unmold the brick of cookie dough from the pan and place it on a cutting board. Cut the brick into three bars, each 8 × 2½ × 1¼ inches. (The bars will be just a little more than 2½ inches wide.) Wrap two of the bars and return them to the refrigerator while you cut the first. Place it on a cutting board and slice the cookies about ¼ inch thick. **7** As you cut the cookies, place them on the prepared pans an inch apart in all directions. Just before putting the pans in the oven, sprinkle the tops of the cookies generously with the cinnamon sugar. **8** Bake the cookies for about 15 minutes, or until they are golden and firm. **9** Slide the papers onto racks. The cookies will become crisp as they cool. Repeat with the remaining bars of dough. **10** Store the cookies between sheets of parchment or wax paper in a tin or plastic container with a tight-fitting cover.

NOTE If you don't want to bake all the cookies at once, wrap and freeze one or two of the bars of dough for up to a month. When you want to bake them, thaw the bar(s) of dough overnight in the refrigerator and proceed with the recipe.

OLD-FASHIONED MOLASSES SLICES

THE DARK, AROMATIC FLAVOR
of molasses makes these crisp cookies
perfect for the first cool days of autumn.

Makes about 50 cookies

2¼ cups all-purpose flour

1 teaspoon baking powder

1 teaspoon ground cinnamon

½ teaspoon ground ginger

¼ teaspoon ground cloves

⅔ cup molasses

6 tablespoons (¾ stick) unsalted butter,
cut into 8 pieces

2 or 3 cookie sheets or jelly roll pans covered
with parchment or foil

1 In a bowl, combine the flour, baking powder,
and spices; stir well to mix. **2** Place the
molasses and butter in a large saucepan over low
heat; stir occasionally until the butter melts and
the mixture comes to a simmer. Remove from the
heat and cool to room temperature. **3** Use a
large rubber spatula to stir the flour mixture
thoroughly into the cooled molasses and butter

mixture. **4** Scrape the dough onto a lightly
floured work surface and shape and squeeze it
into a rough cylinder, about 10 inches long and
2 inches in diameter. **5** Roll a piece of parchment or wax paper around the dough and
tighten the paper by pressing it in with the side
of a cookie sheet or a piece of stiff cardboard, as
in the illustration on page 76. Chill the dough
until firm. Or, at this stage, it can be double-
wrapped in plastic, frozen, and kept for up to
several weeks. **6** When you are ready to bake
the cookies, set the racks in the upper and lower
thirds of the oven and preheat to 350 degrees.
Slice the cookies about 5 to an inch, rotating
the roll often so it doesn't become squashed
from the weight of the knife. **7** Arrange the
cookies on the prepared pans about an inch
apart in all directions and bake them for about
10 to 12 minutes, until they have puffed somewhat and become dull and feel firm to the touch.
Slide the papers from the pans onto racks.
8 After the cookies have cooled, store them
between sheets of parchment or wax paper in a
tin or plastic container with a tight-fitting cover.

ORANGE SPICE REFRIGERATOR WAFERS

THIS IS A COMBINATION OF TWO OF MY favorite flavors. Sometimes I add ½ teaspoon of freshly ground white pepper to the spice blend for a little punch.

Makes about 60 thin cookies

1½ cups all-purpose flour

1 teaspoon baking soda

1 teaspoon ground cinnamon

1 teaspoon ground ginger

¼ teaspoon ground cloves

8 tablespoons (1 stick) unsalted butter, softened

½ cup granulated sugar

¼ cup firmly packed light brown sugar

Finely grated zest of 1 large orange

½ teaspoon orange extract

1 large egg

3 or 4 cookie sheets or jelly roll pans lined with parchment or foil (you will need to cool and reuse them)

1 In a bowl, combine the flour, baking soda, and spices; stir well to mix. **2** In the bowl of a standing electric mixer fitted with the paddle attachment, beat together the butter and both sugars on medium speed until well mixed, about a minute. Then beat in the orange zest and extract. **3** Beat in the egg until well incorporated and the mixture is smooth. Scrape the bowl and beater well, then beat in the flour mixture. **4** Scrape the dough onto a lightly floured work surface and shape and squeeze it into a rough cylinder, about 10 inches long and 2 inches in diameter. **5** Roll a piece of parchment or wax paper around the dough and tighten the paper by pressing it in with the side of a cookie sheet or a piece of stiff cardboard, as in the illustration on page 76. Chill the dough until firm. Or, at this stage, it can be double-wrapped in plastic, frozen, and kept for up to several weeks. **6** When you are ready to bake the cookies, set the racks in the upper and lower thirds of the oven and preheat to 350 degrees. Cut the cookies six slices per inch, rotating the roll often so it doesn't become squashed from the weight of the knife. **7** Arrange the cookies on the prepared pans about 2 inches apart in all directions and bake for about 12 to 15 minutes, until they have puffed somewhat and become dull and feel firm to the touch. Slide the papers from the pans onto racks. **8** After the cookies have cooled, store them between layers of parchment or wax paper in a tin or plastic container with a tight-fitting cover.

ZALETI BOLOGNESI

I SAW THE LEGENDARY ITALIAN BAKER and teacher Margherita Simili prepare these when she came to give a class at Peter Kump's New York Cooking School in the late eighties. Though unfortunately I long ago lost Margherita's recipe, my re-creation here is very much like hers in flavor and texture. Zaleti (*gialetti* in Italian) means "little yellow things" in Emilian dialect.

Stone-ground cornmeal will assure you of a better cornmeal flavor. Most other cornmeal has been degerminated so it keeps but loses a lot of corn flavor in the process.

Makes about 60 thin cookies

1½ cups all-purpose flour

1½ cups stone-ground yellow cornmeal

¼ teaspoon salt

1 teaspoon baking powder

12 tablespoons (1½ sticks) unsalted butter, softened

½ cup sugar

1 teaspoon vanilla extract

2 large eggs

2 or 3 cookie sheets or jelly roll pans covered with parchment or foil

1 In a bowl, combine the flour, cornmeal, salt, and baking powder; stir well to mix. **2** In the bowl of a standing electric mixer fitted with the paddle attachment, beat together the butter and sugar on medium speed until soft and light, about 3 or 4 minutes. Beat in the vanilla, then the eggs, one at a time, beating until smooth after each addition. On low speed, beat in the dry ingredients. **3** Scrape the dough onto a lightly floured work surface and shape and squeeze it into two rough cylinders, each about 8 inches long and 2 inches in diameter. **4** Roll a piece of parchment or wax paper around each piece of dough and tighten it by pressing it in with the side of a cookie sheet or a piece of stiff cardboard, as in the illustration on page 76. Chill the dough until firm. Or, at this stage, it can be double-wrapped in plastic, frozen, and kept for up to several weeks. **5** When you are ready to bake the cookies, set the racks in the upper and lower thirds of the oven and preheat to 350 degrees. Slice the cookies ¼ inch thick, rotating the roll often so it doesn't become squashed from the weight of the knife. **6** Arrange the cookies on the prepared pans about an inch apart in all directions and bake them for about 10 to 12 minutes, until they have puffed somewhat and become dull and feel firm to the touch. Slide the papers from the pans onto racks. **7** After the cookies have cooled, store them between sheets of parchment or wax paper in a tin or plastic container with a tight-fitting cover.

DARK CHOCOLATE SABLÉS

THIS IS AN EXTREMELY DARK AND chocolaty cookie for one made with cocoa powder rather than melted chocolate. Though the cookie is splendid on its own, I also like to add nuts or chocolate chips to the dough, just for variety.

Makes about 40 cookies

1½ cups all-purpose flour

⅓ cup alkalized (Dutch process) cocoa powder, sifted after measuring

½ teaspoon baking soda

⅛ teaspoon salt

8 tablespoons (1 stick) unsalted butter, softened

½ cup sugar

1 teaspoon vanilla extract

1 large egg

2 cookie sheets or jelly roll pans lined with parchment or foil

1 In a bowl, combine the flour, cocoa, baking soda, and salt; stir well to mix. **2** In the bowl of a standing electric mixer fitted with the paddle attachment, beat together the butter and sugar on medium speed until well mixed and fluffy, about 4 or 5 minutes, then beat in the vanilla and egg. Continue beating until the mixture is very smooth, about 2 minutes longer. **3** Scrape the bowl and beater well and beat in the flour mixture. **4** Scrape the dough onto a lightly floured work surface and shape and squeeze it into a rough cylinder, about 10 inches long and 2 inches in diameter. **5** Roll a piece of parchment or wax paper around the dough and tighten the paper by pressing it in with the side of a cookie sheet or a piece of stiff cardboard, as in the illustration on page 76. Chill the dough until firm. Or, at this stage, it can be double-wrapped in plastic, frozen, and kept for up to several weeks. **6** When you are ready to bake the cookies, set the racks in the upper and lower thirds of the oven and preheat to 350 degrees. Slice the cookies ¼ inch thick, rotating the roll of dough often as you slice so it doesn't become squashed from the weight of the knife. **7** Arrange the cookies on the prepared pans about an inch apart in all directions and bake them for about 10 to 12 minutes, until they have puffed somewhat and become dull and feel firm to the touch. Slide the papers from the pans onto racks. **8** After the cookies have cooled, store them between sheets of parchment or foil in a tin or plastic container with a tight-fitting cover.

CHOCOLATE MINT WAFERS

I LIKE THE CHOCOLATE-MINT COMBI-
nation and dress up these cookies by streaking
them with Sugar-Based Chocolate Glaze for
Cookies (page 319), or sandwiching them with
Fluffy Egg White Icing (page 314).

Makes about 90 cookies

2 cups all-purpose flour

1 teaspoon baking powder

½ teaspoon salt

**⅔ cup alkalized (Dutch process) cocoa powder,
sifted after measuring**

12 tablespoons (1½ sticks) unsalted butter, softened

1 cup sugar

1 large egg

4 tablespoons white or green crème de menthe

**3 or 4 cookie sheets or jelly roll pans lined with parch-
ment or foil (you will need to cool and reuse them)**

1 In a bowl, combine the flour, baking powder,
salt, and cocoa; stir well to mix. **2** In the bowl of
a standing electric mixer fitted with the paddle
attachment, beat together the butter and sugar
on medium speed until well mixed, about a
minute. **3** Beat in the egg until it is well incorporated and the mixture is smooth. Scrape the
bowl and beater well and beat in half the flour

mixture. Beat in the crème de menthe. Scrape
the bowl and beater, and finally, beat in the rest
of the flour mixture. **4** Scrape the dough onto
a lightly floured work surface and shape and
squeeze it into a rough cylinder, about 12 inches
long and 2 inches in diameter. **5** Roll a piece of
parchment or wax paper around the dough and
tighten it by pressing it in with the side of a
cookie sheet or a piece of stiff cardboard, as in
the illustration on page 76. Chill the dough until
firm. Or, at this stage, it can be double-wrapped
in plastic, frozen, and kept for up to several
weeks. **6** When you are ready to bake the cookies, set the racks in the upper and lower thirds of
the oven and preheat to 350 degrees. Slice the
cookies ⅛ inch thick, rotating the dough often so
it doesn't become squashed from the weight of
the knife. **7** Arrange the cookies on the prepared pans about an inch apart in all directions
and bake them for about 10 to 12 minutes, until
they have puffed somewhat and become dull and
feel firm to the touch. Slide the papers from the
pans onto racks. **8** After the cookies have
cooled, store them between sheets of parchment
or wax paper in a tin or plastic container with a
tight-fitting cover.

CHOCOLATE WALNUT SLICES

THIS CRISP, NUTTY CHOCOLATE TREAT comes from Phil Krampetz, co-proprietor of the Cultured Cup, Dallas's best tea store.

Makes about 40 cookies

1¾ **cups all-purpose flour**

½ **teaspoon baking powder**

¼ **teaspoon salt**

8 **tablespoons (1 stick) unsalted butter, softened**

¾ **cup sugar**

1 **large egg**

2 **ounces unsweetened chocolate, melted and cooled**

1 **teaspoon vanilla extract**

4 **ounces (about 1 cup) coarsely chopped walnut pieces**

2 **or 3 cookie sheets or jelly roll pans lined with parchment or foil (you will need to cool and reuse them)**

1 In a bowl, combine the flour, baking powder, and salt; stir well to mix. **2** In the bowl of a standing electric mixer fitted with the paddle attachment, beat the butter and sugar together on medium speed until well mixed, about a minute. **3** Beat in the egg until it is well incorporated and the mixture is smooth, then beat in the chocolate and vanilla. Scrape the bowl and beater well and beat in the flour mixture followed immediately by the walnuts. **4** Scrape the dough onto a lightly floured work surface and shape and squeeze it into a rough cylinder, about 10 inches long and 2 inches in diameter. **5** Roll a piece of parchment or wax paper around the dough and tighten it by pressing it in with the side of a cookie sheet or a piece of stiff cardboard, as in the illustration on page 76. Chill the dough until firm. Or, at this stage, it can be double-wrapped in plastic, frozen, and kept for up to several weeks. **6** When you are ready to bake the cookies, set the racks in the upper and lower thirds of the oven and preheat to 350 degrees. Slice the cookies ¼ inch thick, rotating the dough often so it doesn't become squashed from the weight of the knife. **7** Arrange the cookies on the prepared pans about an inch apart in all directions and bake them for about 10 to 12 minutes, until they have puffed somewhat and become dull and feel firm to the touch. Slide the papers from the pans onto racks. **8** After the cookies have cooled, store them between sheets of parchment or wax paper in a tin or plastic container with a tight-fitting cover.

CHECKERBOARD COOKIES

THIS FUN COOKIE IS EASY TO MAKE when you have equal amounts of vanilla and chocolate doughs. Follow the directions below exactly, especially with regard to the chilling times, and your reward will be perfect checkerboard cookies.

Makes about 100 cookies

1 batch French Vanilla Sablés (page 77)

1 batch Dark Chocolate Sablés (page 89)

1 egg white for adhering the dough

3 or 4 cookie sheets or jelly roll pans lined with parchment or foil

1 Press the French Vanilla Sablés dough into a 1-inch-thick square, then wrap and chill. Do the same with the Dark Chocolate Sablés dough. Chill the doughs for several hours or up to several days. **2** When you are ready to form the cookies, remove the vanilla dough from the refrigerator, unwrap it, and on a floured surface roll it

out to an 8 × 12-inch rectangle, about ⅜ inch thick. Slide the dough onto a cookie sheet, cover it with plastic wrap, and chill it until firm again, about 30 minutes. Repeat with the chocolate dough. The dough may remain chilled for several days at this point as long as you have not already chilled it for a long time; if it is adequately covered, it won't dry out. **3** Remove the vanilla dough from the refrigerator and paint it with lightly beaten egg white. Slide the chocolate dough over it and put a jelly roll pan or cookie sheet on top of the stack of dough. Gently press the pan down so the two layers of dough adhere. **4** Immediately cut the layered dough in half, making two 8 × 6-inch rectangles. Paint the top of one rectangle with egg white and place the second one over it. You now have four alternating layers of vanilla and chocolate dough. Repeat the gentle pressing with the pan, then wrap and chill the dough several hours before continuing. **5** Remove the dough from the refrigerator and place it on a cutting board. Using a long sharp knife, cut the dough across the 6-inch side into sixteen ⅜-inch-thick slices. **6** Place one of the slices of dough cut side down on the work surface, so that the four alternating stripes of dough are facing upward. Paint the dough with egg white and stack another slice of dough on top of it, making sure that the slices alternate: If the first slice is chocolate, white, chocolate, white

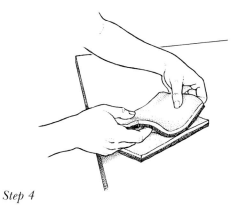

Step 4

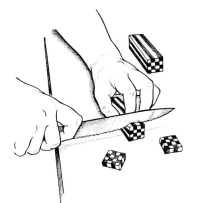

Step 6

Step 8

from left to right, turn the second slice so it is white, chocolate, white, chocolate from left to right. Moisten the top slice and stack another slice on top of it. Again make sure they alternate in colors. Moisten the top slice and stack a fourth and final slice on top of it, again making the colors alternate. Repeat with the remaining slices of dough. You will have four stacks. **7** Gently press each side of each stack of dough to square it and wrap and refrigrate for several hours. They may be well wrapped and frozen at this point—defrost in the refrigerator before continuing. **8** When you are ready to bake the cookies, set the racks in the upper and lower thirds of the oven and preheat to 350 degrees. Slice the cookies ¼ inch thick, turning the stack of dough often so it doesn't become squashed from the weight of the knife. **9** Arrange the cookies on the prepared pans about an inch apart in all directions and bake them for about 10 to 12 minutes, until they have puffed somewhat and become dull and feel firm to the touch. Slide the papers from the pans onto racks. **10** After the cookies have cooled, store them between sheets of parchment or wax paper in a tin or plastic container with a tight-fitting cover.

Refrigerator Cookies

SICILIAN FIG PINWHEELS

THERE ARE LOTS OF POPULAR RECIPES around for a refrigerator cookie with a date filling. They gave me the idea of using a Sicilian-inspired fig filling in a similar type cookie. These are perfect for the holidays— they have that requisite spicy flavor we always associate with Christmas cookies.

Makes about 96 cookies

COOKIE DOUGH

2 cups all-purpose flour

⅓ cup sugar

¼ teaspoon salt

½ teaspoon baking powder

8 tablespoons (1 stick) cold unsalted butter, cut into 10 pieces

1 tablespoon finely grated orange zest

2 large eggs

FIG FILLING

One 12-ounce package dried Calimyrna figs, stemmed and diced (about 2 cups)

⅓ cup apricot preserves

2 ounces semisweet chocolate, cut into ¼-inch pieces

½ teaspoon ground cinnamon

¼ teaspoon ground cloves

3 ounces (about ¾ cup) finely chopped walnut pieces

2 or 3 cookie sheets or jelly roll pans covered with parchment or foil

1 For the dough, in the work bowl of a food processor fitted with the steel blade, combine the flour, sugar, salt, and baking powder. Pulse several times to mix. Add the butter and the orange zest and pulse repeatedly at 1-second intervals until the mixture is fine and powdery. Add the eggs through the feed tube and continue to pulse until the dough forms a ball. Scrape the dough onto a lightly floured work surface and shape it into a 6-inch square. Wrap in plastic and chill while you prepare the filling. **2** Place the stemmed and diced figs in a saucepan and cover with water. Bring to a full boil over medium heat. Drain and cool the figs. **3** In the work bowl of a food processor fitted with the steel blade, combine the cooled figs with the remaining filling ingredients except the walnuts. Pulse until the mixture is finely ground, but not a puree. Scrape the filling into a bowl and stir in the walnuts. If the filling is very thick and difficult to spread, stir in 1 to 2 tablespoons water. **4** To form the cookies, remove the dough from the refrigerator and unwrap it. Place it on a floured work surface and knead it briefly until smooth and malleable. Flour the dough and the work surface and roll it out into a 12-inch square. Cut the square in half to make two 6 × 12-inch rectangles. Spread half the filling evenly over each, then roll them up, jelly roll fashion from a long side. Try not to lengthen the rolls as you roll or the eventual sliced cookies will be too small. **5** Wrap each

cylinder in plastic wrap or wax paper. Chill again for from 2 hours to 3 days. **6** When you are ready to bake the cookies, set the racks in the upper and lower thirds of the oven and preheat to 350 degrees. Slice the cookies ¼ inch thick, rotating the roll often so it doesn't become squashed from the weight of the knife.
7 Arrange the cookies on the prepared pans about an inch apart in all directions and bake them for about 12 to 15 minutes, until they are no longer shiny and the bottoms are light brown. Slide the papers from the pans onto racks. **8** After the cookies have cooled, store them between sheets of parchment or wax paper in a tin or plastic container with a tight-fitting cover.

LINZER ROLL

THIS UNUSUAL COOKIE IS ADAPTED from *Continental Confectionery* by Walter Bach-mann (Maclaren and Sons, Limited, London, 1950). Bachmann, a Swiss pastry chef, lived in London and in the 1950s published many books about professional baking and cooking.

The dough is reminiscent of that used for a Linzertorte (see Viennese Linzer Squares, page 23), but this takes the idea and whirls it into a spiral with raspberry jam delineating the curves. A spectacular-looking cookie.

Makes about 40 cookies

8 tablespoons (1 stick) unsalted butter, softened

½ cup confectioners' sugar

½ teaspoon vanilla extract

1 large egg yolk

½ teaspoon finely grated lemon zest

Pinch ground cloves

1½ cups all-purpose flour

1 cup seedless raspberry jam (or one 12-ounce jar)

2 or 3 cookie sheets or jelly roll pans covered with parchment or foil

(continued)

1 In the bowl of a standing electric mixer fitted with the paddle attachment, beat the butter and confectioners' sugar on medium speed until soft and light, about 3 minutes. Beat in the vanilla, then the egg yolk, zest, and cloves. Continue beating until very light, about 3 minutes longer. Stop and scrape down the bowl and beater, then on low speed beat in the flour. **2** Scrape the dough onto a piece of plastic wrap. Press the dough into an 8-inch square and wrap it well. Chill the dough an hour or two until firm.

3 For the raspberry filling, measure the jam into a medium saucepan and stir it up with a wooden spoon. Place over low heat and bring to a simmer, stirring occasionally. Allow the jam to simmer and reduce for about 5 minutes. Scrape the reduced jam into a small bowl. **4** After the dough has chilled, unwrap it and place it on a floured work surface. Lightly flour the dough and press and pound it gently with a rolling pin to soften it. Roll the dough out into a 10-inch square. Spread each rectangle of dough evenly with the cooled reduced jam, then roll each up from a long end, jelly roll style, into a tight cylinder. Try not to stretch or lengthen the cylinder as you roll it or the cookies will be too small. **5** Wrap and chill the cylinders. **6** When you are ready to bake the cookies, set the racks in the upper and lower thirds of the oven and preheat to 350 degrees. Slice the cookies ¼ inch thick, rotating the dough often so it doesn't become squashed from the weight of the knife. **7** Arrange the cookies on the prepared pans about an inch apart in all directions and bake them for about 12 to 15 minutes, until they have puffed somewhat and become dull and feel firm to the touch. Slide the papers from the pans to racks to cool. **8** After the cookies have cooled, store them between sheets of parchment or wax paper in a tin or plastic container with a tight-fitting cover.

LEMON FRUIT SWIRLS

THIS DELICIOUS AND BEAUTIFUL cookie comes from my friend, veteran baker and award-winning author Flo Braker. Back in the mid-eighties, Flo's book *The Simple Art of Perfect Baking* (Chapters Paperback, 1992) was the first serious and detailed book about fancy European and American pastries to be published in the United States; it opened the door for the rest of us who write about that subject.

Makes about 100 thin cookies

2½ cups all-purpose flour

1 cup sugar

¼ teaspoon salt

16 tablespoons (2 sticks) unsalted butter, cut into ½-inch-thick slices

1 large egg

1 teaspoon vanilla extract

4 teaspoons finely grated lemon zest

1 cup finely chopped dried apricots

½ cup finely chopped pecan pieces

3 or 4 cookie sheets or jelly roll pans covered with parchment or foil

1 In the bowl of a food processor fitted with the steel blade, combine the flour, sugar, and salt. Pulse several times to mix. Add the butter all at once and pulse repeatedly until the mixture becomes the consistency of cornmeal. **2** Whisk the egg with the vanilla and lemon zest in a small bowl. With the motor running, pour the egg mixture through the feed tube and process just until the dough forms a ball. **3** Divide the dough into two equal pieces. Place one half in a bowl and stir in the chopped fruit and pecans. **4** Roll out one piece of dough at a time between sheets of wax paper into an 8 × 16-inch rectangle. Slide the pieces of dough onto a cookie sheet and chill them until firm—2 hours to 3 days, if necessary. **5** To form the dough into cookie logs, remove both pieces of dough from the refrigerator and peel off both top pieces of paper. Using a small pastry brush, paint the plain lemon dough lightly with water, then turn the fruited dough over on top of it. Peel the paper off the fruited dough and press the two doughs gently together. **6** Beginning with a long side of the dough stack, roll it up into a tight cylinder, without stretching it or making it thinner. Cut the log in half and wrap each half in plastic wrap or wax paper. Chill again for from 2 hours to 3 days. **7** When you are ready to bake the cookies, set the racks in the upper and lower thirds of the oven and preheat to 350 degrees. Slice the cookies ⅛ inch thick, rotating the dough often so it doesn't become squashed from the weight of the knife. **8** Arrange the cookies on the prepared pans about an inch apart in all directions and bake them for about 12 to 15 minutes, until they are no longer shiny and the bottoms are light brown. Slide the papers from the pans onto racks. **9** After the cookies have cooled, store them between sheets of parchment or wax paper in a tin or plastic container with a tight-fitting cover.

TWO-TONE PEANUT BUTTER THINS

PINWHEEL COOKIES OF PLAIN CHOCOLATE and vanilla doughs are a traditional favorite. This combination of plain and chocolate peanut butter doughs improves on a good thing.

Makes about 40 cookies

2 ounces bittersweet chocolate, cut into ¼-inch pieces

2 tablespoons water

2 cups all-purpose flour

½ teaspoon baking powder

½ teaspoon salt

8 tablespoons (1 stick) unsalted butter, softened

1 cup firmly packed light brown sugar

⅔ cup creamy peanut butter

1 large egg

2 or 3 cookie sheets or jelly roll pans covered with parchment or foil

1 Put the chocolate and water in a heatproof bowl. Bring a small pan of water to a boil, then turn off the heat and set the bowl over the hot water. Stir occasionally until the chocolate has melted; remove from the hot water and set aside to cool. **2** In a bowl, combine the flour with the baking powder and salt; stir well to mix. **3** In a standing electric mixer fitted with the paddle attachment, beat the butter and the

brown sugar together on medium speed until light, about 2 minutes. Beat in the peanut butter and the egg, beating smooth after each addition. 4 Remove the bowl from the mixer and stir in the flour mixture with a large rubber spatula. Remove a little more than half the dough from the bowl and set it aside. Add the cooled chocolate mixture to the dough left in the bowl and stir it in thoroughly. 5 On a floured piece of foil or wax paper, pat each piece of dough into an 8-inch square. If the dough is extremely soft and sticky, slide the paper onto a cookie sheet and chill briefly. 6 Use a pastry brush to paint the square of chocolate dough with water. Top it with the square of plain dough. Starting anywhere, roll up the two doughs as you would a jelly roll, keeping the roll straight and even. Roll the dough onto a piece of plastic wrap, wrap, and chill. (You may leave the dough chilled for several days or even freeze it at this point. If you have frozen the dough, defrost in the refrigerator before proceeding with the recipe.) 7 When you are ready to bake the cookies, set the racks in the upper and lower thirds of the oven and preheat to 350 degrees. Slice the roll about every $\frac{3}{16}$ inch and arrange each cookie on the prepared pans about 2 inches from the next one and from the edges of the pan. Bake for about 12 to 15 minutes, until the cookies are firm and very lightly colored. Cool on the pans on racks. 8 Keep the cookies between sheets of parchment or wax paper in a tin or plastic container with a tight-fitting cover.

ROLLED COOKIES

Scottish Shortbread

Chocolate Shortbread

Accidental Cookie Dough

Petit Beurre Cookies

Orange Cream Cookies

Sour Cream Diamonds

Pecan Sand Tarts

Crispy St. Nicholas Cookies

Chocolate Rings

Old-fashioned Molasses Cookies

Gingerbread People

Berner Hasselnuss Staengeli
(Swiss Hazelnut Bars
from Berne)

Utziger Hasselnuss Leckerli
(Swiss Hazelnut Cookies from
the Château of Utzigen)

Arnhem Cookies

Apricot Almond Ruglach

ROLLED COOKIES ARE ALL MADE FROM DOUGHS THAT ARE USUALLY CHILLED after mixing, then rolled out on a floured surface with a rolling pin, cut into shapes, and baked.

HINTS FOR ROLLED COOKIES

1 When you are ready to chill the dough, form it into a rectangular cake about ½ inch thick. In that shape the dough will chill quickly and will also be easier to roll because you will be starting with a fairly thin piece.

2 Always place chilled dough on a floured work surface and also lightly flour the dough itself. Use pinches of flour on the work surface and the dough. When you use pinches of flour, you may reflour the dough and work surface as often as necessary and not worry about adding too much flour to the dough. But if you use handfuls of flour, the dough will happily absorb it (which you don't want because handfuls of flour toughen the dough by making it dry and tasteless). **3** If the dough is chilled too hard, pound it gently with the rolling pin to soften it. Don't just slam away, pound in precise strokes close together over the top of the dough. Pounding dough in this way softens it and also makes it thinner. Rolling the hard, thick, chilled dough might make it break apart. **4** Roll out only small pieces of chilled dough. A large piece of dough may soften too much before it is all cut and be difficult to handle. It is far better to roll out small pieces of dough and cut them rapidly, than risk ruining a whole batch of dough by having to reroll it. **5** After cutting out the cookies, save all the scraps and gently mass them together; chill again before rolling out. You'll find that if you allow the scraps to chill before you roll them out again, the second batch of cookies will be just as tender as the first. To avoid having more scraps, use a knife or pizza cutter to cut the rolled sheet of scraps into squares or rectangles. Another way to deal with scraps is to form them as refrigerator cookies: gently knead them into a cylinder and wrap and chill as in directions for making refrigerator cookies. When it is cold, slice and bake the cookies—this method will also leave no scraps. **6** Don't place rolled cookies too close together on the baking pans—although they do not spread, they still puff a little and, if they are too close, could stick together.

Rolled Cookies

SCOTTISH SHORTBREAD

THIS REALLY EASY VERSION OF THIS cookie is also the best one I have ever tasted. I've had the recipe for years and it comes from Peggy Pinckley, a native of Scotland, who now lives in Springfield, Missouri. I met Peggy in the late 1980s when she came to an afternoon demonstration class I was teaching at Peter Kump's. After class she invited me to come to teach at her school, the Parisian Pantry. I visited Springfield and taught several times at the school, which no longer exists.

Many recipes for shortbreads contain rice flour—a starch like cornstarch—and there are those who think that shortbreads without rice flour are not "the real thing." Industrially made shortbreads contain rice flour to weaken the flour—that is, to lower its protein content. In large industrial batches it takes a long time to incorporate the flour and all-purpose flour would be too strong—it would make the dough tough and elastic. In the small batches we make at home using a home-model electric mixer to beat in the flour, no such danger exists.

A note about butter: All the flavor in your shortbreads will come from the butter. You can make sure that the butter you are using is perfectly fresh with this little test. Unwrap a stick of the butter and use a table knife to scrape an inch-long shaving off one side of the stick. The butter revealed under the scraping should be the same color. If the outside is darker than the inside it means that the butter has oxidized—has been exposed to air and has become stale—and it won't have the same fresh taste as butter that is a uniformly light color inside and out.

Makes about 36 cookies,
depending on how large they are cut

20 tablespoons (2½ sticks) unsalted butter, softened

⅔ cup sugar

3¼ cups all-purpose flour

2 or 3 cookie sheets or jelly roll pans covered with parchment or foil

1 Set racks in the upper and lower thirds of the oven and preheat to 325 degrees. **2** In the bowl of a standing electric mixer fitted with the paddle attachment, beat the butter and sugar on medium speed for 5 to 10 minutes, or until the mixture becomes light in color and very soft and fluffy. **3** Remove the bowl from the mixer and fold in the flour by hand. The dough will be soft. **4** Place a handful of the dough at a time on a lightly floured work surface. Use the floured palm of your hand to press out the dough until it is about ⅜ inch thick—don't make the dough too thin. If the dough seems to be sticking, run a long thin knife or spatula under it to loosen it: whatever you do, do not use a lot of flour or the shortbreads will be dry and tough. Cut out the shortbreads using a fluted round cutter anywhere from 2 to 4 inches in diameter, dipped in flour. With a spatula or pancake turner transfer them to the prepared pans, spacing them about 1½ inches apart—they don't spread, but they puff a little. **5** Continue until all the dough has been cut and you have a large pile of scraps. Continue pressing out and cutting the scraps until they have all been used. The key here is to use very little flour on the work surface and on the dough. This way the last shortbread you cut out will be just as tender and fragile as the first. **6** Bake the shortbreads about 15 to 20 minutes, making sure they are just a very pale golden color. Slide papers from pans onto racks. **7** Pack the cooled cookies between sheets of parchment or wax paper in a tin or plastic container with a tight-fitting cover.

VARIATION

BROWN SUGAR SHORTBREAD: Substitute light brown sugar for all or half the sugar.

Rolled Cookies

CHOCOLATE SHORTBREAD

THIS IS AN INTERESTING VARIATION of the classic Scottish shortbread. One word of caution: Unlike the plain shortbread dough on page 104, this dough needs to chill thoroughly before being rolled.

These are wonderful plain and also good sandwiched with melted milk chocolate or any of the filling suggestions on pages 307–320.

Makes about 40 cookies

2⅓ cups all-purpose flour

¼ teaspoon salt

16 tablespoons (2 sticks) unsalted butter, softened

6 ounces semisweet chocolate, melted and cooled

2 or 3 cookie sheets or jelly roll pans covered with parchment or foil

1 Mix the flour with the salt in a medium bowl. **2** In another bowl, stir the softened butter with a rubber spatula until it is smooth. Scrape the chocolate into the butter and continue mixing until the dough is all one color. Fold in the flour to make a smooth, soft dough. **3** Scrape the dough onto a piece of plastic wrap and press it into a square or rectangle about ½ inch thick. Wrap and chill the dough until it is firm, about an hour or two. **4** When you are ready to bake the cookies, set racks in the upper and lower thirds of the oven and preheat to 350 degrees. **5** On a lightly floured surface, roll out a third of the dough at a time until it is between ⅛ and ¼ inch thick. Cut the cookies with a fluted cutter between 2 and 3 inches in diameter, dipping it frequently in flour. Place the cookies, as they are cut, on the prepared pans about an inch apart in all directions. Repeat with the remaining chilled dough. Save, press together, chill, and reroll all the scraps to make more cookies. **6** Bake the shortbreads about 15 to 20 minutes, or until they become dull and dry-looking and feel slightly firm when pressed with a fingertip. Place the pans on racks to cool the cookies. If you overbake these cookies, they will be lethally dry. **7** Pack the cooled cookies between sheets of parchment or wax paper in a tin or plastic container with a tight-fitting cover.

ACCIDENTAL COOKIE DOUGH

THIS IS A PERFECT DOUGH FOR COOKIES you might want to decorate (see pages 307–320). The accident in the title happened when I was making a triple batch of cookie dough for little tartlet shells—a dough that is very fragile after it is baked and sometimes a little difficult to work with. I multiplied the 1¼ cups of flour called for by three and mistakenly came up with 5 cups of flour. I didn't question my math until I saw that the dough was firmer and drier than usual. Not wanting to waste the ingredients, I decided to try the dough with too much flour in it and, to my surprise, it was just as delicate, though not as fragile. The tarts were every bit as tender and flavorful as they had always been. Because I was curious I tried this easier-to-work-with dough for some cookies and I was very happy with the results. This recipe is for half my triple batch. I wish all mistakes would provide such happy endings.

Makes about 30 cookies,
depending on the size of the cutter

12 tablespoons (1½ sticks) unsalted butter, softened

⅓ cup granulated sugar

¼ teaspoon salt

1½ teaspoons vanilla extract

2 large egg yolks

2½ cups all-purpose flour

Confectioners' sugar for sprinkling

2 cookie sheets or jelly roll pans covered with parchment or foil

1 In the bowl of a standing electric mixer fitted with the paddle attachment, beat together the butter, sugar, salt, and vanilla extract on medium speed until very soft, fluffy, and light-colored, about 5 minutes. **2** Beat in the egg yolks, one at a time, beating smooth after each addition. **3** Lower the speed and beat in the flour. Continue beating until the flour is completely absorbed. **4** Remove the bowl from the mixer and give the dough a final mixing with a large rubber spatula, scraping it firmly away from the inside of the bowl. **5** Place the dough on a piece of plastic wrap and form it into a square or rectangle about ½ inch thick. Wrap the dough and chill it until you are ready to use it—a minimum of 1 hour and up to 3 days. **6** When you are ready to bake the cookies, set racks in the upper and lower thirds of the oven and preheat to 325 degrees. **7** Divide the dough into three parts and place one on a floured work surface. Press and pound the dough gently with a rolling pin to soften it, then roll out the dough into a 10-inch square. Cut the dough with a floured 3-inch cutter, then place each cookie immediately on one of the prepared pans, leaving about an inch around it in all directions. (If you don't have a lot of pans, you can transfer the cookies to pieces of parchment or foil and stack up the paper. Then, when you have removed baked cookies on paper from a pan, you can replace it with one of the prepared sheets of unbaked cookies.) Repeat with the remaining pieces of dough. Reserve the scraps. Press them together, chill again, then roll out for a second time (see page 103). **8** Bake the cookies for about 15 to 20 minutes, or until they are light golden all over. **9** Slide the papers onto racks. **10** Pack the cooled cookies between sheets of parchment or wax paper in a tin or plastic container with a tight-fitting cover. Dust lightly with confectioners' sugar before serving.

PETIT BEURRE COOKIES

THIS COOKIE WAS POPULAR WHEN I was a child. Those were industrially made; these, baked at home, are even better. They're perfect cookie jar cookies because they stay really crisp if you keep them stored airtight.

Makes about 48 cookies

3½ cups all-purpose flour

½ cup cornstarch

¼ teaspoon salt

½ teaspoon baking powder

½ teaspoon baking soda

12 tablespoons (1½ sticks) unsalted butter, softened

1 cup sugar

3 large egg yolks

½ cup milk

2 cookie sheets or jelly roll pans covered with parchment or foil

1 In a bowl combine the flour, cornstarch, salt, baking powder, and baking soda; stir well to mix. **2** In the bowl of a standing electric mixer fitted with the paddle attachment, beat together the butter and sugar on medium speed for about a minute. Beat in the egg yolks, one at a time, beating smooth after each addition. **3** Stop the mixer and scrape the bowl and beater. On low speed, add half the flour mixture. After the dry ingredients have been absorbed, beat in all the milk. Stop the mixer, scrape the bowl and beater; on low speed, add the remaining flour mixture. **4** Scrape the dough onto a piece of plastic wrap. Press the dough into a rectangle about ½ inch thick. Wrap and chill for several hours or for up to 3 days. **5** When you are ready to bake the cookies, set racks in the upper and lower thirds of the oven and preheat to 325 degrees. **6** Place the dough on a floured work surface and lightly flour the dough. Press and pound the dough gently with a rolling pin to soften, then roll it out into a 12-inch square. Cut the square in half, then roll each half to a 9- x 12-inch rectangle. With the tines of a fork, pierce the dough at ½-inch intervals. **7** Use a pizza wheel to cut each rectangle into three 3-inch strips, then cut across the strips at 1½-inch intervals to make 48 rectangular cookies. **8** Use a narrow spatula to transfer the cookies to the prepared pan. Leave about an inch in all directions around each cookie. **9** Bake the cookies for about 15 to 20 minutes, or until they are light golden all over. **10** Slide the papers onto racks. **11** Store the cooled cookies between sheets of parchment or wax paper in a tin or plastic container with a tight-fitting cover.

Rolled Cookies

ORANGE CREAM COOKIES

THIS ORANGE-SCENTED COOKIE COMES from Toba Garrett, our resident cake (and cookie) decorating expert at Peter Kump's. Toba uses these cookies as one of the bases in her popular class on decorating cookies.

Makes about 30 to 40 cookies

3½ cups all-purpose flour

1½ teaspoons baking powder

¼ teaspoon salt

16 tablespoons (2 sticks) unsalted butter, softened

1 cup sugar

1 large egg

1 tablespoon finely grated orange zest (grate off the zest before squeezing the juice)

1 tablespoon strained orange juice

2 tablespoons heavy whipping cream

2 or 3 cookie sheets or jelly roll pans covered with parchment or foil

1 Set racks in the upper and lower thirds of the oven and preheat to 350 degrees. **2** In a bowl, combine the flour, baking powder, and salt; stir well to mix. **3** In the bowl of a standing electric mixer fitted with the paddle attachment, beat together the butter and sugar on medium speed until fluffy and light-colored, about 5 minutes. Add the egg and orange zest, beating until smooth. **4** Lower the mixer speed and beat in half the flour mixture, then beat in all the orange juice and cream, one at a time. Beat in half the remaining flour. Stop the mixer and stir in the remaining flour by hand, working it in with a large rubber spatula. **5** Scrape the dough onto a floured work surface and pat it into a rough rectangle. Cut the dough in quarters. Wrap three of them and set them aside. **6** Roll out the dough on a floured surface until it is about ⅛ inch thick. To cut the cookies, use a fluted cutter between 2 and 3 inches in diameter, or decorative cutters. Whatever cutter you use, dip it frequently in flour. Place the cookies as they are cut on the prepared pans, leaving about an inch around each in all directions. Repeat with the remaining dough. Save, press together, chill, and reroll the scraps to make more cookies. **7** Bake the cookies for about 15 to 20 minutes, or until they first become dull and dry-looking and feel slightly firm when pressed with a fingertip. Be careful not to overbake these cookies or they will be very dry. Slide the papers from the pans onto racks. **8** Store the cooled cookies between sheets of parchment or wax paper in a tin or plastic container with a tight-fitting cover.

VARIATION

LEMON CREAM COOKIES: Substitute lemon zest and juice for the orange.

SOUR CREAM DIAMONDS

THESE RICH COOKIES CAN BE CUT OUT in a variety of ways. Diamonds, as in the directions below, are always pretty, but you can also cut them with any kind of decorative cutter you wish. They also make good bases for the icings and glazes on pages 307–320.

Makes about 70 cookies

2½ cups all-purpose flour

¼ teaspoon salt

1 teaspoon baking powder

½ teaspoon baking soda

16 tablespoons (2 sticks) unsalted butter, softened

1 cup granulated sugar

1 teaspoon vanilla extract

1 large egg

½ cup sour cream

Granulated sugar for finishing

2 or 3 cookie sheets or jelly roll pans covered with parchment or foil

1 Set racks in the upper and lower thirds of the oven and preheat to 350 degrees. **2** In a bowl, combine the flour, salt, baking powder, and baking soda; stir well to mix. **3** In the bowl of an electric mixer fitted with the paddle attachment, beat together the butter and sugar on medium speed until well mixed, about a minute. Beat in the vanilla and the egg and continue beating until smooth. **4** Stop the mixer and scrape down the bowl and beater with a rubber spatula. On low speed, beat in half the flour mixture, then the sour cream. Stop the mixer and scrape again, then beat in the remaining flour. **5** Scrape the dough onto a floured work surface and pat it into a rough rectangle. Cut the dough in quarters, wrap them, and chill for 1 hour. **6** Roll out a piece of dough on a floured surface until it is about ⅛ inch thick. To cut the cookies, use a fluted diamond-shaped cutter between 2 and 3 inches long, or any decorative cutters. Just be sure you dip the cutters frequently in flour. As soon as the cookies are cut, place them on the prepared pans and sprinkle lightly with granulated sugar. Leave about an inch around each in all directions. Repeat with the remaining dough. Save, press together, chill, and reroll the scraps to make more cookies. **7** Bake the cookies about 15 to 20 minutes, or until they become dull and dry-looking and feel slightly firm when pressed with a fingertip. If you overbake the cookies, they will be very dry. Slide the papers from the pans onto racks. **8** Store the cooled cookies between sheets of parchment or wax paper in a tin or plastic container with a tight-fitting cover.

VARIATION

BUTTERMILK COOKIES: Substitute buttermilk for the sour cream.

PECAN SAND TARTS

SUPPOSEDLY THESE COOKIES GOT THEIR name from their postbaking coating of sugar, which gives them a sandy texture. This recipe comes from a great friend and cookie lover, Peggy Tagliarino.

Makes about 50 cookies,
depending on how large you cut them

16 tablespoons (2 sticks) unsalted butter, softened

½ **cup sugar**

½ **teaspoon salt**

1 large egg

1 teaspoon vanilla extract

4 ounces (about 1 cup) pecan pieces, finely ground in the food processor

2½ **cups all-purpose flour**

Sugar for coating the baked cookies

2 or 3 cookie sheets or jelly roll pans covered with parchment or foil

1 Set racks in the upper and lower thirds of the oven and preheat to 325 degrees. **2** In the bowl of a standing electric mixer fitted with the paddle attachment, beat together the butter, sugar, and salt on medium speed for 5 to 10 minutes, until very light, fluffy, and whitened. **3** Beat in the egg and vanilla and continue beating until smooth. Lower the mixer speed and beat in the pecans. Then beat in the flour, about a third at a time, scraping the bowl and beater between each addition. **4** Scrape the dough out onto a floured work surface and divide into three pieces. **5** Flour one piece of dough and roll it out about ⅜ inch thick, moving it continually so it doesn't stick to the surface. If it does stick, slide a long, thin-bladed knife or a long spatula under the dough to detach it. Cut the dough with a 2-inch fluted cutter and place the cookies on a prepared pan, about an inch apart on all sides. Repeat with the remaining dough. Save all the scraps until the end, then reroll them and cut more cookies. **6** Bake the cookies about 20 or 25 minutes, until they are light golden on the bottom but still very pale on top. Slide the papers from the pans onto racks. **7** After the cookies have cooled, carefully roll them in granulated sugar. **8** Store the cooled cookies between sheets of parchment or wax paper in a tin or plastic container with a tight-fitting cover.

CRISPY ST. NICHOLAS COOKIES

So what could be wrong with a cookie named after my patron saint? These are a typical Hungarian Christmas cookie; the recipe comes from my friend Nancy Berzinec.

Makes about 36 cookies,
depending on the size of the cutter used

2½ cups all-purpose flour

1 teaspoon ground cinnamon

½ teaspoon baking powder

½ teaspoon salt

8 tablespoons (1 stick) unsalted butter, softened

1 cup sugar

1 large egg

2 teaspoons finely grated lemon zest

2 or 3 cookie sheets or jelly roll pans covered with parchment or foil

1 In a bowl, combine the flour, cinnamon, baking powder, and salt; stir well to mix. **2** In the bowl of a standing electric mixer fitted with the paddle attachment, beat together on medium speed the butter and sugar until light and whitened, about 5 minutes. Beat in the egg and lemon zest and continue beating until smooth and light, another 2 minutes. **3** Scrape down the bowl and beater with a large rubber spatula and, on low speed, add the flour mixture. Continue mixing until the dough is smooth. **4** Remove the bowl from the mixer and complete the mixing with a large rubber spatula. **5** Scrape the dough onto a piece of plastic wrap and press it into a square or rectangle about ½ inch thick. Wrap and chill the dough until it is firm, about an hour or two. **6** When you are ready to bake the cookies, set racks in the upper and lower thirds of the oven and preheat to 350 degrees. **7** On a floured surface, roll out a third of the dough at a time until it is about ⅛ inch thick. Use a fluted cutter between 2 and 3 inches in diameter, or any kind of decorative cutter you wish. Just be sure to dip it frequently in flour. As they are cut, place the cookies on the prepared pans about an inch apart in all directions. Repeat with the remaining dough. Save, press together, chill, and reroll the scraps to make more cookies. **8** Bake the cookies about 15 to 20 minutes, or until they first become dull and dry-looking and feel slightly firm when pressed with a fingertip. If you overbake the cookies, they will be very dry. Slide the papers from the pans onto racks. **9** Store the cooled cookies between sheets of parchment or wax paper in a tin or plastic container with a tight-fitting cover.

CHOCOLATE RINGS

I LIKE THE WAY THESE RING-SHAPED cookies look. You may use a doughnut cutter or simply cut round cookies, then cut out the centers. These are especially beautiful when streaked with Sugar-Based Chocolate Glaze for Cookies (page 319) and a few pinches of finely chopped pistachios.

Makes about 35 cookies,
depending on the size cutter used

2 cups all-purpose flour

⅓ cup unsweetened cocoa powder,
sifted after measuring

16 tablespoons (2 sticks) unsalted butter, softened

½ cup sugar

1 teaspoon vanilla extract

3 large egg yolks

2 cookie sheets or jelly roll pans covered
with parchment or foil

1 In a bowl, combine the flour and cocoa; stir well to mix. **2** In the bowl of a standing electric mixer fitted with the paddle attachment, beat together on medium speed the butter and sugar until soft, fluffy, and whitened, between 5 and 10 minutes. Beat in the vanilla and egg yolks, one at a time, beating smooth after each addition. **3** Stop the mixer and scrape down the bowl and beater. On low speed, add the flour and beat in thoroughly. **4** Remove the bowl from the mixer and complete the mixing with a large rubber spatula. **5** Scrape the dough onto a piece of plastic wrap and press it into a rectangle about ½ inch thick. Wrap, then chill the dough until firm, about 2 hours or for up to 3 days. **6** When you are ready to bake the cookies, set racks in the upper and lower thirds of the oven and preheat to 325 degrees. **7** Divide the dough into three parts and place one on a floured work surface. Refrigerate the remaining dough until needed. Press and pound the dough gently with the rolling pin to soften it, then roll the dough out to a 10-inch square. Cut the dough with a doughnut cutter or a floured 3-inch cutter. As each cookie is cut, place it immediately on one of the pre-pared pans, about an inch apart in all directions. If you used a plain round cutter, after the cookies are on the pans, cut their centers out with a small cutter about 1 inch in diameter or the wide end of a pastry tube. Add the cutout centers to the scraps to be rerolled. Save, press together, chill, and reroll the scraps to make more cookies.

8 Bake the cookies for about 15 to 20 minutes, or until they are dull in appearance and feel firm to the touch of a fingertip. **9** Slide the papers from the pans onto racks. **10** Store the cooled cookies between sheets of parchment or wax paper in a tin or plastic container with a tight-fitting cover.

OLD-FASHIONED MOLASSES COOKIES

THESE ARE ONE OF THE FEW AMERICAN cookies I remember my maternal grandmother, Clotilda Lo Conte, baking when I was a child. In fact, I still have the tattered 1930s molasses company recipe pamphlet from which she got the recipe.

These are a little less delicate than the Gingerbread People on page 117, but for all practical purposes the recipes may be used interchangeably.

Makes about 36 cookies,
depending on the size cutter used

3 cups all-purpose flour

1 teaspoon salt

1 teaspoon baking soda

1 teaspoon ground cinnamon

1 teaspoon ground ginger

½ teaspoon ground cloves

12 tablespoons (1½ sticks) unsalted butter, softened

⅓ cup sugar

⅔ cup molasses

2 or 3 cookie sheets or jelly roll pans lined with parchment or foil

(continued)

1 In a large bowl, combine the flour, salt, soda, and spices; stir well to mix. **2** In the bowl of a standing electric mixer fitted with the paddle attachment, beat together, on medium speed, the butter and sugar until well mixed, about a minute. Lower the speed and beat in a third of the flour mixture, then half the molasses; stop and scrape the bowl and beater. Beat in another third of the flour, then the remaining molasses; stop and scrape again. Finally, beat in the remaining flour. **3** Remove the bowl from the mixer and stir up the dough, scraping it from around the inside of the bowl with a large rubber spatula. **4** Place the dough on a piece of plastic wrap and form it into a square or rectangle about ½ inch thick. Wrap the dough and chill it until you are ready to use it—1 hour or up to 3 days. **5** When you are ready to bake the cookies, set racks in the upper and lower thirds of the oven and preheat to 375 degrees. **6** Divide the dough into three parts and place one on a floured work surface. Refrigerate the remaining dough until needed. Press and pound the dough gently with the rolling pin to soften it, then roll it out into a 10-inch square. Use a floured 3- to 4-inch cutter to cut the dough. As each cookie is cut, place it immediately on one of the prepared pans, leaving about 1½ inches between each cookie in all directions. (If you don't have a lot of pans, you can place the cookies on pieces of parchment or foil and stack up the papers. When one pan of cookies is baked, slide the paper off the pan onto a rack and replace with a paper of unbaked cookies.) Repeat with the remaining pieces of dough. Save, press together, chill, and reroll the scraps to make more cookies. **7** Bake the cookies for about 10 to 15 minutes, or until they are light golden all over. **8** Slide the papers from the pans onto racks. **9** Store the cooled cookies between sheets of parchment or wax paper in a tin or plastic container with a tight-fitting cover.

GINGERBREAD PEOPLE

OF COURSE YOU DON'T HAVE TO CUT these cookies into any particular shape, but if you want to make gingerbread people this is the recipe to use. And the cookies are ideal for decorating—I usually use Royal Icing for that purpose. A bonus: This dough is so tender you can roll and reroll the scraps without having to worry that the last batch of cookies you roll will be tough.

This recipe makes a lot of dough—but it's easy to halve if you need less.

Makes about 30 large cookies,
depending on the size cutter used

5 cups all-purpose flour

4 teaspoons ground ginger

1 tablespoon ground cinnamon

1 teaspoon freshly grated nutmeg

½ teaspoon ground cloves

1 teaspoon salt

½ teaspoon baking soda

16 tablespoons (2 sticks) unsalted butter, softened

⅔ cup firmly packed dark brown sugar

2 large eggs

⅔ cup molasses

Royal Icing (page 312)

Raisins, nut meats, and candies
for decorating (optional)

2 or 3 cookie sheets or jelly roll pans
covered with parchment or foil

(continued)

1 In a large bowl, combine the flour, spices, salt, and baking soda; stir well to mix. **2** In the bowl of a standing electric mixer fitted with the paddle attachment, beat together the butter and brown sugar on medium speed until well mixed, about 1 minute. Beat in the eggs, one at a time, beating smooth after each addition. Scrape down the bowl and beater. **3** Lower the speed and beat in about half the flour mixture. Beat in all the molasses, then scrape the bowl and beater. Add the remaining flour mixture, about a cup at a time, and beat after each addition until it has all been absorbed. **4** Remove the bowl from the mixer and give the dough a final mixing with a large rubber spatula. Scrape half the dough onto a large piece of plastic wrap and press it to about a ½-inch thickness. Wrap the dough securely and repeat with the remaining dough. Chill the dough for at least 2 hours or for up to 3 days. **5** When you are ready to bake the cookies, set racks in the upper and lower thirds of the oven and preheat to 350 degrees. **6** Unwrap one of the pieces of dough and cut it in half. Rewrap one of the halves and return it to the refrigerator. **7** On a floured surface, roll out the dough until it is about ¼ inch thick. Use a floured gingerbread "man" or "woman" cutter to cut the cookies. As they are cut, place the cut cookies on the prepared pans about an inch apart in all directions. Repeat with remaining dough. Save, press together, and reroll the scraps to make more cookies (they don't need to be chilled before rerolling). **8** Bake the cookies about 12 to 15 minutes, or until they become dull and dry-looking and feel slightly firm when pressed with a fingertip. If you overbake the cookies, they will be very dry. Slide the papers from the pans onto racks to cool. **9** After the cookies have cooled decorate them with the Royal Icing and other decorating ingredients if desired. **10** Store the cooled cookies between sheets of parchment or wax paper in a tin or plastic container with a tight-fitting cover.

BERNER HASSELNUSS STAENGELI

Swiss Hazelnut Bars from Berne

THIS IS A TYPICALLY SWISS RECIPE shared by my friend, cooking teacher and caterer Thea Cvijanovich. Thea was born in Berne, Switzerland, and this recipe is like many from the region. Though I don't think these were originally made without flour for religious reasons, they make a great Passover cookie.

Makes about 48 cookies

4½ cups (about 18 ounces) whole unblanched hazelnuts

1½ cups sugar, plus more for rolling out the dough

Finely grated zest of 1 lemon

1 teaspoon ground cinnamon

4 large egg whites (a little more than ½ cup)

2 cookie sheets or jelly roll pans covered with parchment or foil

1 In the work bowl of a food processor fitted with the steel blade, combine the hazelnuts and half the sugar. Pulse repeatedly at 1-second intervals until finely ground. Add the lemon zest and cinnamon and pulse again. **2** In a large bowl, whisk the egg whites to break them up. Whisk in the remaining sugar in a stream. Add the hazel-nut mixture and with a large rubber spatula combine the ingredients to form a very firm dough. Cover the bowl with plastic wrap and set it aside to let the dough mature for about 30 minutes. (This resting time is to get all the sugar melted so that the dough doesn't change consistency while it is being rolled or baked.) **3** When you are ready to bake the cookies, set racks in the upper and lower thirds of the oven and preheat to 350 degrees. **4** Scatter granulated sugar on a work surface and scrape the dough onto it. Use the palm of your hand to flatten the dough and scatter sugar over it. Roll out and press the dough until it is about ¼ inch thick—it should make a 12-inch square. Using a ruler for accuracy, cut the dough into 1-inch wide strips. Then cut across at 3-inch intervals to make 48 cookies. **5** Transfer the cookies to the prepared pans, leaving about an inch all around each. Bake the cookies for about 15 to 20 minutes, until they are slightly puffed but still soft to the touch of a fingertip. Cool on the pans on racks. **6** Store the cooled cookies between sheets of parchment or wax paper in a tin or plastic container with a tight-fitting cover.

Utziger Hasselnuss Leckerli

Swiss Hazelnut Cookies from the Château of Utzigen

This traditional recipe also came to me from Thea Cvijanovich, a native of Berne. I met Thea when I was teaching in Winston-Salem, North Carolina, where she lives and does catering. The ingredients for these seem similar to those of the *Berner Hasselnuss Staengeli* (Swiss Hazelnut Bars from Berne) on page 119, but the texture and flavor are entirely different.

Makes about 32 cookies

Utziger Hasselnuss Leckerli (LEFT)
and Berner Hasselnuss Staengeli, page 119

6 ounces (about 1½ cups) whole unblanched hazelnuts

6 ounces (about 1½ cups) whole unblanched almonds

1 cup granulated sugar

2 tablespoons candied orange rind, chopped very fine

2 tablespoons candied lemon rind, chopped very fine

1½ teaspoons ground cinnamon

½ teaspoon ground star anise or aniseed

3 tablespoons flour

2 large egg whites

1 tablespoon strained lemon juice

1 tablespoon honey

Confectioners' sugar for rolling out the dough

GLAZE

½ cup confectioners' sugar mixed with
2 tablespoons kirsch or lemon juice

2 cookie sheets or jelly roll pans covered
with parchment or foil

1 Set a rack in the middle level of the oven and preheat to 325 degrees. 2 In the work bowl of a food processor fitted with the steel blade, combine the hazelnuts and almonds and pulse at 1-second intervals until finely ground. Stop the machine occasionally and scrape down the inside bottom of the bowl with a metal spatula or table knife to loosen any ground nuts caking there. When the nuts are finely ground, pour them into a large roasting pan; place the pan in the oven and toast the nuts until they are golden brown, stirring often with a large wide spatula or pancake turner. Be careful—ground nuts burn a lot more quickly than whole ones. 3 Remove the ground nuts from the oven and pour them onto a clean pan or work surface to cool. Turn off the oven. 4 When the nuts are cool, place them in a large bowl and stir in the sugar, candied fruit, spices, and flour. In another bowl, whisk together the egg whites, lemon juice, and honey, and using a rubber spatula, scrape this into the nut mixture. Fold the ingredients together until they form a stiff dough. Cover the bowl with plastic wrap and allow the dough to rest an hour.

5 When you are ready to bake the cookies, set a rack in the upper third of the oven and preheat to 425 degrees. It is traditional to bake these cookies with mostly top heat, so only one pan at a time will be baked—but they bake quickly, so the whole procedure doesn't take too long. 6 Strew the work surface with confectioners' sugar and place the dough on it. Sprinkle the dough with more confectioners' sugar and press and roll out the dough into a 12-inch square about ¼ inch thick. Cut the dough into 1½-inch strips with a knife or pizza wheel, then cut across at 3-inch intervals. Straight lines will make rectangles, diagonal ones will make diamonds. As the cookies are cut, place them on the prepared pans, leaving about an inch around all the sides. While the cookies are baking prepare the glaze. 7 Bake for about 8 to 10 minutes, or until the cookies puff slightly and look dry. Remove the cookies from the oven and immediately brush with the glaze. Cool on the pans on racks. 8 Store the cooled cookies between sheets of parchment or wax paper in a tin or plastic container with a tight-fitting cover.

ARNHEM COOKIES

THE RECIPE FOR THIS INTRIGUING
Dutch cookie was recently given to me by my
friend, baking expert Marion Cunningham.
Not only is she the author of *The Fannie Farmer
Baking Book* (Knopf, 1984), she is also one of
the guiding lights of the Bakers Dozen, an
association of professional and avocational bakers in the San Francisco Bay area.

These crunchy cookies come from a simple recipe. They are essentially a plain bread
dough with butter worked into it, then coated
with sanding sugar (see Sources). They have a
wonderfully crunchy exterior and a great flavor
of butter and caramel—what could be better?

Makes about seventy-five 1 × 2-inch cookies

1½ cups all-purpose flour

½ cup plus 1 tablespoon milk

1 teaspoon active dry yeast

⅛ teaspoon salt

8 tablespoons (1 stick) unsalted butter,
cut into 8 equal pieces

About 1 cup sanding sugar

3 or 4 cookie sheets or jelly roll pans
lined with parchment or foil

1 In the bowl of a standing electric mixer fitted
with the dough hook, combine the flour, milk,
yeast, and salt. Stir together by hand, then place
the bowl on the mixer and beat on high speed
until well combined and fairly smooth. The
dough should be very stiff—it may even be necessary to hold the bowl down to keep it from pop-
ping off the machine. **2** With the mixer still
running on high speed, add one piece of butter,
then beat for a full minute. Add the second piece
of butter and beat for another full minute. Continue in the same manner until all the butter has
been added, stirring or scraping down the bowl
occasionally. The dough will look smooth and
satiny. **3** Scrape the dough out into a plastic
bag. Close and seal the bag but leave some space
in the bag at the top for the dough to expand.
Refrigerate for 2 hours or as long as overnight
before continuing. **4** When you are ready to
bake the cookies, set racks in the upper and
lower thirds of the oven and preheat to 275
degrees. **5** Sprinkle the work surface generously with some of the sanding sugar. Remove the
dough from the refrigerator and cut it in half.
Place half on the sugar-coated surface, then
return the other half to the bag and the refrigerator. Sprinkle the dough in front of you with
more sugar and begin rolling it. Keep sprinkling
the dough and the work surface with more sugar,
as needed, to prevent the dough from sticking.

Continue rolling until the dough is about ⅛ inch thick. **6** Use an oval cookie cutter to cut out the dough, or cut with a knife or pizza wheel into 1 × 2-inch rectangles. Place the cut cookies an inch apart all around on the prepared pans. Repeat with the remaining dough. **7** Bake the cookies for about 25 to 30 minutes. Watch them carefully toward the end of the baking time to make sure they do not burn. When baked, they should be puffy and blistered in places, and a light brown color. **8** Slide the papers from the pans onto racks. **9** Store the cooled cookies between sheets of parchment or wax paper in a tin or plastic container with a tight-fitting cover.

APRICOT ALMOND RUGLACH

IF YOU'VE NEVER TRIED RUGLACH, NOW is the time. It's one of the world's best cookies, made from a rich cream cheese wrapped around sugar, nuts, and jam. The cookies always caramelize a little while they're baking, creating a combination of sweet, buttery flavors not duplicated in any other cookie I know. I could make (and eat!) ruglach once a week.

This version comes from my friend Bonnie Stern, Canada's top food authority. It is from her book *Desserts* (Random House of Canada, 1998).

Makes about 24 cookies

CREAM CHEESE PASTRY

1 cup all-purpose flour

8 tablespoons (1 stick) cold unsalted butter, cut into 12 pieces

4 ounces cold cream cheese, cut into 12 pieces

FILLING

¼ cup apricot jam

2 ounces (about ½ cup) chopped toasted almonds

¼ cup sugar

1 teaspoon finely grated lemon zest

TOPPING

1 egg

¼ cup sugar

1 ounce (about ¼ cup) chopped almonds

2 cookie sheets or jelly roll pans covered with parchment or foil

(continued)

Rolled Cookies

1 Set racks in the upper and lower thirds of the oven and preheat to 350 degrees. **2** In the work bowl of a food processor fitted with the steel blade, combine the flour, butter, and cream cheese. Pulse until the dough forms a ball. Remove the dough from the work bowl and divide into two pieces. Place each on a piece of plastic wrap and press each out into a 6-inch disk. Wrap in plastic and refrigerate while preparing the filling. **3** To make the filling, stir the jam until it is spreadable; stir together the almonds, sugar, and zest in a bowl. **4** Remove one of the pieces of dough from the refrigerator and place it on a lightly floured surface. Flour the dough and roll it out into a 9- to 10-inch circle. Using a pizza wheel, cut the circle in twelve equal wedges. Spread with half the jam and evenly scatter on half the almond mixture. Roll up each triangle of dough into a small crescent from the outside inward. As the ruglach are formed, place them on the prepared pan. Repeat with the other piece of dough and the remaining filling. **5** To make the topping, beat the egg in a small bowl until well broken up. In another bowl, mix the sugar and almonds. Brush the top of each pastry with beaten egg, then sprinkle with the almond sugar. **6** Bake for about 30 minutes, or until golden and slightly caramelized. Slide the papers from the pans to racks. **7** Ruglach are best on the day they are baked, but they will certainly keep between sheets of parchment or wax paper in a tin or plastic container with a tight-fitting cover.

PIPED COOKIES

Langues de Chat
("Sid and Sis" Cat's Tongues)

Canary's Tongues

Champagne Fingers

Almond Batons

Hazelnut Fingers

Cigarettes

Ladyfingers

Butter Almond Fingers

Spritz Cookies

W's

Philip Portwood's
Bar Mitzvah Cookies

Chocolate-Filled Stars

Cherry Rosette Butter Cookies

Chocolate Peanut S Cookies

Swiss Chocolate Rings

Cinnamon Shells

Paste di Meliga
(Italian Cornmeal Butter
Cookies from Piemonte)

Swiss Raisin Drops

MERINGUES

Walnut Boulders

Coffee Pecan Meringues

Hazelnut Sticks

Chocolate Meringue Wreaths

Virgules (Commas)

VERSATILE PIPED COOKIES ARE AS DECORATIVE AS THEY ARE DELICIOUS.
The name refers to the process of making them. They either are made extruded in decorative designs from a cookie press or are piped out of a pastry bag. We'll consider each separately.

COOKIE PRESS COOKIES: A cookie press is a hand-operated extruding machine. It is a cylinder with a metal die at one end (presses come with a variety of these, each creating different designs). The dough is held in the cylinder and pushed down and through the die by a plate at the top when the handle is pressed. Cookie presses work the way a gun does: One pull of the trigger pushes a uniform quantity of dough through the die every time—all the cookies emerge the same size.

PIPED COOKIES: Not as precise as pressed cookies, they are formed by squeezing the dough through a pastry bag. The shape and design come from whatever plain or decorative tube you put on the end. Firm doughs are the easiest to pipe because they hold their shape and the bag must be firmly squeezed to force them through. Looser mixtures, such as the batter for ladyfingers, are a little more difficult to pipe because the flow is more difficult to control.

MERINGUES: The ones in this chapter are all piped cookies, although some meringues may be spooned out onto the pans like drop cookies.

HINTS FOR PIPED COOKIES

1 Follow the instructions on pages 128–29 for piping and you will get good results even on the first try. **2** Use a nylon and plastic-coated canvas bag. Disposable bags are good, but sometimes they split if you try to use them to pipe a firm dough. **3** For best results, use the size and type tube specified in the recipe. A smaller tube could crush delicate mixtures and cause them to liquefy or, if the dough is firm, may make it impossible to pipe. Conversely, if you use too large a tube, a soft mixture may flow through it too quickly and if the dough is firm the result will be gigantic cookies.

The cookies in the following recipes will keep for a week or so. Freeze them for longer storage.

How to Pipe

The purpose of a pastry bag is to make the process of shaping cookies easier, though many first-timers find it awkward. Follow the simple rules below and you won't have trouble.

1 Inserting the tube into the bag: When you insert the tube, make sure it is firmly seated in the narrow end of the bag. If the batter you are going to pipe is soft and thin, close off the end of the bag before you begin to fill it. Twist some material from right behind the wide end of the tube and press it into the tube

Step 2

Step 1

from the outside, as in illustration 1. This will keep the batter from leaking out as you are pouring it in. This is not necessary if the dough is firm. 2 Filling the bag: From the wide end of the bag fold back about the top third to the outside and hold it in your nonwriting hand, under the cuff, fingers poised around it as if they were holding a glass. (See illustration 2.) Use your writing hand to fill the bag, not more than half full. Or stand the bag in a large jar or measuring cup and fold the top of the bag down over the outside. This way you can use both hands to fill. 3 Closing the top of the bag: After you have filled half (or less) of the bag, twist the top right above the batter or dough. This closes off the top of the bag so the batter will only come out the end with the tube. 4 Opening the bottom of the bag: Right before you start piping, undo the twisted fabric closing the bottom of the bag. 5 Beginning to pipe: Always hold the bag in the hand you use to write. (If you are left-handed and write back-handed, pipe the same way.) Hold the bag only at the top and, with one hand, grip the top of the bag as though it were an orange half you are about to press over a hand juicer. Use only the index finger of your other hand against the side of the bag to steady it. Do not grip the bag with both hands. 6 Piping half-spheres: To pipe most cookies, hold the bag perpendicular to the pan with the tube about an inch above the surface. Tighten your writing hand to squeeze out some batter or dough. When the cookie is the size you want it, stop squeezing and pull the bag away straight upward. This is the same method you would use to pipe stars or simple flower shapes with a star tube. **7** Piping fingers: To make a long shape, hold the bag at a 45-degree angle to the pan and touch the tube to the surface. Begin to squeeze gently as you pull the tube toward you. When the line of batter on the pan is as long as the recipe states, stop squeezing, then lift the bag away, but back over the shape you have just piped. Don't pull the bag away, or you risk leaving a tail. **8** Piping shells or teardrops: This is done the same way as the fingers above, but to leave a pointed shape gradually release the pressure as you pipe. **9** Cleaning the bag and tube: As soon as you finish piping, remove the tube from the bag, wash it in hot, soapy water, and dry it thoroughly. Wash the

Step 7

bag in hot soapy water and rinse it thoroughly. Sometimes I send a pastry bag through the dishwasher cycle stretched around several of the prongs, wide end down, on the upper rack. Occasionally wash pastry bags in the washing machine with detergent and bleach when you are doing other kitchen laundry.

LANGUES DE CHAT
"Sid and Sis" Cat's Tongues

THESE COOKIES ARE A FAVORITE throughout Europe. The loose batter is piped through a small tube; it spreads and becomes thin and delicate in the oven. To make sure the cookies don't become distorted, I rub the foil lining flat with a soft cloth or paper towel. Then it's easy to brush the foil with soft, not melted, butter.

To get best results with this recipe, measure the egg white very accurately. If three egg whites are less than ½ cup, beat a fourth in a small bowl with a fork until it breaks up and add enough to the measuring cup to make exactly ½ cup.

Sid and Sis are my two black cats, ages 16 and 11, respectively.

Makes about 150 cookies

6 tablespoons (¾ stick) unsalted butter, softened

1¼ cups confectioners' sugar

1 teaspoon vanilla extract

½ cup egg white (from about 3 to 4 large eggs)

1 cup all-purpose flour

4 cookie sheets or jelly roll pans lined with buttered foil

1 Set racks in the upper and lower thirds of the oven and preheat to 400 degrees. **2** In the bowl of a standing electric mixer fitted with the paddle attachment, beat together on medium speed the butter, confectioners' sugar, and vanilla until well mixed and smooth, about 2 minutes. **3** Add the egg whites in about five or six additions, beating smooth after each. **4** Remove the bowl from the mixer and with a large rubber spatula stir in the flour. **5** Fit a pastry bag with a ¼-inch plain tube (Ateco #802). Fill the pastry bag and pipe the batter in 2½-inch fingers. Leave about 1½ inches all around each to allow for spreading. **6** Bake for about 6 or 7 minutes, or until the cookies have spread and are golden around the edges. **7** Slide the foil sheets from the pans to racks. Carefully pry off the cooled cookies. **8** Store the cookies between sheets of parchment or wax paper in a tin or plastic container with a tight-fitting cover.

CANARY'S TONGUES

THESE, AS THE NAME IMPLIES, ARE tinier and more delicate than cat's tongues. I like them without any flavoring so that the unadulterated taste of butter really comes through.

Makes about 100 very thin cookies

1 cup all-purpose flour

¼ teaspoon baking powder

8 tablespoons (1 stick) unsalted butter, softened

½ cup sugar

1 large egg

3 cookie sheets or jelly roll pans lined with buttered foil (see Headnote, opposite)

1 Set racks in the upper and lower thirds of the oven and preheat to 325 degrees. **2** Combine the flour and baking powder in a bowl; stir well to mix. **3** In the bowl of a standing electric mixer fitted with the paddle attachment, beat together the butter and sugar on medium speed until soft and light, about 5 minutes. Add the egg, beating until smooth. **4** Remove the bowl from the mixer and incorporate the flour mixture by hand with a large rubber spatula. **5** Fit a pastry bag with a ¼-inch plain tube (Ateco #802). Pipe out 1½-inch-long cookies about an inch apart on the prepared pans. **6** Bake for about 15 minutes, until the cookies are light golden and a little darker at the edge. **7** Slide the papers onto racks—be careful, these cookies are fragile. **8** Store the cooled cookies between sheets of parchment or wax paper in a tin or plastic container with a tight-fitting cover.

CHAMPAGNE FINGERS

THIS IS A FREESTANDING VERSION OF this classic cookie. The dough is piped out onto flat pans, rather than baked in a mold. I learned to make these in the early seventies when I was working at the Monte Carlo Sporting Club with pastry chef Alexandre Frolla. Though these cookies are delicate and fragile, the same batter makes very good Christmas tree decorations. Just use a smaller tube to pipe it out into letters, numbers, and geometric shapes.

Makes about 50 cookies

4 large eggs

Pinch salt

1 teaspoon vanilla extract or lemon extract

1 cup granulated sugar, plus more for coating the cookies

2 cups all-purpose flour

3 cookie sheets or jelly roll pans covered with parchment or foil

1 Half-fill a medium saucepan with water and bring to a boil over medium heat. Reduce to a simmer. **2** Combine the eggs, salt, extract, and sugar in the bowl of an electric mixer but use a hand whisk to mix smooth. Place the bowl over the pan of simmering water and whisk gently until the mixture is lukewarm, about 100 degrees, all in all about 1 minute. **3** Place the bowl on the mixer fitted with the whisk attachment and whip on medium speed until the mixture has cooled and increased in volume. This will be in about 5 or 6 minutes. Stop the mixer and try to draw a line about 3 inches long and ¼ inch deep in the egg foam with a fingertip; if it holds its shape, it's ready. **4** Remove the bowl from the mixer and in three or four additions sift over and fold in the flour with a rubber spatula. **5** Fit a pastry bag with a ½-inch plain tube

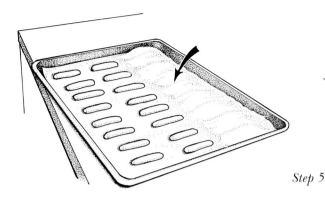

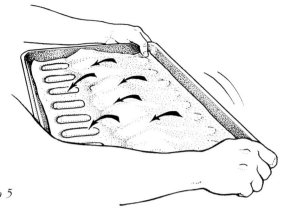

Step 5

(Ateco #806). Pipe the batter dough onto the prepared pans in 2½- to 3-inch fingers, leaving about an inch all around. After all the cookies are piped, cover one row of piped fingers with granulated sugar. Shake the sugar toward you until all the fingers are coated, as in the illustration. Remember to hold down the corners of the paper with your thumbs, or the paper with the cookies attached will slide off the pan. Shake the excess sugar off the pan onto a sheet of wax paper and reuse for the next batch. Let the cookies dry, uncovered, for at least 4 hours at room temperature—overnight is best, so that the sugar coating adheres. **6** When you are ready to bake the cookies, set racks in the upper and lower thirds of the oven and preheat to 325 degrees.

7 Bake the cookies for about 15 to 20 minutes, or until they are firm and light golden color.

8 Slide the papers from the pans onto racks.

9 Store the cooled cookies between sheets of parchment or wax paper in a tin or plastic container with a tight-fitting cover.

VARIATION

ANISE DISKS: This old-fashioned Alsatian and Swiss cookie deserves to be better known. To make them, substitute 2 teaspoons anise extract for the vanilla extract. Pipe the cookies as 1½-inch disks. Sugar them the same way as the champagne fingers or not, as you wish. Let the cookies dry, uncovered, at room temperature for 24 hours before baking them. They are very delicate.

Piped Cookies

ALMOND BATONS

SOMETIMES REFERRED TO AS BATONS Rothschild, these are light and elegant cookies. Made from the same batter as Champagne Fingers, these are covered with ground almonds instead of sugar and the bottoms are iced with tempered chocolate or, if you prefer, Sugar-Based Chocolate Glaze for Cookies (page 319).

Makes about 50 cookies

1 batch batter for Champagne Fingers (page 132)

8 ounces (about 2 cups) whole blanched almonds, finely ground in the food processor

Tempered Chocolate (page 317), for finishing

3 cookie sheets or jelly roll pans covered with parchment or foil

1 Set racks in upper and lower thirds of oven and preheat to 325 degrees. **2** Prepare the batter and pipe the cookies as on pages 132–33. Cover the cookies completely with ground almonds and shake off the excess, as in the illustration on page 133. Do not let the cookies rest, but bake them immediately. **3** Bake the cookies for about 20 to 25 minutes, or until they are firm and a light golden color. **4** Slide the papers from the pans onto racks. **5** When the cookies have cooled, line them up, almond side down, on a clean pan. Spread the flat sides thinly with the tempered chocolate and allow the chocolate to set. **6** Store the cooled cookies between sheets of parchment or wax paper in a tin or plastic container with a tight-fitting cover.

Hazelnut Fingers

THESE COOKIES ARE JUST AS GOOD
when made with almonds, walnuts, or pecans.
They may also be used to make sandwiches
with a filling of melted milk white or dark
chocolate, Ganache for Filling Cookies (page
320), or some reduced, strained apricot
preserves.

Makes about 50 cookies

8 tablespoons (1 stick) unsalted butter, softened

½ cup sugar

1 teaspoon vanilla extract

2 egg whites

4 ounces (about 1 cup) whole unblanched hazelnuts, finely ground in the food processor

½ cup all-purpose flour

Two cookie sheets or jelly roll pans covered with parchment or foil

1 Set racks in the upper and lower thirds of the oven and preheat to 350 degrees. **2** In the bowl of a standing electric mixer fitted with the paddle attachment, beat together the butter and sugar on medium speed until soft and light, about 5 minutes. Add the vanilla. **3** Add the egg whites, one at a time, and continue beating until very creamy. Remove the bowl from the mixer and stir the hazelnuts and flour into the batter. **4** Scrape the batter into a pastry bag fitted with a ½-inch tube (Ateco #806). Position the bag at a 45-degree angle to the pan, with the bottom of the tube touching the paper. Squeeze and pull the tube toward you about 2 inches, then release the pressure and pull the tube away and up to avoid leaving a tail on the cookie. Place the fingers about an inch apart in all directions. **5** Bake for about 10 to 12 minutes, or until the cookies have spread, become matte-looking, and are colored around the edges. **6** Slide the papers from the pans onto racks. **7** Store the cooled cookies between sheets of parchment or wax paper in a tin or plastic container with a tight-fitting cover.

CIGARETTES

Now that smoking has become such an unpopular vice, I hesitated to include this cookie. Of course, the only similarity is in the shape.

Cigarette cookies are made by piping batter onto a pan, then rolling the baked cookie around the handle of a wooden spoon to make a cylinder. They may be left as they are or filled with butter cream or ganache. Luscious cookie, discredited name. Many thanks to my friend Ellen Baumwoll, proprietor of Bijoux Doux in Manhattan, for this recipe.

Makes about 50 cookies

12 tablespoons (1½ sticks) unsalted butter, softened

1½ cups confectioners' sugar

1 teaspoon vanilla extract

Pinch salt

4 large egg whites, freshly separated

1¼ cups all-purpose flour

4 or 5 cookie sheets or jelly roll pans covered with buttered foil (see Headnote, page 130)

1 Set a rack in the middle level of the oven and preheat to 375 degrees. **2** In the bowl of a standing electric mixer fitted with the paddle attachment, combine the butter, sugar, vanilla, and salt. Beat on medium speed until well mixed, about a minute. Beat in the egg whites, a tablespoon or so at a time, beating smooth after each addition. **3** Remove the bowl from the mixer and mix in the flour with a large rubber spatula. **4** Using a pastry bag fitted with a ½-inch plain tube (Ateco #806), pipe 1½-inch mounds of batter onto one of the prepared pans. Pipe six to a pan, about 4 to 5 inches apart. Use a small offset spatula to spread the batter out into 3½-inch disks. **5** Bake the pan of cookies for about 5 to 7 minutes, or until they are golden on the edges, dry and firm. Have several wooden spoons with handles of the same diameter ready and on a baking pan for easy handling on the stove, so you can roll the cookies quickly. Have another pan ready to receive the rolled cookies. Take the pan from the oven and remove one cookie with a thin spatula; immediately roll it around the handle of one of the spoons. Slide the cookie off the spoon handle almost immediately or it may stick. Place the rolled cookie carefully on the waiting pan. Repeat with the remaining cookies on the pan. If some of the cookies harden before you can roll them, return the pan to the oven for a very short time, to reheat and soften the cookies. Then roll them. To reuse a pan, make sure it has cooled completely, then reline it with fresh foil and butter it again before proceeding. **6** Store the cooled cookies between sheets of parchment or wax paper in a tin or plastic container with a tight-fitting cover.

NOTE This piped cookie must be spread with a small offset spatula, using much the same technique as for *Tulipes* (page 212). Only spread six or so on each pan or you won't have enough time after they come out of the oven to roll them before they harden. Don't try to bake more than one pan at a time or the process will turn into a nightmare and you'll end up burning more cookies than you roll. This is best as a two-person job.

VARIATION

FILLED CIGARETTES: Fill the cookies with any of the butter or chocolate-based fillings on pages 307–320, and press the ends into chopped toasted almonds or chopped pistachios.

LADYFINGERS

USE THESE LIGHT, TENDER COOKIES AS
the basis of a fancy dessert such as tiramisù
or a charlotte, or serve them with berries and
cream or any plain fruit dessert.

Makes about 40 cookies

1 teaspoon vanilla extract

½ cup granulated sugar

4 large eggs, separated

Pinch salt

1 cup cake flour

Confectioners' sugar for sprinkling

**2 or 3 cookie sheets or jelly roll pans
covered with parchment or foil**

1 Set racks in the upper and lower thirds of the
oven and preheat to 350 degrees. **2** In the bowl
of a standing electric mixer, whisk the vanilla
extract and ¼ cup granulated sugar into the yolks.
Place the bowl on the mixer stand fitted with the
whisk attachment and whip on medium speed until
light and lemon-colored, about 3 or 4 minutes.
Remove the bowl from the mixer. **3** If you only
have one bowl for your mixer, scrape the yolk
mixture into another bowl and wash the mixer
bowl and whisk attachment with hot, soapy water;
rinse and dry them. In a clean, dry mixer bowl,
combine the egg whites and salt. Place on the
mixer and with a clean whisk attachment whip
the egg whites on medium speed until they are
white, opaque, and beginning to hold their
shape. Increase the mixer speed to maximum
and continue to beat as you add the remaining ¼
cup granulated sugar in a slow stream. Beat until
the egg whites hold a firm peak. **4** Remove the
bowl from the mixer and with a rubber spatula fold
the yolks into the whites. Sift over and fold in the
flour in three or four additions. Remember to
scrape down to the bottom of the bowl as you fold
in the flour to make sure none is accumulating
there. **5** Using about half the batter at a time,
half-fill a pastry bag fitted with a ½-inch plain tube
(Ateco #806). Pipe 3-inch-long fingers onto the
prepared pans, leaving an inch around each in all
directions. Sift a heavy coating of confectioners'
sugar over the fingers. **6** Bake the cookies for
about 15 minutes, or until they are well risen and
firm and the exposed surfaces are a deep golden
color. **7** Slide the papers onto racks. **8** Store the
cooled cookies between sheets of parchment or
wax paper in a tin or plastic container with a tight-
fitting cover.

BUTTER ALMOND FINGERS

THESE COOKIES BRING OUT THE DELICACY of an almond-butter combination better than any other cookie I know. The covering of sliced almonds on these crisp, delicate cookies gives them a little extra crunch. Marilyn Miller was kind enough to share this recipe for which I had been searching for years.

Makes about 120 small cookies

18 tablespoons (2¼ sticks) unsalted butter, softened

1¼ cups sugar

⅛ teaspoon salt

1 teaspoon vanilla extract

1 large egg

2½ cups all-purpose flour

8 ounces (about 2 cups) blanched sliced almonds for covering the outside of the cookies

3 cookie sheets or jelly roll pans covered with parchment or foil

1 Set racks in the upper and lower thirds of the oven and preheat to 350 degrees. 2 In the bowl of a standing electric mixer fitted with the paddle attachment, beat the butter, sugar, salt, and vanilla on medium speed until soft and light, about 5 minutes. 3 Add the egg and continue beating until smooth. 4 Lower the speed and add the flour in several additions, beating smooth after each. 5 Remove the bowl from the mixer and with a large rubber spatula, give the dough a final mixing. 6 Using a pastry bag fitted with a ⅜-inch plain tube (Ateco #804), pipe the dough into 2½- to 3-inch fingers on the prepared pans. Leave about an inch around each cookie in all directions. After the cookies are all piped, sprinkle them with the sliced almonds, then with your fingertips gently press the almonds into the cookies. 7 Bake for about 15 to 20 minutes, until the cookies are firm and the almonds are a light golden color. 8 Slide the papers from the pans onto racks. 9 Store the cooled cookies between sheets of parchment or wax paper in a tin or plastic container with a tight-fitting cover.

SPRITZ COOKIES

THESE ARE A CLASSIC. THE GERMAN verb *spritzen* means "to squirt" and it is also the term used for piping with a pastry bag. Though these cookies may be formed in that way, this recipe is really meant for use with a cookie press. Look around at garage sales for the old-fashioned ones with a screw mechanism. I got my spiffy new Swiss cookie press at Williams-Sonoma and was assured that the store always carries them.

Makes about 75 cookies,
according to the size die used

16 tablespoons (2 sticks) unsalted butter, softened

¾ cup sugar

¼ teaspoon salt

1 teaspoon vanilla extract

3 large egg yolks

2½ cups all-purpose flour

2 or 3 cookie sheets or jelly roll pans covered with parchment or foil

1 Set racks in the upper and lower thirds of the oven and preheat to 375 degrees. **2** In the bowl of a standing electric mixer fitted with the paddle attachment, beat together on medium speed the butter, sugar, salt, and vanilla until very light and fluffy, about 5 minutes. Beat in the egg yolks, one at a time, beating smooth after each addition. **3** Scrape down the side of the bowl and beater. On low speed, add the flour and mix only until it is completely absorbed. Remove the bowl from the mixer and finish mixing the dough with a large rubber spatula. **4** Insert a die into the cookie press, then fill it with about a quarter of the dough. Press the cookies out onto the prepared pans, leaving an inch all around between cookies. **5** Bake the cookies for 10 to 12 minutes, or just until they are a very pale golden color. **6** Slide the papers from the pans onto racks. **7** Store the cooled cookies between sheets of parchment or wax paper in a tin or plastic container with a tight-fitting cover.

NOTE

Spritz cookies, depending upon their shape, are often decorated with bits of candied fruit, raisins, or nuts. They may also be made into sandwiches with ganache (page 320) or with melted milk chocolate. Some may be dipped partially or halfway in chocolate (page 317) or Sugar-Based Chocolate Glaze for Cookies (page 319). Dipped cookies may also have the dipped ends further dipped in chopped nuts or shaved chocolate.

W's

These pretty cookies are the signature cookie of Wittamer, the best pastry shop in Brussels. The traditional shape is a wavy W, but of course they may be piped in any shape. The recipe is adapted from *Les heures et les jours Wittamer* ("*The Hours and Days at Wittamer*") by Jean Pierre Gabriel (Editions Lannoo, 1994).

This recipe uses a typically European method: scraping out and using the seeds of a vanilla bean rather than vanilla extract.

Makes about 30 cookies

14 tablespoons (1¾ sticks) unsalted butter, softened

⅓ cup granulated sugar

½ vanilla bean, split, or 1 teaspoon vanilla extract

1 large egg white

2 cups all-purpose flour

Confectioners' sugar for sprinkling

2 cookie sheets or jelly roll pans covered with parchment or foil

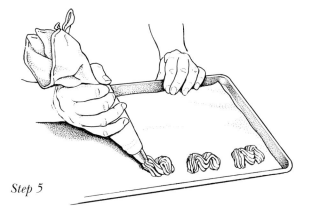

Step 5

1 Set racks in the upper and lower thirds of the oven and preheat to 350 degrees. **2** In the bowl of a standing electric mixer fitted with the paddle attachment, combine the butter and granulated sugar. **3** Use the point of a paring knife to remove the black seeds from the inside of the piece of vanilla bean and add them to the bowl. Beat on medium speed until well mixed, about 2 minutes. Add the egg white and continue to beat until smooth. **4** Lower the mixer speed and beat in the flour, just until it is absorbed. Remove the bowl from the mixer and finish mixing the dough with a large rubber spatula. **5** Using a pastry bag fitted with a ½-inch star tube (Ateco #824), pipe the dough onto the prepared pans in a series of W's (or whatever initial or shape you prefer). Leave about an inch in all directions around each, as in the illustration. **6** Bake the cookies for about 15 minutes, or until they are firm and very light golden. Slide the papers from the pans onto racks. **7** Just before serving the cookies, dust them with confectioners' sugar. **8** Store the cooled cookies between sheets of parchment or wax paper in a tin or plastic container with a tight-fitting cover.

Piped Cookies

PHILIP PORTWOOD'S BAR MITZVAH COOKIES

THESE WERE CREATED IN DALLAS BY Kyra Effren for the bar mitzvah of the son of our mutual friend, Sheri Portwood. Better than a standard spritz-type cookie, these are enriched with cream cheese and are especially fragile because of the combination of flour and cornstarch. To dot the center of the cookies with chocolate, I like to invert a chocolate chip—it fits just perfectly and leaves the center of the cookie with a perfect circle of chocolate.

Makes about 100 cookies

2 cups all-purpose flour

⅔ cup cornstarch

¼ teaspoon salt

16 tablespoons (2 sticks) unsalted butter, softened

4 ounces cream cheese, at room temperature

1 cup sugar

Finely grated zest of 2 medium lemons

1 tablespoon strained lemon juice

1 large egg yolk

Semisweet chocolate chips for finishing

2 cookie sheets or jelly roll pans covered with parchment or foil

1 Set racks in the upper and lower thirds of the oven and preheat to 350 degrees. **2** In a mixing bowl, combine the flour, cornstarch, and salt; stir well to mix. **3** In the bowl of a standing electric mixer fitted with the paddle attachment, beat together the butter, cream cheese, and sugar on medium speed until very light and fluffy, abut 5 minutes. Add the lemon zest, lemon juice, and egg yolk, and continue to beat until smooth. **4** Stop the mixer and scrape down the sides of bowl and the beater. On low speed, add the flour mixture, and beat only until the dry ingredients are absorbed. Remove the bowl from the mixer and finish mixing the dough with a large rubber spatula. **5** Using a pastry bag fitted with a ½-inch star tube (Ateco #824) pipe out 1-inch rosettes or stars about 2 inches apart in all directions. After all the cookies are on the pan, pop an inverted chocolate chip into the center of each cookie. **6** Bake the cookies for 12 to 15 minutes, or until they are golden and firm. **7** Slide the papers from the pans onto racks. **8** Store the cooled cookies between sheets of parchment or wax paper in a tin or plastic container with a tight-fitting cover.

CHOCOLATE-FILLED STARS

THESE COOKIES MAY BE PIPED WITH a star tube or put through a cookie press with any daisy-like die you have. They are indented in the center before baking, like thumbprint cookies, and after baking the dimples may be filled with Sugar-Based Chocolate Glaze for Cookies or Ganache for Filling Cookies.

Makes about 100 cookies,
depending on the size piped

2⅓ cups all-purpose flour

½ teaspoon salt

¼ teaspoon baking soda

10 tablespoons (1¼ sticks) unsalted butter, softened

½ cup firmly packed dark brown sugar

½ cup granulated sugar

1½ teaspoons vanilla extract

1 large egg

1 large egg yolk

Sugar-Based Chocolate Glaze for Cookies (page 319) or Ganache for Filling Cookies (page 320)

3 cookie sheets or jelly roll pans covered with parchment or foil

1 Set racks in the upper and lower thirds of the oven and preheat to 350 degrees. **2** In a bowl, combine the flour, salt, and baking soda; stir well to mix. **3** In the bowl of a standing electric mixer fitted with the paddle attachment, beat together the butter, brown sugar, and granulated sugar on medium speed until soft and light, about 5 minutes. Add the vanilla extract, whole egg, and egg yolk, beating smooth after each addition. **4** Lower the speed and beat in the flour mixture only until the flour is absorbed. Remove the bowl from mixer and give the dough a final mixing with a large rubber spatula. **5** Using a pastry bag fitted with a ½-inch star tube (Ateco #824) or a cookie press fitted with a star or daisy-shaped die, pipe out 1-inch-round cookies. If you are using a pastry bag, make rosettes or stars. After all the cookies are on the pan, with your index finger indent the center of each to make room for the filling. **6** Bake the cookies for 12 to 15 minutes, or until they are golden and firm. Slide the papers from the pans onto racks. **7** After the cookies have cooled, fill them with the chocolate glaze or ganache. Use a pastry bag fitted with a small plain tube, a paper cone, or the snipped corner of a nonpleated plastic bag. Let the filling set before packing up the cookies. **8** Store the cooled cookies between sheets of parchment or wax paper in a tin or plastic container with a tight-fitting cover.

Piped Cookies

CHERRY ROSETTE BUTTER COOKIES

THESE CHERRY-CENTERED COOKIES were part of every assortment of bakery cookies I remember from my childhood. They were always the ones I fished out first. I still do if no one is looking. If you don't like candied cherries, you may substitute a whole blanched almond or a pecan half. Dip the nut in a little beaten egg white so it sticks to the cookie dough.

Makes about 100 cookies

2⅓ cups all-purpose flour

¼ teaspoon salt

¼ teaspoon baking powder

10 tablespoons (1¼ sticks) unsalted butter, softened

1 cup sugar

1 teaspoon vanilla extract

½ teaspoon lemon extract

1 large egg

1 large egg yolk

100 halves or quarters of candied cherries for finishing the cookies

3 cookie sheets or jelly roll pans covered with parchment or foil

1 Set racks in the upper and lower thirds of the oven and preheat to 350 degrees. **2** In a bowl, combine the flour, salt, and baking powder; stir well to mix. **3** In the bowl of a standing electric mixer fitted with the paddle attachment, beat together on medium speed the butter and sugar until soft and light, about 5 minutes. Add the vanilla and lemon extracts, the whole egg, and the egg yolk, beating smooth after each addition. **4** Lower the speed and beat in the flour mixture, only until the flour is absorbed. Remove the bowl from the mixer and give the dough a final mixing with a large rubber spatula. **5** Using a pastry bag fitted with a ½-inch star tube (Ateco #824) or a cookie press fitted with a star or daisy-shaped die, pipe out 1-inch-round cookies. If you are using a pastry bag, make rosettes or stars. After all the cookies are on the pans, place a half or quarter cherry, rounded side up, in the center of each. **6** Bake the cookies for 12 to 15 minutes, or until they are golden and firm. Slide the papers from the pans onto racks. **7** Store the cooled cookies between sheets of parchment or wax paper in a tin or plastic container with a tight-fitting cover.

CHOCOLATE PEANUT S COOKIES

ALWAYS A TEMPTING COMBINATION, this peanut butter and chocolate cookie looks fancy but is actually quite easy to make. Though the directions in the recipe specify a star tube for piping out S's, this is a good recipe to use for trying the grooved-top ribbon die of your cookie press. If you use the ribbon die, press out flat, rectangular cookies. Thanks to Brenda van Horn for this delicious recipe.

Makes about 50 cookies

COOKIE DOUGH

1¼ cups all-purpose flour

2 teaspoons baking powder

⅛ teaspoon salt

8 tablespoons (1 stick) unsalted butter, softened

½ cup creamy peanut butter

½ cup firmly packed light brown sugar

½ cup granulated sugar

1 teaspoon vanilla extract

1 large egg

3 ounces bittersweet chocolate, finely grated (about 1 cup)

FINISHING

6 ounces bittersweet chocolate, melted and cooled

4 tablespoons (½ stick) unsalted butter, softened

1½ cups honey-roasted peanuts, finely chopped, but not ground

3 cookie sheets or jelly roll pans covered with parchment or foil

1 Set racks in the upper and lower thirds of the oven and preheat to 375 degrees. **2** In a bowl, combine the flour, baking powder, and salt; stir well to mix. **3** In the bowl of a standing electric mixer fitted with the paddle attachment, beat together on medium speed the butter, peanut butter, and sugars until well mixed and light, about 2 minutes. Add the vanilla and egg and beat until smooth. **4** Lower the speed and beat in the flour mixture and chocolate. Remove the bowl from the mixer and complete the mixing of the dough with a large rubber spatula. **5** Use a pastry bag fitted with a ½-inch star tube (Ateco #824) to pipe 2½-inch-long S shapes, about an inch apart all around, on the prepared pans. Or use a cookie press fitted with the grooved-top ribbon die and press the dough out flat in 2- to 3-inch rectangles. Bake the cookies for about 10 to 12 minutes, or until they are firm and a lightly golden. **6** Slide the papers from the pans onto racks. **7** To prepare the chocolate mixture, in a small bowl stir the chocolate and butter together until smooth. Have the chopped peanuts ready in another bowl nearby. Dip both ends of each cooled cookie in the chocolate mixture, then into the peanuts. Place the cookies on a parchment or foil-covered pan as they are finished. Leave at a cool room temperature for several hours to allow the chocolate to set. **8** Store the cookies between sheets of parchment or wax paper in a tin or plastic container with a tight-fitting cover.

SWISS CHOCOLATE RINGS

THESE ARE A POPULAR MILDLY CHOCO-late and crumbly textured Swiss cookie. The streaks of chocolate not only dress up the cookies, but also add a bit more chocolate flavor.

Makes about 35 cookies

1¾ cups all-purpose flour

2 tablespoons unsweetened cocoa powder, sifted after measuring

10 tablespoons (1¼ sticks) unsalted butter, softened

⅔ cup sugar

½ vanilla bean, split, or 1 teaspoon vanilla extract

1 large egg white

FINISHING

Sugar-Based Chocolate Glaze for Cookies (page 319)

1 ounce (about ¼ cup) sliced almonds, toasted and chopped

2 cookie sheets or jelly roll pans covered with parchment or foil

1 Set racks in the upper and lower thirds of the oven and preheat to 375 degrees. 2 Combine the flour and cocoa powder in a small bowl; stir well to mix. 3 In the bowl of a standing electric mixer fitted with the paddle attachment, combine the butter and sugar. Use the point of a paring knife to remove the black seeds from the inside of the piece of vanilla bean and add them to the bowl. (If using vanilla extract add it now.) Beat on medium speed until soft and light, about 5 minutes. Beat in the egg white and continue beating until smooth. 4 Lower the speed and add the flour mixture. Beat only until smooth. Remove the bowl from the mixer and finish mixing the dough with a large rubber spatula. 5 Using a pastry bag fitted with a ½-inch plain tube (Ateco #806), pipe the dough into 2½- to 3-inch-diameter circles on the prepared pans. Keep the tube close to the pan so that you pipe a flat circle as opposed to a cylindrical one. Leave about an inch around the cookies in all direc-

tions. 6 Bake the cookies for about 15 to 20 minutes, until they are firm and dull in appearance. Slide the papers from the pans onto racks. 7 After the cookies have cooled completely, use a paper cone, a squeeze bottle, or the snipped corner of a nonpleated plastic bag to streak them with the glaze. Sprinkle sparingly with the almonds quickly, while the glaze is still wet. 8 Store the cooled cookies between sheets of parchment or wax paper in a tin or plastic container with a tight-fitting cover.

Piped Cookies

CINNAMON SHELLS

THESE DAINTY SHELLS ARE ANOTHER popular Swiss cookie. They too are often piped in S shapes, but of course they may also be piped as straight sticks. Cinnamon is traditional to flavor these, but the same amount of another spice such as ginger or nutmeg would make an interesting variation. This dough works well in a cookie press.

Makes about 100 piped cookies,
slightly less when using a cookie press

1⅔ cups all-purpose flour, 2 cups flour
if using a press

¼ teaspoon salt

1 teaspoon ground cinnamon

12 tablespoons (1½ sticks) unsalted butter, softened

½ cup sugar

1 large egg yolk

2 cookie sheets or jelly roll pans
covered with parchment or foil

1 Set racks in the upper and lower thirds of the oven and preheat to 375 degrees. **2** In a bowl, combine the flour, salt, and cinnamon; stir well to mix. **3** In the bowl of a standing electric mixer fitted with the paddle attachment, beat together on medium speed the butter and sugar until soft and very light and fluffy, about 5 minutes. Add the egg yolk and continue beating until smooth. **4** Lower the speed and beat in the flour mixture. Beat only until the mixture forms a dough. Remove the bowl from the mixer and give a final mixing with a large rubber spatula. **5** Using a pastry bag fitted with a ½-inch star tube (Ateco #824), pipe the dough onto the prepared pans in 1-inch shells, leaving about an inch all around each cookie. **6** Bake the cookies for about 12 to 15 minutes, or until they are golden. Slide the papers from the pans onto racks. **7** Store the cooled cookies between sheets of parchment or wax paper in a tin or plastic container with a tight-fitting cover.

PASTE DI MELIGA

Italian Cornmeal Butter Cookies from Piemonte

I RECENTLY HAD THE OCCASION TO spend a long weekend in Asti in the Piedmont area of northern Italy. Of course, the first thing I did was to take a walk and look at all the pastry shops. There was one cookie in all of them: a delicately flavored but coarse-textured piped butter cookie with delicious tastes of cornmeal and vanilla. I came home and experimented with duplicating them. This recipe is the result.

Makes about 20 cookies

10 tablespoons (1¼ sticks) unsalted butter, softened

½ cup sugar

1 teaspoon vanilla extract

2 large egg yolks

1 cup all-purpose flour

⅔ cup stone-ground yellow cornmeal

**2 cookie sheets or jelly roll pans
covered with parchment or foil**

1 Set racks in the upper and lower thirds of the oven and preheat to 325 degrees. **2** In the bowl of a standing electric mixer fitted with the paddle attachment, beat together on medium speed the butter, sugar, and vanilla until very soft, fluffy, and whitened, about 5 minutes. **3** Add the egg yolks, one at a time, beating smooth after each addition. **4** Remove the bowl from the mixer and use a large rubber spatula to stir in the flour and cornmeal by hand. **5** Using a pastry bag fitted with a ½-inch star tube, (Ateco #824), pipe the cookie dough onto the prepared pans in double S curves about 2½ inches long, as in the illustration. Leave about 1½ inches around each cookie in all directions. These spread quite a bit. **6** Bake the cookies for about 15 minutes, or until they are firm and very light golden. **7** Slide the papers from the pans onto racks. **8** Store the cooled cookies between sheets of parchment or wax paper in a tin or plastic container with a tight-fitting cover.

Step 5

Swiss Raisin Drops

This unusual recipe makes a flat, buttery cookie dotted with chopped raisins. It is adapted from the bible of Swiss pastry art, *Swiss Bakery and Confectionery* by Walter Bachmann (Maclaren and Sons Limited, London, 1949).

Makes about 130 cookies

12 tablespoons (1½ sticks) unsalted butter, softened

¾ cup sugar

½ teaspoon lemon extract

3 large eggs

3 large egg yolks

2¼ cups all-purpose flour

6 ounces (about 1¼ cups) dark raisins, coarsely chopped

3 cookie sheets or jelly roll pans covered with parchment or foil

1 Set racks in the upper and lower thirds of the oven and preheat to 350 degrees. **2** In the bowl of a standing electric mixer fitted with the paddle attachment, beat together on medium speed the butter, sugar, and lemon extract until very light and fluffy, about 5 minutes. **3** In a bowl, whisk the eggs and yolks just until they are broken up. **4** Add about a third of the egg mixture to the butter mixture in the mixer bowl. Beat until it is absorbed and the batter is smooth again. Lower the mixer speed and add a third of the flour. Add half the remaining eggs, then half the remaining flour. When they are incorporated, beat in the remaining eggs, then the remaining flour. Beat in the raisins. **5** Remove the bowl from the mixer and finish mixing the batter by hand with a large rubber spatula. **6** Using a pastry bag fitted with a ½-inch plain tube (Ateco #806), pipe 1½-inch disks onto the prepared pans. Leave about 1½ inches around each cookie on all sides. **7** Bake the cookies for about 15 minutes, until they are firm and golden on edges. **8** Slide the papers from the pans onto racks. **9** Store the cooled cookies between sheets of parchment or wax paper in a tin or plastic container with a tight-fitting cover.

MERINGUES

IN THE RECIPES FOR TRUE MERINGUES THE EGG WHITE IS COMBINED WITH AT least twice its weight in sugar. The meringues in this section all follow those proportions but they are made in two ways: the ordinary meringue method or the Swiss meringue method.

To make ordinary meringue, whip egg whites until they start to hold their shape then begin adding the first half of the sugar slowly. When it is incorporated, fold the second half of the sugar in gently with a rubber spatula. Nuts are often added with the second half of the sugar and occasionally a little cornstarch for greater stability.

To make Swiss meringue, combine the egg whites and all the sugar in the bowl of an electric mixer. Place the bowl over a pan of simmering water and whisk gently by hand until the egg whites are hot and the sugar is dissolved. The best way to test this is with a fingertip: If you immerse the tip of your index finger in hot egg whites, you will instinctively withdraw it immediately. Rub that fingertip against the thumb of the same hand—if you can't feel any sugar granules the meringue is ready to be whipped. Whip the meringue by machine with the whip attachment until it has risen in volume and cooled to room temperature.

HINTS FOR MERINGUES

1 Separate eggs when they are cold—the whites are more viscous and hold together better when cold. 2 When separating the eggs, be careful not to break the yolks: a little yolk in the egg white will prevent it from whipping to a good volume and this, in turn, causes the meringue to be watery and unable to hold its shape. 3 Before whipping cold egg whites for ordinary meringue, stand the mixer bowl with the whites in it in several inches of warm tap water. This will warm the egg whites slightly so they will whip up better and more quickly. 4 No matter what type of meringue you are preparing, beware of overbeating and overmixing. Meringue gets overbeaten when you have left it too long in the mixer and it whips up until it gets a dry, grainy consistency. Meringue gets overmixed when you are folding other ingredients into the whipped egg whites. Fold gently and thoroughly, but not for so long or so hard that the folding deflates the mixture and renders it useless.

STORING BAKED MERINGUES

If you live in a humid climate, even the most carefully stored meringues may become soggy. If this happens, scatter the meringues on a parchment or foil-covered cookie sheet and bake them for about 30 minutes at your oven's lowest temperature setting. They will be crisp again after they cool.

Piped Cookies

WALNUT BOULDERS

This is an amazing variation on meringue cookies. They are giant kiss shapes filled with pieces of walnut and chewy raisins. The nuts and fruit make an excellent contrast to the crisp meringue.

Makes about 80 cookies

4 large egg whites (a bit more than ½ cup)

Pinch salt

1 cup sugar

4 ounces (about 1 cup) walnut pieces, chopped into ¼-inch pieces

1 cup dark raisins, chopped into ¼-inch pieces

2 tablespoons cornstarch

2 cookie sheets or jelly roll pans covered with parchment or foil

1 Set racks in the upper and lower thirds of the oven and preheat to 300 degrees. **2** In the bowl of a standing electric mixer fitted with the whip attachment, whip the egg whites and salt on medium speed for about 3 or 4 minutes or until white and opaque and beginning to hold their shape. **3** In a bowl, stir ½ cup sugar with the walnuts, raisins, and cornstarch. **4** When the egg whites are ready, increase the mixer speed to the maximum and add the remaining ½ cup sugar a tablespoon at a time. Beat until the egg whites are stiff but not dry. **5** Remove the bowl from the mixer and add the nut and raisin mixture. With a large rubber spatula fold it in thoroughly. **6** Using a pastry bag without a tube, pipe out kiss shapes 1½ inches in diameter on the prepared pans, leaving an inch all around each. **7** Bake the meringues for about 30 minutes, or until they are firm on the outside and still somewhat soft within. The best way to tell is to poke one with a fingertip—if there is only a wet area the size of a hazelnut in the center, they are ready. They will finish crisping as they cool. **8** Cool the meringues on the pans on racks. **9** Store the cooled cookies between sheets of parchment or wax paper in a tin or plastic container with a tight-fitting cover. (Store them only one-layer deep if you want to preserve the points on top.)

COFFEE PECAN MERINGUES

THESE CRISP MERINGUE FINGERS HAVE
an intriguing coffee flavor that puts them
definitely into the realm of "adult" cookies.
They're perfect with ice cream or any other
creamy dessert.

Makes about 80 cookies

4 large egg whites (a bit more than ½ cup)

Pinch salt

1 cup granulated sugar

**4 ounces (about 1 cup) pecan pieces, finely ground
in the food processor**

½ teaspoon ground cinnamon

2 teaspoons instant espresso powder

2 tablespoons cornstarch

Confectioners' sugar for sprinkling

**2 cookie sheets or jelly roll pans
covered with parchment or foil**

1 Set racks in the upper and lower thirds of the
oven and preheat to 300 degrees. **2** In the bowl
of a standing electric mixer fitted with the whip
attachment, whip together the egg whites and salt
on medium speed for about 3 or 4 minutes or
until white and opaque and beginning to hold
their shape. **3** In a small bowl, stir ½ cup of the
granulated sugar together with the pecans, cinnamon, coffee, and cornstarch. **4** When the egg
whites are ready, increase the mixer speed to the
maximum and add the remaining ½ cup granulated sugar a tablespoon at a time. Beat until the
egg whites are stiff but not dry. **5** Remove the
bowl from the mixer and add the pecan mixture.
Fold it in thoroughly with a large rubber spatula.
6 Using a pastry bag fitted with a ½-inch plain
tube (Ateco #806), pipe out 3-inch-long fingers
on the prepared pans, leaving about an inch
around each cookie. Dust the meringues with
confectioners' sugar. **7** Bake the meringues for
about 30 to 35 minutes, or until they are firm on
the outside and still somewhat soft within. The
best way to tell is to poke one with a fingertip—if
there is only a wet area the size of a hazelnut in
the center, they are ready. They will finish crisping as they cool. **8** Cool the meringues on the
pans on racks. **9** Store the cooled cookies
between sheets of parchment or wax paper in a
tin or plastic container with a tight-fitting cover.

Piped Cookies

Hazelnut Sticks

These easy nut meringues are among the most fragile of all cookies. Use them to accompany any creamy dessert or serve them after dinner with coffee.

Makes about 75 cookies

4 large egg whites (a bit more than ½ cup)

Pinch salt

1 cup sugar

4 ounces (about 1 cup) whole unblanched hazelnuts, finely ground in the food processor

2 tablespoons cornstarch

Tempered Chocolate for Dipping and Streaking Cookies (page 317) or Untempered Chocolate for Dipping and Streaking Cookies (page 318) for finishing

2 cookie sheets or jelly roll pans covered with parchment or foil

1 Set racks in the upper and lower thirds of the oven and preheat to 300 degrees. 2 In the bowl of a standing electric mixer fitted with the whip attachment, whip together the egg whites and salt on medium speed for about 3 or 4 minutes or until they are white and opaque and beginning to hold their shape. 3 In a small bowl, stir ½ cup of the sugar together with the ground hazelnuts and the cornstarch. 4 When the egg whites are ready, increase the mixer speed to the maximum and add the remaining ½ cup sugar a tablespoon at a time. Beat until the egg whites are stiff but not dry. 5 Remove the bowl from the mixer and add the hazelnut mixture. Fold it in thoroughly with a large rubber spatula. 6 Using a pastry bag fitted with a ½-inch plain tube (Ateco #806), pipe out 3-inch-long fingers on the prepared pans, leaving about an inch around each cookie. 7 Bake the meringues for about 30 minutes, or until they are firm. They will finish crisping as they cool. 8 Cool the meringues on the pans on racks. 9 Dip each end of the cooled sticks in chocolate, then replace the sticks on the paper-lined pans to set. 10 Store the cookies between sheets of parchment or wax paper in a tin or plastic container with a tight-fitting cover.

CHOCOLATE MERINGUE WREATHS

THESE RING-SHAPED COOKIES ARE
good at any time of the year, but always seem
so festive at the holidays. They keep well in
a tin, but are really best on the day they are
baked when they are still a little soft and
chewy in the center.

Makes about 30 cookies

½ cup egg whites (from about 3 or 4 large eggs)
Pinch salt
1¼ cups sugar
**6 ounces bittersweet (not unsweetened) chocolate,
melted and cooled**
Unsweetened cocoa for sprinkling
**2 or 3 cookie sheets or jelly roll pans covered
with parchment or foil**

1 Set racks in the upper and lower thirds of
the oven and preheat to 300 degrees. **2** Half-
fill a medium saucepan with water and on moderate heat, bring to a boil. Lower the heat so the
water simmers. **3** In the bowl of a standing
electric mixer, combine the egg whites, salt, and
all the sugar. Whisk by hand just to mix. Place
the bowl over the pan of water, and whisking
constantly, but slowly, heat the meringue, until
the egg white is hot and the sugar is dissolved,
about 3 or 4 minutes. **4** Place the bowl on the
mixer fitted with the whip and whip until the
meringue has cooled and increased in volume,
about 5 minutes. **5** Remove the bowl from
the mixer and use a large rubber spatula to
fold in the chocolate. **6** Using a pastry bag
fitted with a ½-inch star tube (Ateco #824),
pipe 2½- to 3-inch rings onto the prepared pans,
leaving about 1½ inches around each cookie.
Use a shaker or a small strainer to sprinkle the
meringues lightly with the cocoa. **7** Bake the
meringues for about 10 or 12 minutes, or until
they are dry on the outside and still somewhat
moist within. **8** Cool the cookies on the pans
on racks. **9** Store the cooled cookies between
sheets of parchment or wax paper in a tin or
plastic container with a tight-fitting cover.

VIRGULES
Commas

WHEN I WORKED AT THE SPORTING
Club in Monte Carlo in the early seventies,
these cookies were a specialty of Michel
Defino, the second-in-command pastry chef.
Michel used to sandwich these with praline
paste mixed with an equal weight of butter,
but I prefer chocolate.

Makes about 60 sandwiched cookies

ALMOND MERINGUE

4 large egg whites (a bit more than ½ cup)

Pinch salt

1 cup sugar

**4 ounces (about 1 cup) whole unblanched almonds
or hazelnuts, finely ground in the food processor**

2 tablespoons cornstarch

Unsweetened cocoa powder for sprinkling

CHOCOLATE FILLING

4 tablespoons (½ stick) unsalted butter, softened

**6 ounces semisweet or bittersweet chocolate,
melted and cooled**

**2 cookie sheets or jelly roll pans
covered with parchment or foil**

1 Set racks in the upper and lower thirds of the
oven and preheat to 300 degrees. **2** In the bowl
of an electric mixer fitted with the whip attachment, whip together the egg whites and salt on
medium speed for about 3 or 4 minutes or until
white and opaque and beginning to hold their
shape. **3** In a small bowl, stir ½ cup of the sugar
together with the ground almonds or hazelnuts
and the cornstarch. **4** When the egg whites are
ready, increase the mixer speed to the maximum
and add the remaining ½ cup sugar, a tablespoon
at a time. Beat until the egg whites are stiff but
not dry. **5** Remove the bowl from the mixer
and add the almond or hazelnut mixture. Fold
it in thoroughly with a large rubber spatula.
6 Using a pastry bag fitted with a ½-inch star
tube (Ateco #824), pipe out pairs of 2-inch-long

Step 6

comma shapes onto the prepared pans, as in the illustration. Leave about 1½ inches all around each cookie. Use a shaker or a small strainer to sprinkle the meringues very lightly with the cocoa. **7** Bake the meringues for about 30 minutes, or until they are firm on the outside and still somewhat soft within. They will finish crisping as they cool. **8** Cool the meringues on the pans on racks. **9** While they are cooling mix together the butter and the chocolate with a small rubber spatula. Use a paper cone or a nonpleated plastic bag snipped in one corner to pipe the chocolate filing on the flat side of one of each pair of the commas. Press the pair together and repeat with the remaining meringues. **10** Store the cookies between sheets of parchment or wax paper in a tin or plastic container with a tight-fitting cover.

MACAROONS

Old-fashioned Chewy Macaroons

Cherry Macaroon Rosettes

Gommés
("Gummed" or Glazed Macaroons)

Little Italy Pine Nut Macaroons

Richard Sax's Spumetti

Brown Sugar Pecan Macaroons

All-American
Coconut Macaroons

Golden Coconut Macaroons

Smooth French Macaroons

French Coffee Macaroons

French Hazelnut Macaroons

French Coconut Macaroons

MACAROONS ARE CHEWY, EGG-WHITE-BASED CONFECTIONS, THE SOFT COUSINS OF crisp meringues. For most Americans, coconut comes to mind if the word "macaroon" is mentioned. In fact, coconut macaroons are a fairly recent variation on an old theme.

Almost all European countries with strong sweet baking traditions have a macaroon particular to them. Italy has several different types of amaretti (little bitter things), named for the aromatic presence of bitter almonds that gives the macaroons that characteristically perfumed flavor. French macaroons are smooth-surfaced and elegant-looking. They come in many colors and flavors and are often sandwiched, flat sides together, around a little butter cream or jam in a similar or contrasting flavor.

Older recipes for macaroons tend to be more meringue-like. They call for more egg whites than contemporary recipes, so the macaroons they make are both lighter and at the same time less richly moist after baking. It seems contradictory—that macaroons with more egg white actually bake drier. Macaroon mixtures with less egg white rise less and consequently don't have as much surface to dry out to retain their structure. Therefore, they are baked a shorter time and remain moister after baking. Macaroons with more egg white have to be baked longer to keep their shape and consequently are drier.

Most macaroons are formed by being piped. Review the instructions for piping on pages 128–29.

HINTS FOR MACAROONS

1 If a recipe calls for almond paste, always use the type that comes in a can. Two brands are best: Solo and American. Avoid other brands. They may have water or excessive amounts of sugar added and either will make your macaroons collapse during baking. **2** Never beat macaroon mixtures very long. Even almond paste macaroons should be mixed only until the paste holds together. If there is a tiny lump or two of unmixed almond paste in the mixture, it will bake smooth. **3** Always bake macaroons immediately if you have moistened their surface. If the surface of the macaroons has not been moistened before baking the cookies, always allow them to dry. This may take from 30 minutes to 2 hours, according to individual recipes. **4** If macaroons are supposed to remain moist-textured, don't overbake or they will be hard as well as dry. **5** If macaroons are supposed to be crisp, don't underbake or they will collapse as they cool.

Macaroons

Old-fashioned
Chewy Macaroons

These are the kind of macaroons I remember from my childhood. They came from the Italian pastry shops in our neighborhood in Newark, New Jersey. They were moist and chewy and had a distinctive crackled surface. It turns out they are easy to duplicate but you must use the type of almond paste that comes in a can.

Makes about 50 macaroons

8 ounces canned almond paste, cut into ½-inch pieces

¾ cup granulated sugar, plus more for sprinkling before baking

⅓ cup confectioners' sugar

2 large egg whites

2 cookie sheets or jelly roll pans covered with parchment or foil

1 Set racks in the upper and lower thirds of the oven and preheat to 375 degrees. 2 In the bowl of a standing electric mixer fitted with the paddle attachment, beat together the almond paste and half the granulated sugar on low speed for about 3 or 4 minutes, until the almond paste is reduced to fine crumbs. Add the remaining ⅜ cup granulated sugar and the confectioners' sugar and continue to beat another 3 or 4 minutes. 3 Whisk the egg whites slightly to make them break up, then with the mixer still on low speed beat in about a quarter of them. As soon as the first quantity of egg white is absorbed, add more, and continue until all the egg white has been added and the macaroon paste is smooth and sticking to the bottom of the bowl. But the second it reaches that state, turn off the mixer. If beaten for too long the macaroons will puff and sink in the oven. All the adding and mixing should take about a minute. 4 Because the macaroon paste is firm and difficult to pipe, only put a little at a time into the pastry bag fitted with a ½-inch plain tube (Ateco #806). Pipe out 1-inch spheres onto the prepared pans and continue to add macaroon paste to the bag until all the cookies have been piped. 5 Fold a clean flat-weave kitchen towel the long way into a strip about 2 inches wide. Fill a small bowl with water. Wet the cloth and wring it out only slightly, so that some water is still dripping. Hold one end of the strip in each hand and drop the wet cloth onto the piped macaroons to flatten and moisten them. Repeat until all the macaroons have been moistened. 6 Sprinkle the moistened surfaces with granulated sugar and bake them immediately. 7 Bake

the macaroons for about 15 to 20 minutes, or until they are golden and firm on the outside but still soft within. **8** Cool the macaroons on the pans on racks. **9** Store the macaroons between sheets of parchment or wax paper in a tin or plastic container with a tight-fitting cover.

CHERRY MACAROON ROSETTES

THESE ARE A POPULAR MACAROON variation. If you don't like candied cherries substitute a blanched almond dipped in a little egg white to keep it in place.

Makes about 70 small cookies

8 ounces canned almond paste, cut into ½-inch pieces

1 cup sugar

2 large egg whites

1 teaspoon vanilla extract

Halves or quarters of candied cherries

2 cookie sheets or jelly roll pans covered with parchment or foil

1 In the bowl of a standing electric mixer fitted with the paddle attachment, beat together on low speed the almond paste and half the sugar for 3 or 4 minutes, until the almond paste is reduced to fine crumbs. Add the remaining sugar and continue beating another 3 or 4 minutes. **2** Whisk the egg whites slightly with the vanilla to break them up, then with the mixer still on low speed pour in about a quarter of the egg whites. As soon as the first quantity of egg white is absorbed, add more. Continue until all the egg white has been added. Mix until the macaroon paste is smooth and sticking to the bottom of the bowl, but no longer. Too much mixing will make the macaroons puff and sink in the oven. All the adding and mixing should take about a minute. **3** Because the macaroon paste is firm and difficult to pipe, only put a little at a time into the pastry bag fitted with a ½-inch star tube (Ateco #824). Pipe out 1-inch stars onto the prepared pans and continue to add macaroon paste to the bag until all the cookies have been piped. Decorate the center of each with a piece of cherry. **4** Let the macaroons dry, uncovered, at room temperature for an hour before baking them. **5** When you are ready to bake the macaroons, set racks in the upper and lower thirds of the oven and preheat to 375 degrees. **6** Bake the macaroons for about 10 minutes, or until they are golden and firm on the outside but still soft within. **7** Cool the macaroons on the pans on racks. **8** Store the macaroons between sheets of parchment or wax paper in a tin or plastic container with a tight-fitting cover.

GOMMÉS

"Gummed" or Glazed Macaroons

THESE MACAROONS HAVE A DECIDEDLY odd name; it means "gummed" in French. Originally, when these fancy-shaped cookies emerged from the oven they were brushed with a solution of gum arabic to make them shiny. Nowadays we use heated corn syrup to achieve the same results.

Makes about 70 cookies

8 ounces canned almond paste, cut into ½-inch pieces

⅔ cup granulated sugar

½ cup confectioners' sugar

2 large egg whites

1 teaspoon lemon extract

Small pieces of candied fruit or blanched sliced almonds dipped in egg white for finishing the cookies

½ cup light corn syrup for glazing

2 cookie sheets or jelly roll pans covered with parchment or foil

1 In the bowl of a standing electric mixer fitted with the paddle attachment, beat together on low speed the almond paste and all the granulated sugar for 3 or 4 minutes, until the almond paste is reduced to fine crumbs. Add the confectioners' sugar and continue beating another 3 or 4 minutes. **2** Whisk the egg whites slightly with the lemon extract to break them up, then with the mixer still on low speed pour in about a quarter of the egg whites. As soon as the first quantity of egg white is absorbed, add more. Continue until all the egg white has been added. Mix until the macaroon paste is smooth and sticking to the bottom of the bowl, but no longer. Too much mixing will make the macaroons puff and sink in the oven. All the adding and mixing should take about a minute. **3** Because the macaroon paste is firm and difficult to pipe, only put a little at a time into the pastry bag fitted with a ½-inch star tube (Ateco #824). Pipe out 1-inch stars onto the prepared pans and continue to add macaroon paste to the bag until all the cookies have been piped. Decorate the center of each with a piece of candied fruit or a sliced almond. **4** Let the macaroons dry, uncovered, at room temperature for an hour before baking them. **5** When you are ready to bake the macaroons, set racks in the upper and lower thirds of the oven and preheat to 400 degrees. **6** Bake the macaroons for about 10 minutes, or until they are golden and firm on the outside but still soft within. **7** While the macaroons are baking, pour the corn syrup into a small saucepan and heat it over low heat until it is simmering. As soon as the macaroons come out of the oven, brush them with the hot corn syrup. **8** Cool the macaroons on the pans on racks until the corn syrup has dried. **9** Store the macaroons between sheets of parchment or wax paper in a tin or plastic container with a tight-fitting cover.

LITTLE ITALY PINE NUT MACAROONS

THIS OLD RECIPE IS FOR VERY DELICATELY flavored macaroons made famous by the Ferrara pastry shop on Grand Street in New York's Little Italy. Thanks to food journalist Irene Sax for finding and head baker Dennis Canciello for sharing the recipe.

Makes about 60 cookies

½ **cup granulated sugar**

8 ounces (about 2 cups) whole blanched almonds

3 large egg whites

1 cup confectioners' sugar

4 ounces (about 1 cup) raw pine nuts for topping

2 cookie sheets or jelly roll pans
covered with parchment or foil

1 Set racks in the upper and lower thirds of the oven and preheat to 300 degrees. **2** In the work bowl of a food processor fitted with the steel blade, pulse the granulated sugar and almonds repeatedly to grind them very finely. The whole process should take about 3 or 4 minutes. You are finished when there are no discernible pieces of almond. As the machine is grinding, stop it occasionally and scrape around the inside walls and bottom of the work bowl with a narrow metal spatula to dislodge anything caked there. Pour the ground mixture into a mixing bowl. **3** Use a large rubber spatula to work in half the egg whites. Sift over and work in the confectioners' sugar, adding the remaining egg whites little by little, to make a smooth, heavy paste. **4** Using a pastry bag fitted with a ½-inch plain tube (Ateco #806), pipe 1½-inch macaroons onto the prepared pans, leaving about an inch all around each cookie. Top each with pine nuts and gently press them in with your fingertips. **5** Bake the macaroons for about 30 minutes, or until they are golden, risen, and still moist within. If you poke one with a fingertip the center will still be wet. **6** Cool the macaroons on the pans on racks. **7** Store the cooled macaroons between sheets of parchment or wax paper in a tin or plastic container with a tight-fitting cover.

RICHARD SAX'S SPUMETTI

THESE LOVELY ITALIAN MACAROONS are amusingly sometimes known as *brutti ma buoni*: ugly but good. (*Spumetti* actually means "little foamies," referring to their texture.) There are several different ways to prepare this Italian classic, though this is the easiest. The recipe comes from *The Cookie Lover's Cook Book* (HarperPerennial, 1986), by my late friend Richard Sax. The book is long out of print, but worthwhile searching for in used bookstores.

Makes about 30 cookies

6 ounces (about 1½ cups) unblanched hazelnuts

1 cup confectioners' sugar

3 tablespoons unsweetened cocoa powder

¼ teaspoon ground cinnamon

3 large egg whites

Pinch salt

2 or 3 cookie sheets or jelly roll pans covered with parchment or foil

1 Set racks in the upper and lower thirds of the oven and preheat to 350 degrees. 2 Toast the hazelnuts in a small roasting pan for 10 or 15 minutes, or until they are fragrant. Rub the hazelnuts in a towel to remove as much skin as possible, then set them aside in a bowl to cool. Chop coarsely with a knife or in the food processor. 3 Sift ¼ cup of the confectioners' sugar with the cocoa and cinnamon onto a piece of paper. 4 In the bowl of a standing electric mixer fitted with the whip attachment, whip the egg whites and salt on medium speed until they begin to look frothy. Whip in the remaining ¾ cup confectioners' sugar a tablespoon at a time, until the whites hold a firm peak, about 3 or 4 minutes. 5 Remove the bowl from the mixer and fold in the sifted ingredients and the hazelnuts. 6 Use a tablespoon to spoon out the batter onto the prepared pans. Leave about 2 inches around each one. 7 Bake the macaroons for about 20 to 25 minutes, or until they are risen and still soft within. 8 Place the pans on racks to cool. 9 Store the macaroons between sheets of parchment or wax paper in a tin or plastic container with a tight-fitting cover.

Brown Sugar Pecan Macaroons

These treats are as easy to make as they are to consume. The combination of the brown sugar and pecans in this chewy cookie is a perfect one. Thanks to Marilynn and Sheila Brass for this contribution.

Makes about 40 cookies

2 large egg whites

½ teaspoon salt

**2 cups firmly packed dark brown sugar
(or one 1-pound box)**

**8 ounces (about 2 cups) pecan pieces, lightly
toasted and chopped into ¼-inch pieces**

**2 cookie sheets or jelly roll pans covered
with parchment or foil**

1 Set racks in the upper and lower thirds of the oven and preheat to 350 degrees. 2 In the bowl of a standing electric mixer fitted with the whip attachment, whip the egg whites and salt on medium speed until they hold a firm peak, about 2 or 3 minutes. 3 Remove the bowl from the mixer, and with a large rubber spatula, fold in the sugar and the pecans. The egg whites will deflate entirely and the mixture will become sticky and pasty. 4 Using a pastry bag fitted with a ½-inch plain tube (Ateco #806), pipe out 1½-inch macaroons onto the prepared pans. Leave about 2 inches around each cookie. 5 Bake for about 20 minutes, or until the macaroons are puffed and somewhat firm. Cool on the pans on racks. 6 Store the cooled cookies between sheets of parchment or wax paper in a tin or plastic container with a tight-fitting cover.

ALL-AMERICAN COCONUT MACAROONS

THIS IS ANOTHER RECIPE FROM MY friend Kyra Effren, a champion cookie baker. Unsweetened coconut is called for, easier to find in a health food store than in the supermarket.

Makes about 50 cookies

½ cup egg whites (about 3 or 4 large eggs)

Pinch salt

2 teaspoons lemon juice

1 cup sugar

1 teaspoon vanilla extract

5 ounces (about 2 cups) unsweetened shredded coconut

2 cookie sheets or jelly roll pans covered with parchment or foil

1 Set racks in the upper and lower thirds of the oven and preheat to 325 degrees. **2** In the bowl of a standing electric mixer fitted with the whip attachment, whip together on medium speed the egg whites, salt, and lemon juice until white, opaque, and beginning to hold their shape, about 3 or 4 minutes. Increase the speed to the maximum and, 1 tablespoon at a time, add the sugar. Continue to beat until the egg whites are very stiff, but not dry. **3** Whip in the vanilla extract. **4** Remove the bowl from the mixer and with a large rubber spatula, fold in the coconut. **5** Use a teaspoon or a small ice cream scoop to spoon the macaroon paste out onto the prepared pans. Leave about an inch around the cookies in all directions. **6** Bake the macaroons for about 15 to 20 minutes or until they are a golden color, but still moist within. **7** Slide the papers from the pans to racks. **8** Store the cooled cookies between sheets of parchment or wax paper in a tin or plastic container with a tight-fitting cover.

GOLDEN COCONUT MACAROONS

THESE ARE A VARIATION ON THE classic coconut macaroons made with meringue. The whole eggs make them richer and, somehow, a little less sweet. Another wonderful Jayne Sutton recipe.

Makes about 40 macaroons

One 7-ounce package sweetened shredded coconut

2 large eggs

Pinch salt

⅔ cup sugar

1 teaspoon vanilla extract

2 cookie sheets or jelly roll pans covered with parchment or foil

1 Set racks in the upper and lower thirds of the oven and preheat to 350 degrees. **2** In the work bowl of a food processor fitted with the steel blade, pulse the coconut about six or eight times at 1-second intervals to chop, not grind, it. **3** In a medium bowl, whisk the eggs with the salt until they are combined. **4** Whisk in the sugar in a stream, then the vanilla. Fold in the coconut. **5** Drop rounded tablespoons of the macaroons onto the prepared pans. Leave about 2 inches all around between each. **6** Bake for about 12 to 15 minutes, or until the macaroons are a deep golden color and still soft within. **7** Slide the papers from the pans to racks. **8** Store the cooled macaroons between sheets of parchment or wax paper in a tin or plastic container with a tight-fitting cover.

SMOOTH FRENCH MACAROONS

THESE ARE THE BEAUTIFULLY SMOOTH-topped pink macaroons you see at all the best pastry shops in Paris. It's also possible to buy them in New York at François Payard's Patis-serie and Bistro on Lexington Avenue. And because François generously shared his recipe for these popular macaroons, you can make them in your own kitchen. François makes macaroons in pink, yellow, and green—you can use any color you like. The macaroons may be sandwiched with some raspberry jam as they are here, or with a similar or contrasting flavor of butter cream—or even some Ganache for Filling Cookies (see page 320).

Makes about 30 sandwiched macaroons

1½ cups confectioners' sugar

6 ounces (about 1½ cups) whole blanched almonds

4 large egg whites

½ cup granulated sugar

2 tablespoons water

2 tablespoons light corn syrup

Red food coloring

⅔ cup seedless raspberry jam for sandwiching the macaroons

2 cookie sheets or jelly roll pans covered with parchment or foil, plus two more uncovered pans

1 In the work bowl of a food processor fitted with the steel blade, pulse the confectioners' sugar with the almonds repeatedly for 3 or 4 minutes. The nuts should be ground very fine and there shouldn't be any discernible pieces of almond left. As you are grinding, stop the machine occasionally and scrape down around the inside and bottom of the work bowl with the end of a narrow metal spatula to dislodge any of the ground mixture caked there. Pour the ground mixture into a bowl. 2 Half-fill a saucepan with water and bring it to a boil over medium heat. Lower to a simmer. In the bowl of a standing elec-tric mixer combine the egg whites, granulated sugar, and water. Place the bowl on the pan of water and whisk gently until the egg whites are hot and the sugar is dissolved. Place the bowl on the mixer fitted with the whip attachment and beat until cooled and stiff. 3 Gently fold in the almond and sugar mixture and the corn syrup into the meringue. Fold in several drops of food coloring. The macaroon paste should be tinted a deep pink. 4 Using a pastry bag fitted with a ½-inch plain tube (Ateco #806), pipe 1½-inch macaroons onto the prepared pans. Leave about an inch around each cookie in all directions. Let the macaroons dry, uncovered, at room tempera-ture for an hour. 5 When you are ready to bake

the macaroons, set racks in the upper and lower thirds of the oven and preheat to 300 degrees. The macaroons will be baked only in the lower third. Place one empty pan on the upper rack of the oven to protect the macaroons from the top heat, then place another empty pan on the lower rack so that the macaroons will bake on two pans and be protected from the bottom heat. Place a pan of macaroons on the lower pan and bake for 10 to 12 minutes, or until the macaroons are risen and are smooth and crackled around the edges that meet the pan. Remove the pan with the mac-aroons on it to a rack to cool. Place the second pan of macaroons in the oven on the pan that is still on the lower rack and bake the remaining macaroons. **6** While the macaroons are cooling, heat the jam to a simmer in a small saucepan on medium heat, stirring often. **7** After the maca-roons have cooled, detach them from the paper and sandwich them together, using about ¼ tea-spoon of the jam for each pair. **8** Store the sandwiched macaroons between sheets of parch-ment or wax paper in a tin or plastic container with a tight-fitting cover.

FRENCH COFFEE MACAROONS

THESE ARE ANOTHER VARIATION ON
François Payard's classic macaroons on page
172.

Makes about 30 sandwiched macaroons

1½ cups confectioners' sugar

6 ounces (about 1½ cups) whole blanched almonds

4 large egg whites

½ cup granulated sugar

1 tablespoon water

3 tablespoons instant espresso coffee dissolved
in 1 tablespoon hot water

2 tablespoons light corn syrup

1 batch Ganache for Filling Cookies (page 320)

2 cookie sheets or jelly roll pans covered with
parchment or foil, plus two more uncovered pans

1 In the work bowl of a food processor fitted
with the steel blade, pulse the confectioners'
sugar with the almonds repeatedly for 3 or 4
minutes. The nuts should be ground very fine
and there shouldn't be any discernible pieces
of almond left. As you are grinding, stop the
machine occasionally and scrape down around
the inside and bottom of the work bowl with the
end of a narrow metal spatula to dislodge any of
the ground mixture caked there. Pour the
ground mixture into a bowl. **2** Half-fill a
saucepan with water and bring it to a boil over
medium heat. Lower to a simmer. In the bowl of a
standing electric mixer combine the egg whites,
granulated sugar, and water. Place the bowl on the
pan of water and whisk gently until the egg whites
are hot and the sugar is dissolved. Place the bowl
on the mixer fitted with the whip attachment and
beat until cooled and stiff. **3** Gently fold the
almond and sugar mixture and the corn syrup
into the meringue. Fold in the coffee mixture.
The macaroon paste should be tinted a deep
beige. **4** Using a pastry bag fitted with a ½-inch
plain tube (Ateco #806), pipe 1½-inch macaroons onto the prepared pans. Leave about an
inch around each cookie in all directions. Let the
macaroons dry, uncovered, at room temperature
for an hour. **5** When you are ready to bake the
macaroons, set racks in the upper and lower
thirds of the oven and preheat to 300 degrees.
The macaroons will be baked only in the lower
third. Place one empty pan on the upper rack of
the oven to protect the macaroons from the top
heat, then place another empty pan on the lower
rack so that the macaroons will bake on two pans
and be protected from the bottom heat. Place a
pan of macaroons on the lower pan and bake for
10 to 12 minutes, or until the macaroons are risen
and are smooth and crackled around the edges
that meet the pan. Remove the pan with the macaroons on it to a rack to cool. Place the second
pan of macaroons in the oven on the pan that is
still on the lower rack and bake the remaining

macaroons. **6** After the macaroons have cooled, detach them from the paper and sandwich them with about ¼ teaspoon of the ganache for each pair. **7** Store the sandwiched macaroons between sheets of parchment or wax paper in a tin or plastic container with a tight-fitting cover.

FRENCH HAZELNUT MACAROONS

FRANÇOIS PAYARD'S MACAROONS ARE so wonderful it's almost irresistible to keep trying variations. This one has hazelnuts rather than almonds.

Makes about 30 sandwiched macaroons

1½ cups confectioners' sugar

6 ounces (about 1½ cups) whole blanched hazelnuts, plus finely chopped hazelnuts to sprinkle over the macaroons

4 large egg whites

½ cup granulated sugar

2 tablespoons water

2 tablespoons light corn syrup

1 batch Ganache for Filling Cookies (page 320)

2 cookie sheets or jelly roll pans covered with parchment or foil, plus two more uncovered pans

1 In the work bowl of a food processor fitted with the steel blade, pulse the confectioners' sugar with the hazelnuts repeatedly for 3 or 4 minutes. The nuts should be ground very fine and there shouldn't be any discernible pieces of hazelnut left. As you are grinding, stop the machine occa-sionally and scrape down around the inside and bottom of the work bowl with the end of a narrow metal spatula to dislodge any of the ground mixture caked there. Pour the ground mixture into a bowl. **2** Half-fill a saucepan with water and bring it to a boil over medium heat. Lower to a simmer. In the bowl of a standing electric mixer combine the egg whites, granulated sugar, and water. Place the bowl on the pan of water and whisk gently until the egg whites are hot and the sugar is dissolved. Place the bowl on the mixer fitted with the whip attachment and beat until cooled and stiff. **3** Gently fold the hazelnut and sugar mixture and the corn syrup into the meringue. **4** Using a pastry bag fitted with a ½-inch plain tube (Ateco #806), pipe 1½-inch macaroons onto the prepared pans. Leave about an inch around each cookie in all directions. Sprinkle the macaroons with the finely chopped hazelnuts and let them dry, uncovered, at room temperature for an hour. **5** When you are ready to bake the macaroons, set racks in the upper and lower thirds of the oven and preheat to 300 degrees. The macaroons will be baked only in the lower third. Place one empty pan on the upper rack of the oven to protect the macaroons from the top heat, then place another empty pan on the lower rack so that the macaroons will bake on two pans and be protected from the bottom heat. Place a pan of macaroons on the lower pan and bake for 10 to 12 minutes, or until the macaroons are risen and are smooth and crackled around the edges that meet the pan. Remove the pan with the maca-roons on it to a rack to cool. Place the second pan of macaroons in the oven on the pan that is already on the lower rack and bake the remaining macaroons. **6** After the macaroons have cooled, detach them from the paper and sandwich them with about ¼ teaspoon of the ganache for each pair. **7** Store the sandwiched macaroons between sheets of parchment or wax paper in a tin or plastic container with a tight-fitting cover.

FRENCH COCONUT
MACAROONS

THESE ARE ANOTHER VARIATION ON Payard's Smooth French Macaroons (page 172). They are exquisite, a high-class version of the standard American coconut cookie.

Makes about 30 sandwiched macaroons

1½ cups confectioners' sugar, divided

6 ounces (about 2 cups) unsweetened coconut, plus more to sprinkle on the macaroons

4 large egg whites

½ cup granulated sugar

2 tablespoons water

2 tablespoons light corn syrup

1 batch Lemon Curd (page 316) for sandwiching the macaroons

2 cookie sheets or jelly roll pans covered with parchment or foil, plus two more uncovered pans

1 In the work bowl of a food processor fitted with the steel blade, pulse the confectioners' sugar with the coconut repeatedly for 3 or 4 minutes. The coconut should be ground very fine and there shouldn't be any discernible pieces of coconut left. As you are grinding, stop the machine occasionally and scrape down around the inside and bottom of the work bowl with the end of a narrow metal spatula to dis-lodge any of the ground mixture caked there. Pour the ground mixture into a bowl. **2** Half-fill a saucepan with water and bring it to a boil over medium heat. Lower to a simmer. In the bowl of a standing electric mixer combine the egg whites, granulated sugar, and water. Place the bowl on the pan of water and whisk gently until the egg whites are hot and the sugar is dissolved. Place the bowl on the mixer fitted with the whip attachment and beat until cooled and stiff. **3** Gently fold the almond and sugar mixture and the corn syrup into the meringue. **4** Using a pastry bag fitted with a ½-inch plain tube (Ateco #806), pipe 1½-inch macaroons onto the prepared pans. Leave about an inch around each cookie in all directions. Sprinkle the macaroons with more coconut and let them dry, uncovered, at room temperature for an hour. **5** When you are ready to bake the macaroons, set racks in the upper and lower thirds of the oven and preheat to 300 degrees. The macaroons will be baked only in the lower third. Place one empty pan on the upper rack of the oven to protect the macaroons from the top heat, then place another empty pan on the lower rack so that the macaroons will bake on two pans and be protected from the bottom heat. Place a pan of macaroons on the lower pan and bake for 10 to 12 minutes, or until the macaroons are risen and are smooth and crackled around the edges that meet the pan. Remove the pan with the macaroons on it to a rack to cool. Place the second pan of macaroons in the oven on the pan that is still on the lower rack and bake the remaining macaroons. **6** After the macaroons have cooled, detach them from the paper and sandwich them with about ¼ teaspoon of the lemon curd for each pair. **7** Store the sandwiched macaroons between sheets of parchment or wax paper in a tin or plastic container with a tight-fitting cover.

MOLDED COOKIES

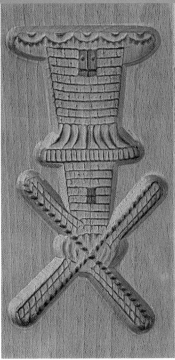

Pecan Butter Balls

Crisp Coconut Cookies

Chocolate Hazelnut Truffles

Kourabiethes
(Greek Almond Cookies)

Macadamia Lime Cookies

Wiener Mandelgipferl
(Little Viennese
Almond Crescents)

Sonja Henies

Crackled Chocolate Cookies

Chinese Almond Cookies

The Good Cook's Gingersnaps

Chunky Peanut Butter Cookies

Mostaccioli Baresi
(Spice Cookies from Bari)

Koulourakia
(Greek Sesame Ring Cookies)

Love Knots

Vanilla Pretzels

Biscotti di Vino
(Red Wine Cookies)

Taralli Dolci di Pasqua
(Easter Ring Cookies)

Buttermilk Fudge Gems

Shortbread Gems

Madeleines
(French Shell Cookies)

Petits Financiers
(Little Financier Cookies)

Tulipes
(Cookie Cup Dessert Shells)

Anisbroetli
(Swiss Anise Cookies)

Badener Chrabeli
(Little Claws from Baden)

Speculaas

MOLDED COOKIES FALL INTO SEVERAL CATEGORIES: SOME ARE MADE BY PRESSING dough into a mold or form or pressing a mold or form onto a piece of dough to imprint a design or shape on it (Swiss and German Springerle and Dutch speculaas are made this way). Others are made by actually baking dough or batter in a plain or decorative mold, like *financiers* and madeleines. Still others are molded by hand into simple or complex shapes, the way a simple gingersnap is rolled into a ball before being placed on the pan to bake.

Whether you want to press a design into the cookie or to bake the dough or batter in a mold, kitchenware stores and mail-order sources make them widely available.

HINTS FOR MOLDED COOKIES

HAND-MOLDED COOKIES

1 Use a small ice cream scoop, measuring spoon, or other consistent measure for the dough to keep the cookies uniform in size. **2** When you are rolling cookie into balls it's better to oil or butter your hands than to flour them. The flour on your hands could bake on the cookies and make an unattractive crust. **3** When a recipe says to roll dough into narrow, pencil-like strands, use very little flour on the work surface or the dough might just slide around rather than rolling into a cylinder. **4** Use a ruler if a recipe calls for cutting dough to specific dimensions. You'll be a lot happier with the resulting neat and uniform cookies.

COOKIES FORMED, BUT NOT BAKED, IN MOLDS

1 Make sure the surface of the dough is lightly floured before you press the mold into it. **2** The face of the mold should also be lightly floured. **3** Press the mold lightly but firmly. Too much pressure may make the dough stick to the mold. **4** Remove the mold before you cut around the cookie. A mold left on dough for a long time might stick. **5** If the molds are sticking, try letting the dough dry at room temperature for 20 minutes before pressing with the mold. **6** If the cookies are to be pressed *into* and emerge from a mold, generously flour the inside of the mold first. Try to form a piece of dough so it is roughly the shape of the cavity in the mold. That way you are less likely to press too much dough into the mold, which could cause it to stick. After the dough is pressed into the mold, trim it even with the top of the form. To ease the dough out of the mold, start by digging loose one corner, then inverting the mold over a baking pan. The cookie should drop out of the mold. If the dough doesn't drop even with a pulled-up corner, hold the mold at a 45-degree angle away from you and gently, but smartly, tap the far end of the mold against the work surface a few times. This should encourage the cookie to drop.

COOKIES BAKED IN MOLDS

1 Prepare molds by buttering and flouring them. Use soft not melted butter and apply it with a brush. It will coat the inside of the mold more thickly. **2** To flour the molds, apply a thin coat of flour and tap it around in the mold so all surfaces are covered. Then turn the mold over and rap it smartly against the work surface to knock out excess flour.
3 After cookies baked in molds emerge from the oven, let them stand a minute or two, then unmold them and arrange them right side up on racks to cool.

COOKIES FORMED IN MOLDS

Some of the most beautiful cookies possible are those given a decorative design or shape by molds. Some molds are designed to be pressed into dough and lifted off. The cookie is cut out around the shape the mold has imprinted. Others are designed to have dough pressed into the cavity and either removed to bake on a pan or left to bake right in the mold. The resulting cookie not only has a design imprinted on it but also the particular shape. Review the hints on page 181 before you start any of the following recipes.

PECAN BUTTER BALLS

THIS RECIPE COMES FROM MY OLD friend Peter Fresulone, who, along with Bill Liederman, was my partner in the Total Heaven Baking Company in the early eighties. We must have sold at least a ton of these cookies a year—they were one of our most popular items. At the time Peter said the recipe had come from his aunt so we always jokingly called them Zi' Rosa's cookies. The joke was that there is absolutely nothing Italian about them.

When Peter went to look for the recipe so that I could reprint it here, he found out that it had actually been given to him by his sister, Carol Pascarella. Belatedly, thanks, Carol, after all these years.

Makes about 50 cookies

16 tablespoons (2 sticks) unsalted butter, softened

⅓ cup granulated sugar

½ teaspoon salt

1 teaspoon vanilla extract

1 tablespoon water (or dark rum, bourbon, or brandy)

2 cups all-purpose flour

8 ounces (about 2 cups) pecan pieces, finely chopped, but not ground, in the food processor

1 cup confectioners' sugar for finishing

2 cookie sheets or jelly roll pans covered with parchment or foil

1 Set racks in the upper and lower thirds of the oven and preheat to 325 degrees. 2 In the bowl of a standing electric mixer fitted with the paddle attachment, beat together on medium speed the butter, granulated sugar, and salt until soft and fairly light, about 3 minutes. 3 Beat in the vanilla and water and continue beating until smooth. 4 Remove the bowl from the mixer and stir in the flour and pecans with a large rubber spatula. Keep mixing until the dough holds together. 5 Use a small ice cream or melon ball scoop to separate pieces of the dough for the cookies. Roll the dough between the palms of your hands to make a ball and place on the baking pan leaving about an inch around each. They don't spread, but they do puff slightly. Repeat until all the dough has been used. 6 Another method is to roll pieces of the dough under the palms of your hands to make a cylinder about an inch thick. Cut off ¾-inch pieces of the dough and roll as above. 7 Bake the cookies for about 15 to 20 minutes, or until they are firm and golden. Slide the papers from the pans to racks. 8 After they are cold, sift the confectioners' sugar into a shallow bowl and roll the cookies in it. 9 Store the cooled cookies between sheets of parchment or wax paper in a tin or plastic container with a tight-fitting cover.

(continued)

Molded Cookies

VANILLA BALLS: This is an interesting variation on the pecan ball theme sent to me by my friend Sheri Portwood. She uses cream to replace some of the butter, which makes an extremely tender and fragile cookie. I'll just give the ingredient list, because mixing, shaping, and baking are the same as the recipe above with one notable exception. Sheri rolls the cookies in the confectioners' sugar while they're still warm—it makes more sugar stick to the cookies.

Makes about 40 cookies

12 tablespoons (1½ sticks) unsalted butter, softened

⅓ cup confectioners' sugar, plus 1 cup for finishing

1 teaspoon vanilla extract

¼ cup heavy whipping cream

1¾ cups all-purpose flour

3 ounces (about ¾ cup) lightly toasted pecans or other nuts, finely chopped, but not ground, in the food processor

CRISP COCONUT COOKIES

THIS INTRIGUING COOKIE CAME TO ME by way of Carrie Fisher. The one from Carlisle, Pennsylvania, not the movie star. At first glance, it doesn't seem different from other recipes of the same type. But in this recipe bicarbonate of ammonia is used as the leavening. That not only makes the cookies puff beautifully while they are baking, but also leaves them extremely crisp after they have cooled.

Baker's ammonia is available in most Chinese grocery stores and in German, Middle

Eastern, and Greek specialty stores. See Sources at the end of the book for mail order.

If you have never used baker's ammonia, don't be surprised if the cookies smell and taste like ammonia when you take them out of the oven; the aroma will dissipate when they cool.

If you can't find the ammonia and want to try these cookies, you can always substitute baking powder—the taste will be the same, but the cookies will not have the same crisp texture.

Makes about 40 cookies

2 cups all-purpose flour

1 teaspoon bicarbonate of ammonia, finely crushed, if necessary

Pinch salt

16 tablespoons (2 sticks) unsalted butter, softened

⅓ cup sugar

1 teaspoon vanilla extract

1 cup firmly packed sweetened, shredded coconut, finely chopped, but not ground in the food processor

2 cookie sheets or jelly roll pans lined with parchment or foil

1 Set racks in the upper and lower thirds of the oven and preheat to 325 degrees. **2** Combine the flour, ammonia, and salt in a bowl; stir well to mix. **3** In the bowl of a standing electric mixer fitted with the paddle attachment, beat together on medium speed the butter, sugar, and vanilla extract until soft and smooth, about 2 or 3 min-utes. Stop the mixer and scrape down the bowl and beater. **4** On low speed, beat in the flour mixture, then the coconut. Remove the bowl from the mixer and complete the mixing with a large rubber spatula. **5** Use a small ice cream scoop to portion out 1-inch-diameter pieces of dough. Roll into perfect balls between the palms of your hands. Place the balls of dough on the prepared pans. Leave about 3 inches all around each cookie to allow for spreading. **6** Bake the cookies for about 12 to 15 minutes, or until they have spread and puffed and are firm to the touch. If you open the oven to check on the cookies while they are baking, be sure to avert your face to avoid inhaling the ammonia fumes. Slide the papers from the pans to racks. **7** Store the cooled cookies between sheets of parchment or wax paper in a tin or plastic container with a tight-fitting cover.

CHOCOLATE HAZELNUT TRUFFLES

THIS CHOCOLATE VERSION OF A NUT ball cookie is as rich and satisfying as a chocolate truffle. Hazelnuts pair perfectly with the chocolate, but pecans or walnuts would be excellent choices as well. If the two different quantities of nuts listed in the ingredients seem confusing, the chopped toasted nuts—the first—are incorporated into the cookie dough, and the ground, untoasted ones are to roll the cookies in before you bake.

Makes about 50 cookies

1⅔ cups all-purpose flour

½ teaspoon salt

½ teaspoon ground cinnamon

12 tablespoons (1½ sticks) unsalted butter, softened

1 cup sugar

2 ounces unsweetened chocolate, melted and cooled

1 large egg

6 ounces (about 1½ cups) hazelnuts, toasted and skinned (see page xv), finely chopped but not ground

6 ounces (about 1½ cups) raw unblanched hazelnuts, finely ground in the food processor

2 cookie sheets or jelly roll pans covered with parchment or foil

1 Set racks in the upper and lower thirds of the oven and preheat to 350 degrees. **2** In a bowl, combine the flour, salt, and cinnamon; stir well to mix. **3** In the bowl of a standing electric mixer fitted with the paddle attachment, beat together on medium speed the butter and sugar until well mixed, about 1 minute. **4** Stop the mixer and scrape the cool melted chocolate into the bowl. Beat again until it is just mixed in, then beat in the egg. Continue beating until smooth, about another minute. **5** Stop the mixer and scrape down the bowl and beater. Add the dry ingredients and the toasted chopped hazelnuts, and mix on lowest speed until the mixture forms a dough. **6** Remove the bowl from the mixer and complete the mixing with a large rubber spatula. **7** Place the raw ground hazelnuts in a shallow bowl. With a small ice cream scoop or measuring spoon, scoop out a piece of cookie dough. Roll it between the palms of your hands to make a neat sphere, then roll the ball in the ground hazelnuts to coat the outside. Place an inch apart on the prepared pans. **8** Bake the cookies about 12 to 15 minutes, or until firm and well colored on the bottom. Cool on the pans on racks. **9** Store the cooled cookies between sheets of parchment or wax paper in a tin or plastic container with a tight-fitting cover.

KOURABIETHES
Greek Almond Cookies

THESE CRUMBLY, FRAGRANT COOKIES, staples of the Greek baking repertoire, are perhaps the world's best-known Greek sweet. The delicate texture comes from the large quantity of butter and the ground nuts added to the dough. Michelle Tampakis, my Greek connection, shared this recipe.

Makes about 30 cookies

16 tablespoons (2 sticks) unsalted butter, softened

¼ cup confectioners' sugar, plus more for finishing

1 large egg yolk

1 tablespoon Metaxa (Greek brandy) or other brandy

Pinch ground cloves

2 ounces (about ½ cup) blanched almonds, finely ground in the food processor

2½ cups all-purpose flour

2 cookie sheets or jelly roll pans covered with parchment or foil

1 Set racks in the upper and lower thirds of the oven and preheat to 300 degrees. **2** In the bowl of a standing electric mixer fitted with the paddle attachment, beat together on medium speed the butter and confectioners' sugar until well mixed, about 1 minute. **3** Beat in the egg yolk, brandy, and cloves and continue beating until smooth. **4** Lower the mixer speed and beat in the almonds, then the flour. **5** Remove the bowl from the mixer and complete the mixing with a large rubber spatula. **6** With a small ice cream scoop or measuring spoon, scoop out a piece of dough. Roll it into a ball between the palms of your hands, then pinch the ends to make a football shape. Place on the prepared pans. Repeat, making sure the pieces are all the same size. Leave about an inch all around each cookie. **7** Bake the cookies for about 15 to 20 minutes, until they are firm and beginning to color only on the bottom. Place the pans on racks, then immediately sift a thick coat of confectioners' sugar over the hot cookies. (These cookies are too fragile to move while they are hot.) Allow them to cool completely, then sift over another coat of confectioners' sugar. **8** Store the cooled cookies between sheets of parchment or wax paper in a tin or plastic container with a tight-fitting cover.

Molded Cookies

MACADAMIA LIME COOKIES

AN UNLIKELY COMBINATION OF FLAVORS yields an excellent and easy cookie. If macadamias are difficult to find, substitute blanched almonds or even pecans. If key limes are available, by all means use them. The cookies will be extremely tangy and fragrant.

Makes about 40 cookies

2 cups all-purpose flour

1 teaspoon baking powder

Pinch salt

12 tablespoons (1½ sticks) unsalted butter, softened

1 cup sugar

4 tablespoons strained lime juice

3 ounces (about ¾ cup) macadamia nuts, chopped, but not ground, in the food processor (see Note)

Sugar for rolling the cookies before baking

2 cookie sheets or jelly roll pans covered with parchment or foil

1 Set the racks in the upper and lower thirds of the oven and preheat to 350 degrees. **2** In a bowl, combine the flour, baking powder, and salt; stir well to mix. **3** In the bowl of a standing electric mixer fitted with the paddle attachment, beat together on medium speed the butter and sugar until light, about 3 minutes. Lower the speed and beat in half the lime juice, then half the flour mixture. Stop the mixer and scrape the bowl and beater. Beat in the remaining lime juice, the chopped nuts, then the remaining flour. **4** Remove the bowl from the mixer and use a large rubber spatula to finish mixing the dough. **5** Place the sugar for rolling the cookies in a shallow bowl. Use an ice cream scoop or measuring spoon to scoop the dough into equal pieces. Roll between the palms of your hands to form a ball, then roll the ball of dough through the sugar. Place on the prepared pans. Repeat, making sure the pieces of dough are all the same size. Leave about 2 inches all around each cookie. **6** Bake the cookies for about 15 to 20 minutes, until they are golden and firm. Slide the papers from the pans to racks. **7** Store the cooled cookies between sheets of parchment or wax paper in a tin or plastic container with a tight-fitting cover.

NOTE Most shelled macadamia nuts commonly available are salted. To remove the salt, place the nuts in a strainer and shake them under running hot water. Place them on a pan lined with paper towels and roll them around to dry. This treatment will remove as much of the salt as necessary to use the nuts in a recipe.

WIENER MANDELGIPFERL
Little Viennese Almond Crescents

THESE FRAGILE NUT COOKIES ARE similar to but more delicate than the Pecan Butter Balls on page 183. There are recipes for this cookie that call for either walnuts, hazelnuts, or almonds. I prefer almonds—their delicate flavor seems most in keeping with this very subtle cookie. Thanks to Nancy Berzinec, Paul Kinberg, and Phil Krampetz, who shared their various recipes.

Makes about 48 cookies

18 tablespoons (2¼ sticks) unsalted butter, softened

1 cup confectioners' sugar, plus more for finishing

2 teaspoons vanilla extract

4 ounces (about 1 cup) blanched almonds, finely ground in the food processor

2½ cups all-purpose flour

2 cookie sheets or jelly roll pans covered with parchment or foil

1 Set the racks in the upper and lower thirds of the oven and preheat to 350 degrees. **2** In the bowl of a standing electric mixer fitted with the paddle attachment, beat together on lowest speed the butter and the 1 cup confectioners' sugar until combined. Raise the speed to medium and continue beating until soft and smooth, about 2 minutes. Beat in the vanilla. **3** Lower the speed and beat in the almonds, then the flour. **4** Remove the bowl from the mixer and finish mixing with a large rubber spatula. **5** Scrape the dough onto a floured work surface and divide it into four equal pieces. Use the palms of your hands to roll each into a cylinder. Cut each cylinder into twelve equal pieces. Shape each piece into a 2-inch cylinder, then taper the ends slightly. Place on one of the prepared pans, then curve the ends slightly to make a crescent shape. Repeat with the rest of the dough. **6** Bake the cookies for about 20 to 25 minutes, or until they are firm and very pale. Cool the cookies on the pans on racks (they are too delicate to move when they are hot). When the cookies are cool, sift confectioners' sugar generously over them. **7** Store the cooled cookies between sheets of parchment or wax paper in a tin or plastic container with a tight-fitting cover. Be careful—even cold they are extremely fragile.

SONJA HENIES

NO ONE SEEMS TO KNOW WHY THIS cookie was named for the Norwegian champion skater and movie star of the thirties. The recipe comes from Alexis Grossman, who cuts my hair. One day when I was in her chair we were talking about cookies and she gave me her grandmother's recipe for these. This fragile cookie is covered in walnuts, and has a "thumbprint" or small cavity in the top filled with jam. I don't know if the late movie star ever tasted one of these, but they have star quality of their own.

Makes about 40 cookies

COOKIE DOUGH

16 tablespoons (2 sticks) unsalted butter, softened

¼ cup granulated sugar

¼ cup firmly packed light brown sugar

2 large egg yolks

1 teaspoon vanilla extract

2 cups all-purpose flour

FINISHING

2 large egg whites

4 ounces (about 1 cup) walnut pieces, finely ground in the food processor

½ cup seedless raspberry jam

2 cookie sheets or jelly roll pans covered with parchment or foil

1 In the bowl of a standing electric mixer fitted with the paddle attachment, beat together on medium speed the butter, granulated sugar, and brown sugar until soft, light, and fluffy, about 5 minutes. Beat in the egg yolks and vanilla and continue beating until smooth. **2** Lower the speed and beat in the flour. **3** Remove the bowl from the mixer and finish mixing with a large rubber spatula. Scrape the dough onto a piece of plastic wrap and press it into a rectangle about ½ inch thick. Wrap well and refrigerate about 1 hour. The dough should become more firm, but do not refrigerate so long that the dough hardens. **4** When you are ready to bake the cookies, set racks in the upper and lower thirds of the oven and preheat to 350 degrees. **5** Cut the chilled dough into 1-inch strips. Cut across the strips every ½ inch. Roll each piece into a ball

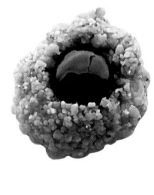

between the palms of your hands. Repeat with all the dough, lining up the balls of dough on your work surface. **6** In a shallow bowl, beat the egg whites until broken up and place the ground walnuts in another shallow bowl nearby. With your left hand, pick up a ball of the dough and roll it around in the egg white. Use the same hand to lift it out of the egg white and place it in the ground walnuts. With your clean right hand, roll the cookie around in the walnuts to coat it evenly, then place it on one of the prepared pans, spacing the cookies about 1 inch apart. **7** After all the cookies have been coated with the walnuts and arranged on the pans, use the end of a wooden spoon handle or a fingertip to press a cavity into the top of each cookie. The indentation should be about half the cookie's depth. Fill the dimple with a little of the jam. **8** Bake the cookies for about 15 to 20 minutes, or until they are a very light golden and somewhat firm. Cool the cookies on the pans on racks. If the jam has boiled out of the cookies, or they just don't seem full enough, bring more jam to a boil in a small saucepan, lower it to a simmer, let it reduce for a minute or two, then use a small spoon to refill the cookies. **9** Store the cooled cookies between sheets of parchment or wax paper in a tin or plastic container with a tight-fitting cover.

CRACKLED CHOCOLATE COOKIES

THESE ATTRACTIVE-LOOKING COOKIES reveal a chocolate core through a coating of confectioners' sugar crackled on the surface. The secret to making these successfully is to chill the dough for a long time—even overnight. When you form the cookies, work quickly so that the sugar-coated balls of dough are still cold when they go into the oven.

Makes about 70 cookies

**8 tablespoons (1 stick) unsalted butter,
cut into 8 pieces**

**4 ounces unsweetened chocolate,
cut into ¼-inch pieces**

2 cups all-purpose flour

2 teaspoons baking powder

¼ teaspoon salt

4 large eggs

2 cups granulated sugar

1 teaspoon vanilla extract

Confectioners' sugar for coating the cookies

**2 or 3 cookie sheets or jelly roll pans
covered with parchment or foil**

1 Melt the butter in a small saucepan over medium heat. Let it get hot and bubble up slightly. Remove from the heat and add the chocolate. Swirl the pan to make sure the chocolate is submerged and allow it to melt for 2 minutes. Whisk smooth. **2** In a bowl, combine the flour, baking powder, and salt; stir well to mix. **3** In a medium bowl, whisk the eggs by hand until broken up. Whisk in the granulated sugar in a stream, then the vanilla. Whisk in the chocolate mixture, then fold in the flour mixture with a rubber spatula. **4** Cover the bowl with plastic wrap and refrigerate the dough at least 4 hours, or overnight. **5** When you are ready to bake the cookies, set the racks in the upper and lower thirds of the oven and preheat to 350 degrees. **6** Place the confectioners' sugar in a shallow bowl. Remove the dough from the refrigerator and use a small ice cream scoop or measuring spoon to divide small pieces of dough and drop them into the confectioners' sugar. Cover them with a thick coating. Roll each piece of dough into a ball between the palms of your hands and place on the prepared pans. Repeat, leaving about 3 inches all around each cookie. **7** Bake the cookies until they are well crackled and firm, about 12 to 15 minutes. Slide the papers from the pans to racks. **8** Store the cooled cookies between sheets of parchment or wax paper in a tin or plastic container with a tight-fitting cover.

CHINESE ALMOND COOKIES

WHEN I WAS A CHILD, MY PATERNAL grandmother, Angelina Maggio Malgieri, would occasionally take me to a Chinese restaurant in downtown Newark. There was egg drop soup, egg rolls, fried rice, and chow mein, and always almond cookies for dessert. These are based on a recipe shared by Jayne Sutton.

By the way, lard is the right fat to use for these, though lard and butter together give a better flavor. Don't substitute vegetable shortening for the lard, or the cookies won't have the right taste or texture.

Makes about 40 cookies

2 cups all-purpose flour

1½ teaspoons baking powder

¼ teaspoon salt

6 tablespoons (¾ stick) unsalted butter, softened

6 tablespoons lard

½ cup sugar, plus ½ cup for covering the cookies before baking

1 teaspoon almond extract

2 large egg whites

1 tablespoon water

Whole blanched almonds for decorating the cookies

3 cookie sheets or jelly roll pans covered with parchment or foil

1 Set the racks in the upper and lower thirds of the oven and preheat to 325 degrees. **2** In a bowl, combine the flour, baking powder, and salt; stir well to mix. **3** In the bowl of a standing electric mixer fitted with the paddle attachment, beat together on medium speed the butter, lard, ½ cup sugar, and almond extract until soft and light, about 2 or 3 minutes. **4** Lower the speed and beat in half the flour mixture. Whisk the egg whites and water together in a small bowl, then beat them in. Stop the mixer and scrape the bowl and beater with a rubber spatula. **5** Beat in the remaining flour mixture. Remove the bowl from mixer and finish mixing with a large rubber spatula. **6** Use a small ice cream scoop to form 1-inch-diameter pieces of dough. Roll the pieces into balls between the palms of your hands, then roll them in the remaining ½ cup sugar. Place the balls of dough on the prepared pans, leaving about 3 inches in all directions to allow for spreading. Repeat until all the dough has been used. Top each cookie with an almond, pressing it in firmly. **7** Bake the cookies for about 12 to 15 minutes, or until they have spread and crackled on the surface and they are firm to the touch. Slide the papers from the pans to racks. **8** Store the cooled cookies between sheets of parchment or wax paper in a tin or plastic container with a tight-fitting cover.

THE GOOD COOK'S GINGERSNAPS

In 1998, I was invited by Pat Adrian, director of the Good Cook division of the Book-of-the-Month Club, to judge its annual office baking contest. There were luscious cakes, pies, and cookies of all types, but these gingersnaps were the hands-down winners. Julie Ellis-Clayton, the winner of the contest, was kind enough to share her recipe with me. It was adapted from a recipe in *The New England Cookbook* (Culinary Arts Institute, no date).

Makes about 40 cookies

2 cups all-purpose flour

2 teaspoons baking soda

½ teaspoon salt

2 teaspoons ground ginger

1 teaspoon ground cinnamon

½ teaspoon ground cloves

12 tablespoons (1½ sticks) unsalted butter

1 cup sugar, plus ½ cup for finishing

1 large egg

¼ cup molasses

2 or 3 cookie sheets or jelly roll pans covered with parchment or foil

1 Set the racks in the upper and lower thirds of the oven and preheat to 350 degrees. **2** Combine the flour, baking soda, salt, and spices in a bowl; stir well to mix. **3** In the bowl of a standing electric mixer fitted with the paddle attachment, beat together on medium speed the butter and 1 cup sugar for about 5 minutes until very light, fluffy, and whitened. Add the egg and continue beating until smooth. **4** Lower the speed and beat in half the dry ingredients, then the molasses. Stop the mixer and scrape down the bowl and beater. Beat in the remaining dry ingredients. **5** Remove the bowl from the mixer and use a large rubber spatula to finish mixing the dough. **6** Place the remaining ½ cup sugar in a shallow bowl. **7** Use a small ice cream scoop to form 1-inch-diameter pieces of dough. Roll the pieces into balls between the palms of your hands, then roll them in the sugar. Place the balls of dough on the prepared pans, leaving about 3 inches all around each, to allow for spreading. **8** Bake the cookies for about 15 to 20 minutes, or until they have spread, colored, the surface has crackled, and they are firm to the touch. Slide the papers from the pans to racks. The cookies become crisp as they cool. **9** Store the cooled cookies between sheets of parchment or wax paper in a tin or plastic container with a tight-fitting cover.

CHUNKY PEANUT BUTTER COOKIES

THESE ARE MY FAVORITE VARIATION ON classic peanut butter cookies. They have a real peanut crunch. My friend Jennifer Migliorelli developed this recipe when she was working as a chef in an American restaurant in Hong Kong.

Makes about fifty 3-inch cookies

8 tablespoons (1 stick) unsalted butter, softened

1 cup firmly packed dark brown sugar

1 cup granulated sugar

½ teaspoon salt

⅔ cup smooth peanut butter

2 large eggs

1½ teaspoons vanilla extract

2½ cups flour

2 teaspoons baking soda

8 ounces (about 2 cups) chopped honey-roasted peanuts

2 or 3 cookie sheets or jelly roll pans lined with parchment or foil

1 Set the racks in the upper and lower thirds of the oven and preheat to 350 degrees. **2** In the bowl of a standing electric mixer fitted with the paddle attachment, beat on medium speed the butter, the sugars, salt, and peanut butter just until smooth. Add the eggs, one at a time. Beat only until smooth after each addition. Beat in the vanilla. **3** Separately, in a small bowl, mix the flour with the baking soda, then beat into the peanut butter mixture, scraping the bowl and beaters. Stir in the peanuts. **4** Roll 1-teaspoon portions of the dough between the palms of your hands to form rough balls and place them on the prepared pans. Leave 3 inches in all directions around each cookie. Flatten the cookies with the bottom of a glass. Bake about 12 to 15 minutes, until the cookies are well risen and golden. **5** Slide the papers from the pans to racks. **6** Store the cookies between layers of wax paper in a tin or plastic container with a tight-fitting cover.

Chunky Peanut Butter Cookie (LEFT)
and The Good Cook's Gingersnap

MOSTACCIOLI BARESI
Spice Cookies from Bari

THESE ARE A VERSION OF APULIAN *mostaccioli* cookies usually made with the almonds left over after making a kind of blancmange called *latte di mandorle* or almond milk, a traditional Apulian Christmas dessert. Thanks to Rose Valenti for the recipe.

Makes about 60 cookies

COOKIE DOUGH

4 ounces (about 1 cup) whole unblanched almonds

⅔ cup granulated sugar

Grated zest of 1 large orange

4 cups all-purpose flour

1 tablespoon sifted cocoa powder

2 teaspoons baking powder

2 teaspoons ground cinnamon

1 teaspoon ground cloves

8 tablespoons (1 stick) cold unsalted butter

4 large eggs

⅓ cup sweet wine or *vino cotto* (see Note)

ICING

One 1-pound box confectioners' sugar (about 4 cups)

¼ cup water

¼ cup orange juice

3 cookie sheets or jelly roll pans covered with parchment or foil

1 Set the racks in the upper and lower thirds of the oven and preheat to 425 degrees. **2** In the work bowl of a food processor fitted with the steel blade, pulse the almonds and sugar repeatedly until the almonds are finely ground. **3** Add the orange zest, flour, cocoa, baking powder, cinnamon, and cloves and pulse several times to mix. **4** Cut the butter into twelve pieces and add it to the work bowl. Pulse until the butter is mixed in—about twenty to twenty-five times. **5** Add the eggs and wine; pulse until the dough is evenly moistened, though it probably will not form one ball. **6** Scrape the dough onto an oiled work surface and roll into a log, 12 inches long. Cut the log into six pieces. **7** Roll each piece of dough into a 12-inch cylinder, flatten slightly with the palm of your hand, then cut each 12-inch cylinder diagonally into ten or eleven pieces and place the pieces on pans about 1 inch apart. **8** Place the pans in the oven and immediately lower the temperature to 400 degrees. Bake the cookies about

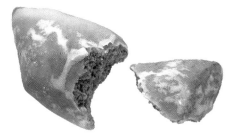

10 to 15 minutes, or until firm and light golden. Slide the papers from the pans to racks. **9** To make the icing, in a saucepan, stir the sugar into the water and orange juice. Heat the icing over low heat until it is warm, stirring often. Add a tablespoon or two of water if the icing is too thick. **10** Add about a third of the cookies to the icing, stirring them gently with a rubber spatula to coat them completely. Transfer the cookies to the paper- or foil-covered pans to dry. Repeat with the remaining cookies, reheating the icing between batches if necessary. **11** Store the iced cookies between sheets of parchment or wax paper in a tin or plastic container with a tight-fitting cover.

NOTE

Vino Cotto: Combine 1 quart red jug wine and 1 cup sugar in an enamel or stainless steel pan. Bring to a boil and simmer until reduced to a thick syrup—about 1½ cups. Pour the wine into a jar and store refrigerated. (*Vino cotto* is a typical southern Italian sweetener made from reduced wine or grape juice. It is used in many old-fashioned recipes of the region.)

Molded Cookies

KOULOURAKIA
Greek Sesame Ring Cookies

THE NAME OF THESE COOKIES MEANS "little rings" in Greek. They are related to the *taralli* on page 205, although these are more buttery. And these are brushed with beaten egg and sprinkled with sesame seeds before baking for a little crunch on the outside of a tender cookie. Thanks to Michelle Tampakis for sharing this recipe.

Makes about 40 cookies

COOKIE DOUGH

4 cups all-purpose flour

2 teaspoons baking powder

16 tablespoons (2 sticks) unsalted butter, softened

¾ cup confectioners' sugar

3 egg yolks

3 tablespoons orange juice

1 tablespoon Metaxa (Greek brandy) or another brandy

EGG WASH

1 large egg, well beaten with 1 pinch salt

Sesame seeds for sprinkling over the cookies before baking

3 or 4 cookies sheets or jelly roll pans covered with parchment or foil

1 Set the racks in the upper and lower thirds of the oven and preheat to 350 degrees. 2 In a bowl, combine the flour and baking powder; stir well to mix. 3 In the bowl of a standing electric mixer fitted with the paddle attachment, beat together on medium speed the butter and confectioners' sugar until well mixed, about a minute. Whisk the egg yolks with the orange juice and brandy in a small bowl. 4 Lower the mixer speed and beat in about a third of the dry ingredients. Then beat in half the egg yolk mixture. Stop the mixer and scrape the bowl and beater with a rubber spatula. Beat in another third of the dry ingredients and the remaining egg yolk mixture. Stop and scrape again. Finally, beat in the remaining dry ingredients. 5 Remove the bowl from the mixer and complete the mixing with a large rubber spatula.

6 Scrape the dough onto a floured work surface and divide it into four equal pieces. Then divide each in half, to make eight pieces. Roll each piece into a 10-inch cylinder then cut the cylinders into 2-inch pieces to make 40 pieces of dough in all. To form the cookies, roll each piece of dough between the palms of your hands until it is a 5-inch strand. Pinch the ends of the dough firmly to make a circle and place the circles on the prepared pans. Leave about 2 inches all around each cookie. 7 Lightly brush the top of each cookie with the egg wash and sprinkle it with a pinch of the sesame seeds. 8 Bake the cookies for about 25 to 30 minutes, or until evenly golden and firm. Slide the papers from the pans to racks. 9 Store the cooled cookies between sheets of parchment or wax paper in a tin or plastic container with a tight-fitting cover.

LOVE KNOTS

I remember my aunt, Kitty Rocco, making these cookies during my childhood. Fortunately, her daughter, my cousin Karen Ludwig, saved all her mother's recipes and gave me this one.

Makes about 60 cookies

COOKIE DOUGH

4½ cups all-purpose flour

4 teaspoons baking powder

6 large eggs

1 cup granulated sugar

8 tablespoons (1 stick) unsalted butter, melted

1 teaspoon lemon extract

ICING

One 1-pound box confectioners' sugar
(about 4 cups)

⅓ cup water

½ teaspoon lemon extract

3 cookie sheets or jelly roll pans lined
with parchment or foil

1 Set the racks in the upper and lower thirds of the oven and preheat to 375 degrees. **2** Combine the flour and baking powder in a bowl; stir well to mix. **3** In a large mixing bowl, whisk the eggs to break them up. Whisk in the granulated sugar in a stream, then whisk in the butter and lemon extract. **4** Add the flour to the egg mixture and use a large rubber spatula to mix it into the liquid until a soft dough forms. **5** Scrape the dough onto a lightly floured work surface and press into a rectangle. Cut the dough into four equal pieces. **6** Roll each piece of dough into a rough cylinder, then cut it into three equal pieces. Repeat with the remaining pieces of dough to make twelve pieces in all. Take one piece of dough and roll it under your palms to a cylinder 10 inches long. Slice the cylinder into 2-inch rolls. To form a cookie, hold one end of a roll in your left hand and make a loop by crossing the right end over it; tuck the right end of the roll under the cookie so it looks like a knot, as in the illustrations. **7** Arrange the cookies on the prepared pans as they are formed, and repeat the dividing and forming with the remaining dough. **8** Bake the cookies for about 10 minutes, until they are lightly colored on the bottom, but still pale on top, and feel firm, but not dry, when they are poked with a fingertip. Slide the papers from the pans to racks. **9** To make the icing, combine the confectioners' sugar, water, and lemon extract in a medium saucepan. Place over low heat and cook, stirring constantly, until the icing is lukewarm—about 100 to 110 degrees. Hold one of the cookies by the bottom and dip the top third into the icing. Let the excess icing drip back into the pan for a few seconds, then place the iced cookie, right side up, on the paper that it baked on. Continue with the other cookies until they are all iced—it may be necessary to reheat the icing once or twice to keep it liquid. **10** Let the icing dry for several hours at room temperature before packing up the cookies. Store the cooled cookies between sheets of parchment or wax paper in a tin or plastic container with a tight-fitting cover.

VARIATION

ANISE LOVE KNOTS: Substitute 1 tablespoon anisette for the lemon extract in the dough and 1 tablespoon anisette for the lemon extract in the icing. Put 1 tablespoon less water into the icing or it will be too thin.

Step 6

VANILLA PRETZELS

THERE ARE VARIOUS TYPES OF COOKIE pretzels, many of which contain ground nuts and are variations on *Wiener Mandelgipferl* (page 189). This recipe makes a more cakey type of cookie, easier to form into the characteristic pretzel shape. These cookies have the further advantage of being tender and sweet, a perfect cookie to dunk in coffee.

Makes about 30 cookies

2¼ cups all-purpose flour

1 teaspoon baking powder

Pinch salt

6 tablespoons (¾ stick) unsalted butter, softened

½ cup granulated sugar

1½ teaspoons vanilla extract

3 large egg yolks

½ cup milk

Confectioners' sugar for finishing

2 or 3 cookie sheets or jelly roll pans covered with parchment or foil

1 In a medium bowl, combine the flour, baking powder, and salt; stir well to mix. **2** In the bowl of a standing electric mixer fitted with the paddle attachment, beat together on medium speed the butter and granulated sugar until soft and light, about 2 minutes. Beat in the vanilla. **3** In a small bowl, whisk the egg yolks and milk together and pour about a third into the mixer. Beat until smooth. **4** Lower the speed and beat in half the dry ingredients. Stop the mixer and scrape the bowl and beater. Beat in the remaining liquid, then the remaining dry ingredients. **5** Remove the bowl from the mixer and finish mixing the dough with a large rubber spatula. **6** Scrape the dough together in the bowl, then cover the bowl with plastic wrap. Refrigerate until the dough is firm, about 3 hours, or overnight. **7** When you are ready to bake the cookies, set the racks in the upper and lower thirds of the oven and preheat to 350 degrees. **8** Scrape the dough onto a floured surface and press it into a rough rectangle. Divide into three equal pieces. Then divide each of those pieces in half, to make six pieces of dough. **9** Flour your hands, then roll each of the pieces of dough into a cylinder. Slice each cylinder into five equal pieces. **10** To shape the cookies, roll one of the pieces of dough under the palms of your hands until it forms a rope about 8 inches long. Fold the rope in half and position it on the prepared pan. To form a pretzel follow the illustration. Leave about 2 inches all around each cookie so it can puff while it bakes. **11** Bake the cookies for about 15 minutes, or until they are golden and firm. Slide the papers from the pans to racks. **12** Dust the cooled cookies lightly with confectioners' sugar just before serving. **13** Store the cookies between sheets of parchment or wax paper in a tin or plastic container with a tight-fitting cover.

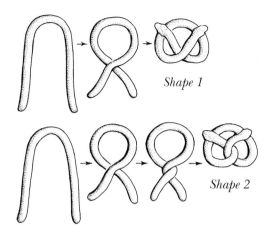

Shape 1

Shape 2

BISCOTTI DI VINO
Red Wine Cookies

THESE ARE NOT THE TWICE-BAKED biscotti, which appear in the next chapter. Here, the word just means "cookie." They are a specialty of my friend Sandy Leonard, who lives in Boston. They are a tender and tasty cookie, unusual in that they contain both wine and olive oil. Make sure you don't use either your best or your most robustly flavored oil for the cookies. Light or pure olive oil both work well.

Makes about 40 cookies

3 cups all-purpose flour

½ cup sugar

1 teaspoon salt

1½ teaspoons baking powder

1 cup red wine

⅓ cup light or pure olive oil, or vegetable oil

2 teaspoons vanilla extract

EGG WASH

1 egg

Pinch salt

3 ounces (about ¾ cup) sliced almonds, crushed, for finishing

3 cookie sheets or jelly roll pans covered with parchment or foil

(continued)

1 In a large bowl, combine the flour, sugar, salt, and baking powder; stir well to mix. **2** In a medium bowl, whisk together the wine, oil, and vanilla extract. Stir the liquid into the dry ingredients with a large rubber spatula and continue mixing until a dough forms. **3** Turn the dough out onto a floured surface and fold it over on itself several times. Use a bench scraper or a spatula or a pancake turner to detach it from the surface. Wrap the dough in plastic wrap and let it rest about an hour at room temperature. **4** When you are ready to bake the cookies, set the racks in the upper and lower thirds of the oven and preheat to 350 degrees. **5** Unwrap the dough and divide it in four equal pieces. Roll each into a cylinder about 10 inches long. Cut each piece into ten 1-inch pieces. Put the pieces of dough off to the left of the work surface and the pans to the right, leaving an area free in front of you. **6** Take one piece of dough and roll it under the palms of your hands into a thin cylinder, the width of a pencil, about 4 or 5 inches long. Pinch the ends together tightly to make a circle. Place the cookie on the prepared pan, making sure the circular shape stays intact. Repeat with the remaining pieces of dough, leaving about 1½ inches all around each cookie. **7** Beat together the egg and salt. Paint each cookie with the egg wash and sprinkle with the almonds. **8** Bake the cookies about 15 or 20 minutes until they are golden and firm. Slide the papers from the pans to racks. **9** Store the cooled cookies between sheets of parchment or wax paper in a tin or plastic container with a tight-fitting cover.

TARALLI DOLCI DI PASQUA
Easter Ring Cookies

THESE LARGE COOKIES ARE A TRADI-
tional southern Italian Easter specialty, though
they are good any time of the year. If you prefer a plainer cookie, omit the icing and brush
the outside with an Egg Wash (page 310).
Thanks to Marie Ciampi for sharing the
recipe on which this is loosely based.

Makes 16 large cookies

COOKIE DOUGH

5½ cups all-purpose flour

1½ tablespoons baking powder

6 eggs

1 cup granulated sugar

12 tablespoons (1½ sticks) unsalted butter, melted

1½ tablespoons vanilla extract

ICING

3 cups confectioners' sugar

4 tablespoons water

1 tablespoon lemon juice

1 teaspoon vanilla extract

Multicolored nonpareils, optional

3 cookie sheets or jelly roll pans covered
with parchment paper or foil

1 Set the racks in the upper and lower third of
the oven and preheat to 350 degrees. 2 In a
medium bowl, combine the flour and baking
powder; stir well to mix. 3 Break the eggs into a
large bowl and whisk them by hand until broken
up. Whisk in the granulated sugar in a stream,
then the melted butter and vanilla, whisking
smooth after each addition. Use a large rubber
spatula to fold in the dry ingredients. 4 Turn
the dough out onto a floured surface and knead
lightly. Divide it into sixteen equal pieces. Roll
each piece under your palms into an 8-inch rope,
then pinch the ends together to form a circle.
Place five or six circles on each pan. 5 Bake the
taralli about 30 minutes, or until well puffed and

Molded Cookies

deep golden. Cool on racks. **6** To make the icing, combine all the icing ingredients in a saucepan and heat gently until lukewarm, stirring often. Hold one of the cookies by the bottom and dip the top third into the icing. Let the excess icing drip back into the pan for a few seconds, then place the iced cookie, right side up, on the paper that it was baked on. Immediately sprinkle with multicolored nonpareils, if desired, before the icing has a chance to dry. Repeat with the other cookies; it may be necessary to reheat the icing before all the cookies are iced. **7** Store the cooled cookies between sheets of parchment or wax paper in a tin or plastic container with a tight-fitting cover.

VARIATION

If you prefer smaller cookies, divide the dough into 32 or 40 pieces. Roll the dough out to only 5 inches before making it into a circle. And bake the cookies only about 20 minutes; because they are smaller they will be done more quickly.

BUTTERMILK FUDGE GEMS

THIS DELIGHTFULLY OLD-FASHIONED cookie is like a rich little cupcake. They are excellent on their own but they are also easy to dress up with a rosette of butter cream (page 315) or streaks of chocolate glaze (page 319).

To bake these, you'll need mini muffin pans with cavities at least an inch deep. The size of these little pans varies somewhat so the yield of the recipe depends on the size of the cavities in your pans.

Thanks to Jayne Sutton for this recipe.

Makes about 48 cookies,
depending on the pans used

3 ounces unsweetened chocolate, cut into ¼-inch pieces

¼ cup boiling water

2 cups all-purpose flour

1¼ cups sugar

½ teaspoon salt

1 teaspoon baking soda

8 tablespoons (1 stick) unsalted butter, melted

1 cup buttermilk or 1 cup milk mixed with 1 teaspoon vinegar

3 large eggs

1 teaspoon vanilla extract

4 mini muffin pans, buttered and floured, then arranged by twos on jelly roll pans

1 Set the racks in the upper and lower thirds of the oven and preheat to 375 degrees. **2** Place the chocolate in a heatproof bowl and pour the boiling water over it. Let stand 2 minutes; stir smooth. **3** Combine the flour, sugar, salt, and baking soda in the bowl of a standing electric mixer; stir well to mix. Add the butter and buttermilk. Place the bowl on the stand and, with the paddle attachment, beat on medium speed until smooth, a minute or two. **4** Stop the mixer and add the chocolate, the eggs, and the vanilla and beat on medium speed again for about a minute, or until the batter is smooth. **5** Remove the bowl from the mixer and finish mixing with a large rubber spatula. To make filling the pans easier, pour some of the batter into a 1- or 2-cup pitcher or measuring cup. **6** Fill the cavities in the mini muffin pans about half full. **7** Bake the cookies for about 15 to 20 minutes, or until they rise and are firm but not hard. **8** Remove the pans from the oven and place them on racks to cool for about 5 minutes. Then unmold the cookies onto racks to finish cooling. **9** Store the cooled cookies between sheets of parchment or wax paper in a tin or plastic container with a tight-fitting cover.

Molded Cookies

SHORTBREAD GEMS

THIS IS ANOTHER COOKIE MADE IN A mini muffin pan. Delicious as is, it may also be indented after it cools slightly to become a container for some reduced jam, Lemon Curd (page 316), or even Ganache for Filling Cookies (page 320). Thanks to Jayne Sutton for another wonderful gem.

Makes about 30 cookies

1¼ cups all-purpose flour

½ cup cornstarch

Pinch salt

16 tablespoons (2 sticks) unsalted butter, softened

¾ cup confectioners' sugar, plus more for finishing

1 teaspoon vanilla extract

2 or 3 mini muffin pans, buttered (most mini muffin pans have 15 cavities, though some have only 12)

1 Set a rack in the middle level of the oven and preheat to 350 degrees. 2 Combine the flour, cornstarch, and salt in a small bowl; stir well to mix. 3 In the bowl of an electric mixer fitted with the paddle attachment, beat together the butter and confectioners' sugar on medium speed until very light, about 3 or 4 minutes. Beat in the vanilla. 4 Lower the speed and beat in the dry ingredients. 5 Remove the bowl from the mixer and use a large rubber spatula to finish mixing. 6 Deposit tablespoon-size pieces of the dough and press them into the cavities of the prepared pans. Fill about two-thirds full. 7 Bake the cookies about 20 minutes, until golden and firm. 8 Place the pans on racks to cool for 10 minutes. 9 If you wish to fill the cookies, after 10 minutes press in the center with the round handle of a wooden spoon. The indentation should only be half the depth of the cookie. 10 Unmold the cookies and turn them right side up again. Dust lightly with confectioners' sugar. (If you are going to fill the cookies, dust with confectioners' sugar before filling.) Fill with the filling of your choice. 11 Store the cooled cookies between sheets of parchment or wax paper in a tin or plastic container with a tight-fitting cover. If the cookies are filled, store them in a single layer.

MADELEINES
French Shell Cookies

THESE LITTLE SHELL-SHAPED CAKES are one of the glories of French baking. Light, delicate, and buttery, they are surprisingly easy to prepare. This recipe calls for two madeleine pans each with twelve cavities. The ones I have are standard and make a 3-inch madeleine. If you only have one pan or your molds are smaller, you can keep reusing the same pan. These bake fairly quickly. If you don't have madeleine pans, try using mini muffin pans (see Buttermilk Fudge Gems, page 207); the madeleines won't look the same, but they will taste as good.

Makes 24 shell-shaped cookies

2 large eggs

Pinch salt

½ cup granulated sugar

Finely grated zest of 1 large orange

1 teaspoon orange flower water, optional

1 cup all-purpose flour

8 tablespoons (1 stick) unsalted butter, melted

Confectioners' sugar for finishing

Two madeleine pans, buttered and floured

1 Set a rack in the middle level of the oven and preheat to 375 degrees. **2** In a medium bowl, by hand, whisk together the eggs and salt until frothy, about 15 seconds. Whisk in the granulated sugar in a stream, then the orange zest and orange flower water, if used. **3** Use a rubber spatula to fold in the flour, then the melted butter. **4** Use a large soup spoon to fill the cavities in the molds about two-thirds full. **5** Bake the madeleines for about 20 minutes, until they are well risen, firm, and a golden color. **6** Remove the pans from the oven and unmold the madeleines immediately onto racks to cool. If you want to reuse the pan, wash it, then butter and flour it again. **7** Dust the madeleines lightly with confectioners' sugar, just before serving. **8** Store the cooled madeleines between sheets of parchment or wax paper in a tin or plastic container with a tight-fitting cover.

(continued)

VARIATIONS

LEMON MADELEINES: Substitute the finely grated zest of one large or two small lemons for the orange zest and ½ teaspoon pure lemon extract for the orange flower water.

CHOCOLATE MADELEINES: Substitute ⅔ cup all-purpose flour and ¼ cup unsweetened cocoa powder, sifted after measuring, for the flour. Omit the orange flower water and replace with 1 teaspoon vanilla extract; do not omit the grated orange zest.

PETITS FINANCIERS
Little Financier Cookies

THESE ARE ONE OF THOSE LITTLE CAKES you always see in fancy pastry shops in France. There are dozens of different ways of preparing them but this recipe is a classic. It is loosely based on one I got in the early eighties from the Pâtisserie Ernest in Cannes.

Individual *financiers* are usually baked in small rectangular molds, but, lacking those, use mini muffin pans.

Makes about 40 cookies

3 ounces (about ¾ cup) whole blanched almonds

3 ounces (about ¾ cup) whole unblanched hazelnuts

1½ cups sugar

1 cup unbleached all-purpose flour

10 tablespoons (1¼ sticks) unsalted butter

2 tablespoons dark rum

2 teaspoons vanilla extract

1 cup egg whites (about 8 large)

Pinch salt

36 individual 1¾ × 3½-inch rectangular molds, buttered and floured, on a jelly roll pan, or 3 or 4 mini muffin pans

1 In the work bowl of a food processor fitted with the steel blade, pulse the almonds, hazelnuts, and ¾ cup of the sugar until the mixture is finely ground. Pour the mixture into a bowl and stir in the flour. **2** In a saucepan over medium heat, melt the butter and continue cooking until it colors a deep golden; add the rum and vanilla extract slowly off the heat to avoid having the butter foam up and out of the pan. Set aside to cool slightly. **3** In the bowl of an electric mixer fitted with the whisk attachment, whip the egg whites and salt on medium speed until they form a very soft peak. Increase the speed to maximum, then whip in the remaining ¾ cup sugar in a very slow stream, continuing to whip the egg whites until they hold a soft peak. **4** Fold the nut mixture into the egg whites, then fold in the butter mixture. Chill the mixture for several hours, or overnight before baking. Then bring the mixture to room temperature, stirring often to deflate it. **5** When you are ready to bake the *financiers*, set a rack in the middle level of the oven and preheat to 350 degrees. Pipe or spoon the batter into the pans, filling them about two-thirds full. Bake the *financiers* about 20 minutes, until well risen and golden. Cool briefly in the pans, then unmold onto a rack to finish cooling. **6** Store the cooled cookies between sheets of parchment or wax paper in a tin or plastic container with a tight-fitting cover.

Molded Cookies

TULIPES
Cookie Cup Dessert Shells

THESE ARE THE BEAUTIFUL COOKIE cups in which to serve such elegant desserts as delicate ice creams, sherbets, and mousses. They are essentially a large, round, paper-thin cookie, removed from the pan immediately after they come out of the oven and molded in a cup or bowl to make them into containers. They aren't particularly difficult to make. The whole trick is just to bake only a few at a time so you can pry them off the pan and mold them quickly, before they begin to harden. This is definitely a two-person job—one to spread the batter on the pans and watch the baking and the other to mold the cookies.

You will notice a striking similarity, both in ingredients and techniques, to Cigarettes (page 136).

Makes 12 to 18 cookie cups,
depending on their diameter

6 tablespoons (¾ stick) unsalted butter, softened

1 cup confectioners' sugar

1 teaspoon vanilla extract

3 large egg whites (between ⅓ and ½ cup)

1 cup all-purpose flour

3 or 4 cookie sheets or jelly roll pans, buttered and the buttered surface coated with flour

6 small bowls, with 6 other smaller bowls or cups that fit into them, arranged on a jelly roll pan

1 Set a rack in the middle level of the oven and preheat to 375 degrees. It's better to bake only one pan of tulipes at a time. **2** In the bowl of a standing electric mixer fitted with the paddle attachment, beat together on medium speed the butter and confectioners' sugar until well mixed and soft, about 1 minute. Continuing to beat on medium speed, add the vanilla, then, about a tablespoon at a time, the egg whites. **3** Remove the bowl from the mixer and stir in the flour with a large rubber spatula. **4** Using a bowl or plate as a guide, mark 5- to 6-inch circles on the floured pans. On one pan, using a small offset spatula or the back of a spoon, spread about a tablespoon of batter in each of the marked circles, filling the circles completely. **5** Bake the cookies for about 7 or 8 minutes, or until they are just a light golden color. While the cookies are baking, bring the pan containing the mold-ing bowls to the stove top. When the cookies are baked, lift one off the pan with a spatula and center it over one of the large bowls. Then use the smaller bowl or cup to press the cookie down into the larger bowl to make a cup or bowl shape. Quickly repeat with the other cookies on the pan. If the cookies cool to the point that they are brittle before you can remove them from the pan, you can return the pan to the oven for a minute to soften the cookies. Don't place another pan in the oven until all the cookies from the first pan are molded. Remove the cups and place the tulipes on a pan. **6** Repeat with the remaining batter. The recipe makes a lot because some burn, some shatter, and some just don't mold successfully, so you need a lot of batter to get enough presentable ones to use. **7** Pack the cooled tulipes in a tin with squares of paper towel between them if you need to stack them. Don't make them more than a day in advance since they break so easily; it's better not to keep them around for too long.

VARIATIONS

CHOCOLATE TULIPES: Substitute ⅔ cup all-purpose flour and 3 tablespoons unsweetened cocoa powder, sifted after measuring, for the flour.

STRIPED TULIPES: Make a batch each of white and chocolate tulipe batters. Spread a tulipe of one color on the prepared pan, then use the other color, forced through a pastry bag with a very small tip, paper cone, or the snipped corner of a nonpleated plastic bag, to make a design on the circle as in the illustrations below. Draw a toothpick through the lines in the direction of the arrows on the designs to "feather" the lines.

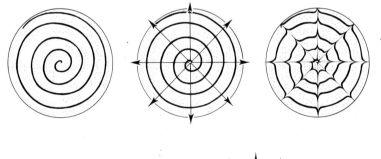

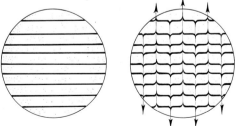

Molded Cookies

ANISBROETLI
Swiss Anise Cookies

THESE ARE EXACTLY THE SAME AS German Springerle—rich anise-flavored dough imprinted with special molds to give the cookies beautiful designs. In Germany, to imprint the dough with designs, they are usually rolled with a special carved rolling pin. The Swiss tend to imprint using individual molds. The Swiss system is more reliable because you are working with only a small portion of the dough at a time. Molds were difficult to find at one time, but now there are many antique-reproduction molds, cast from the Swiss originals, easily available (see Sources). The molds may be carved to represent domestic, architectural, agricultural, or religious scenes. Or the shape of the mold may be the main design—a heart, diamond, flower—and the surface may be decorated with a geometric design.

If you want to try these cookies but don't have any molds, try making the *Badener Chrabeli* on page 217.

Makes 15 to 20 cookies,
depending on the size of the molds

3 cups all-purpose flour

⅔ cup cornstarch

1½ teaspoons baking powder

2 tablespoons aniseed, optional

4 large eggs

2 cups sugar

3 teaspoons anise extract

2 or 3 cookie sheets or jelly roll pans covered with parchment or foil

1 Combine the flour, cornstarch, baking powder, and half the optional aniseed in a bowl; stir well to mix. **2** Half-fill a medium saucepan with water and bring it to a boil over medium heat. Reduce to a simmer. **3** Break the eggs into the bowl of a standing electric mixer and whisk in the sugar by hand. Place the bowl over the pan of simmering water and warm the mixture, whisking constantly, until it is lukewarm (100 to 110 degrees), about a minute or two. Place the bowl on a mixer fitted with the whisk attachment and whip the mixture on medium speed until cooled to room temperature. Whip in the anise extract. **4** Remove the bowl from the mixer and fold in the flour mixture about a third at a time, until a dough forms. **5** Scrape the dough onto a floured work surface and lightly flour the top of the dough. Press the dough into a rectangle and divide it into four parts. **6** Strew the rest of the optional aniseed on the prepared pans. With the palms of your hands, press and pat each piece of dough into an 8-inch square. Keep moving the dough and sprinkling more flour under it so it doesn't stick to the surface. Flour the mold or molds and gently press one into the dough. Cut around the printed dough and use a spatula or pancake turner to transfer it to the prepared pan. Continue with the remaining dough. **7** Allow the cookies to dry, uncovered, at room tempera-ture for 2 or 3 hours. **8** When you are ready to bake the cookies, set the racks in the upper and lower thirds of the oven and preheat to 300 degrees. Bake the cookies for about 20 minutes, until risen and very white on the surface. Do not allow the tops of the cookies to take on any color. They may become a light golden color on the bot-tom. **9** Slide the papers from the pans to racks. **10** Store the cooled cookies between sheets of parchment or wax paper in a tin or plastic con-tainer with a tight-fitting cover.

BADENER CHRABELI
Little Claws from Baden

THIS IS THE SAME DOUGH USED TO prepare *Anisbroetli* (page 215) in an alternate shape. I have no idea of the significance of the claw shape. I suspect that slashing the dough helps it bake through more efficiently. I have seen the same cookies referred to as cockscombs in an old Swiss baking book.

Makes about 48 cookies

½ batch *Anisbroetli* dough (page 215)

2 cookie sheets or jelly roll pans covered with parchment or foil

1 Roll the dough under the palms of your hands to form a cylinder. Divide into six equal parts. **2** Roll one part into a rope about 16 inches long, then cut the rope into eight 2-inch pieces. Repeat with the remaining pieces of dough. **3** Flatten each piece of dough very slightly, then slash one side three or four times with the point of a sharp paring knife, as in the illustration. Arrange each cookie on a pan, curving it into a crescent shape to make the slashes open. **4** Allow the cookies to dry, uncovered, at room temperature for 2 or 3 hours. **5** When you are ready to bake the cookies, set the racks in the upper and lower thirds of the oven and preheat to 300 degrees. Bake the cookies for about 20 minutes, until they have risen and are very white on the surface. Do not allow the tops of the cookies to take on any color. They may become a light golden color on the bottom. **6** Slide the papers from the pans to racks. **7** Store the cooled cookies between sheets of parchment or wax paper in a tin or plastic container with a tight-fitting cover.

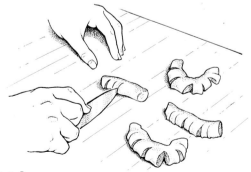

Step 3

SPECULAAS

THESE MOLDED COOKIES ARE POPULAR throughout the Low Countries as well as in Germany. They are called *speculoos* in Belgium and *Speculatius* in Germany, but apart from a few differences in seasonings, they are the same cookies. The name derives from the word for mirror and refers to the fact that the cookie "mirrors" its mold.

This is a traditional Dutch version of the cookie. To make these you will need a speculaas mold—a flat plate with one side carved into a cavity usually representing a knight, a horse and rider, or some elaborately dressed antique figure. Unlike Swiss *Anisbroetli* (page 215), for which the molds are just pressed against the dough to imprint it, speculaas dough is pressed into the mold and emerges in the shape of the figure. If you don't have a special mold, you may use an *Anisbroetli* mold, or just roll the dough out and cut it into rectangles—the cookies will taste just as good.

*Makes about 24 cookies,
depending on the size of the mold used*

(continued)

218

3 cups all-purpose flour

½ teaspoon baking soda

½ teaspoon salt

2 teaspoons ground cinnamon

1½ teaspoons freshly grated nutmeg

1 teaspoon ground coriander

1 teaspoon ground ginger

½ teaspoon ground cloves

¼ teaspoon freshly ground white pepper

12 tablespoons (1½ sticks) unsalted butter, softened

1 cup firmly packed light brown sugar

⅓ cup milk or water

2 or 3 cookie sheets or jelly roll pans
covered with parchment or foil

1 In a bowl, combine the flour, baking soda, salt, and spices; stir well to mix. **2** In the bowl of a standing electric mixer fitted with the paddle attachment, beat together on medium speed the butter and brown sugar until mixed, about 2 minutes. Lower the speed and beat in half the flour mixture. Stop the mixer and scrape down the bowl and beater with a rubber spatula. **3** Beat in the milk, then the remaining flour. Continue to mix until a firm dough forms. **4** Remove the bowl from the mixer and scrape the dough onto a floured work surface. Fold the dough over on itself several times, then place it on a piece of plastic wrap and press it into a rectangle about ½ inch thick. Wrap and chill the dough several hours or overnight. **5** When you are ready to bake the cookies, set the racks in the upper and lower thirds of the oven and preheat

to 350 degrees. **6** Remove the dough from the refrigerator and divide it into twelve pieces. Use one piece of dough at a time; put the rest on a pan and place it in the refrigerator. On a floured work surface, use the palm of your hand to press the piece of dough to roughly the shape of the cavity in the mold. Generously flour the cavity in the mold, then quickly press the dough into the mold, and with a long thin knife, scrape away the excess dough. Invert the mold over the pan and rap the far end of the mold against the pan, holding it at an angle to release the formed cookie, as in the illustration. Reflour the mold and repeat with the remaining pieces of dough. As you accumulate scraps of dough, press them together and chill them to mold again. **7** When all the cookies are formed, bake them for about 15 to 20 minutes, or until they are firm and golden. Slide the papers from the pans to racks. **8** Store the cooled cookies between sheets of parchment or wax paper in a tin or plastic container with a tight-fitting cover.

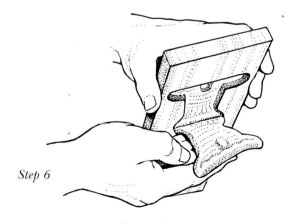

Step 6

BISCOTTI

IF THERE IS ONE COOKIE THAT CAN BE IDENTIFIED DEFINITIVELY WITH AMERICA in the last decade of the twentieth century, it is biscotti. The name biscotti means "twice-cooked" and it refers to the way these cookies are made. First the dough is formed into loaves or logs and baked. Then after these cool, they are sliced and baked again. Many nationalities have twice-baked specialties, though they tend to be a little blander than the Italian version.

Many biscotti are enriched with nuts. The recipes in this chapter don't call for the nuts to be toasted in advance because I find that they toast quite enough during the second baking. Sometimes, as in the case of the Lemon Pistachio Biscotti, you want to avoid having them toast too much or the lovely green color gets lost.

HINTS FOR BISCOTTI

1 If the dough seems soft, it is right. It is meant to be that way. Do not add extra flour to the biscotti doughs in this chapter or the resulting cookies will be cement-like. Review the instructions for measuring flour on page xiii. 2 If you need to flour the work surface to handle the dough more easily, do so. When the dough is safely on the pan just brush off the excess flour with a dry pastry brush.

3 Make sure you bake the biscotti enough the first time around. If the centers of the logs are not baked through, they will compress when you slice them and harden during the second baking. 4 Use a really sharp knife to slice the biscotti. Cutting with a dull knife will make the baked log shatter. 5 The thinner you slice the biscotti, the more pan room you will need for the second baking. I usually count on one cookie sheet or jelly roll pan per log of biscotti. 6 Watch the biscotti carefully during the second baking. Most biscotti have a fairly high sugar content and will burn easily if left unattended. 7 Cool biscotti on their pans—the extra bit of drying time will help make them even crisper. 8 Biscotti are the perfect "keeping" cookie—just be sure to store them airtight and away from humidity.

Biscotti

Cantuccini
Classic Tuscan Biscotti

THESE CLASSIC TUSCAN BISCOTTI ARE very popular all over Italy. They are harder than most biscotti Americans are accustomed to and are made to be dunked in sweet wine or coffee.

Makes about 60 biscotti

2 cups all-purpose flour

¾ cup sugar

1½ teaspoons baking powder

½ teaspoon ground cinnamon

6 ounces (about 1½ cups) whole unblanched almonds

3 large eggs

2 teaspoons vanilla extract

2 cookie sheets or jelly roll pans covered with parchment or foil

1 Set a rack in the middle level of the oven and preheat to 350 degrees. 2 In a bowl, combine the flour, sugar, baking powder, and cinnamon; stir well to mix. Stir in the almonds. 3 In another bowl, whisk the eggs with the vanilla, then use a rubber spatula to stir the eggs into the dry ingredients. Continue to stir until a stiff dough forms.

4 Scrape the dough out onto a lightly floured work surface and divide it in half. Roll each half under the palms of your hands into a cylinder a little shorter than your baking sheet. Place the logs of dough on the baking sheet, making sure they are not too close to each other or to the sides of the pan. Press down gently with the palm of your hand to flatten the logs. 5 Bake for about 25 to 30 minutes, or until the logs are well risen and have also spread to about double their original size. The logs are done if they feel firm when pressed with a fingertip. Place the pan on a rack and let the logs cool completely. 6 Reset the racks in the upper and lower thirds of the oven but leave the temperature at 350 degrees. Place each of the cooled logs on a cutting board and cut it diagonally into slices ⅓ inch thick. Arrange the biscotti on the prepared pans, cut side down. It isn't necessary to leave space between them. Bake the biscotti for about 15 or 20 minutes or until they are well toasted. Cool the pan on a rack. 7 Store the cooled biscotti between sheets of parchment or wax paper in a tin or plastic container with a tight-fitting cover.

LEMON PISTACHIO BISCOTTI

I HAVE ALWAYS LOVED THE COMBINATION of lemon and pistachios. Maybe it's the idea of yellow and green or the fact that the acidity of lemon perfectly tempers the richness of pistachios.

Be careful on the second baking of these biscotti—if they get a little too dark the pistachios will turn brown and you'll lose their lovely green color.

Makes about 60 biscotti

2¼ cups all-purpose flour

¾ cup sugar

1½ teaspoons baking powder

6 ounces (about 1½ cups) unsalted pistachios

3 large eggs

Finely grated zest of 2 medium lemons

3 tablespoons strained lemon juice

1 teaspoon vanilla extract

2 cookie sheets or jelly roll pans covered with parchment or foil

1 Set a rack in the middle level of the oven and preheat to 350 degrees. **2** In a medium bowl, combine the flour, sugar, and baking powder; stir well to mix. Stir in the pistachios. **3** In another bowl, whisk the eggs with the lemon zest, juice, and vanilla. Use a rubber spatula to stir the egg mixture into the dry ingredients. Continue to stir until a stiff dough forms. **4** Scrape the dough onto a lightly floured work surface and divide it in half. Roll each half under the palms of your hands into a cylinder a little shorter than your baking sheet. Place the logs of dough on the baking sheet, making sure they are not too close to each other or to the sides of the pan. With the palm of your hand, press down gently to flatten the logs. **5** Bake for about 25 to 30 minutes, or until the logs are well risen and have spread to about double their size. The logs are done when, pressed with a fingertip, they feel firm. Place the pan on a rack to cool the logs completely. **6** Reset the racks in the upper and lower thirds of the oven. Reduce the oven temperature to 300 degrees. Place each of the cooled logs on a cutting board and cut it into ⅓-inch-thick diagonal slices. Arrange the biscotti on the prepared pans, cut side down. It isn't necessary to leave space between them. Bake the biscotti for about 15 or 20 minutes or until they are dry and lightly golden. Cool on the pan on a rack. **7** Store the cooled biscotti between sheets of parchment or wax paper in a tin or plastic container with a tight-fitting cover.

CHOCOLATE CHUNK BISCOTTI

THESE ARE A VARIATION ON ELLEN Baumwoll's recipe for chocolate biscotti, which appeared in my book *Chocolate*. Here chunks of dark and milk chocolate are added for a subtle richness.

Makes about 60 biscotti

1¾ cups all-purpose flour

⅔ cup unsweetened cocoa powder, sifted after measuring

2 teaspoons baking powder

Pinch salt

1¼ cups sugar

6 ounces bittersweet or semisweet chocolate, cut into ¼-inch pieces

6 ounces milk chocolate, cut into ¼-inch pieces

4 large eggs

1 teaspoon vanilla extract

2 cookie sheets or jelly roll pans covered with parchment or foil

1 Set a rack at the middle level of the oven and preheat to 325 degrees. 2 In a bowl, combine the flour, cocoa, baking powder, and salt; stir well to mix. Stir in the sugar and chocolates. 3 In another bowl, whisk together the eggs and vanilla and using a large rubber spatula stir the eggs into the flour mixture to form a dough. 4 On a lightly floured surface, press the dough together—it will be sticky. Flour your hands and the surface lightly, but do not add any more flour to the dough. Divide the dough in half and roll each half into a log the length of your pan (14 to 18 inches). Place the logs on a pan, making sure they are not too close to each other or to the sides of the pan. Press down gently with the palm of your hand to flatten the logs. (Use a dry brush to remove excess flour, if necessary.) Bake for about 30 minutes, until they are well risen and have also spread to about double in size. The logs are done when, pressed with a fingertip, they feel firm. Cool the logs on the pan. 5 Reset the racks in the upper and lower thirds of the oven. Using a sharp serrated knife, slice the baked logs diagonally about every ¼ to ½ inch. Return the biscotti to the pans, cut side down, and bake up to 20 minutes longer, or until the biscotti are dry and crisp. 6 Store the cooled biscotti between sheets of parchment or wax paper in a tin or plastic container with a tight-fitting cover.

ALMOND AND HAZELNUT BISCOTTI

THIS COMBINATION WORKS PARTICU-
larly well and makes nutty, fragrant biscotti.
Of course you may also make them with all
hazelnuts or all almonds.

Don't be confused by the two quantities
for each nut in the ingredient list. The first is
for ground nuts, the second for whole ones.

Makes about 60 biscotti

2 cups all-purpose flour

⅔ cup sugar

**2 ounces (about ½ cup) whole unblanched almonds,
finely ground in the food processor**

**2 ounces (about ½ cup) whole unblanched hazel-
nuts, finely ground in the food processor**

1 teaspoon baking powder

½ teaspoon baking soda

1 teaspoon ground cinnamon

3 ounces (about ¾ cup) whole unblanched almonds

3 ounces (about ¾ cup) whole unblanched hazelnuts

⅓ cup honey

⅓ cup water (in a 1-cup glass measuring cup)

**2 cookie sheets or jelly roll pans covered
with parchment or foil**

1 Set a rack in the middle level of the oven and
preheat to 350 degrees. **2** In a large bowl, combine the flour, sugar, ground nuts, baking powder,
baking soda, and cinnamon; stir well to mix. Stir
in the whole nuts. **3** Pour the honey into the
water in the measuring cup; you will have ⅔ cup
of the liquid. Stir the water and honey together,
then add them to the bowl. **4** Stir the ingredients together until they form a stiff dough.
5 Scrape the dough onto a lightly floured work
surface and divide it in half. Roll each half under
the palms of your hands into a cylinder a little
shorter than your baking sheet. Place the logs of
dough on the baking sheet, making sure they are
not too close to each other or to the sides of the
pan. With the palm of your hand press down gently
to flatten the logs. **6** Bake the logs of dough for
about 30 minutes, or until they are well risen and
have also spread to about double in size. The logs
are done when, pressed with a fingertip, they feel
firm. Place the pan on a rack to cool the logs completely. **7** Reset the racks in the upper and lower
thirds of the oven but leave the temperature set at
350 degrees. Place each of the cooled logs on a
cutting board and slice it diagonally every ⅓ inch.
Arrange the biscotti on the prepared pans, cut side
down. Bake the biscotti for about 15 or 20 minutes
or until they are well toasted. Cool on the pan on a
rack. **8** Store the cooled biscotti between sheets
of parchment or wax paper in a tin or plastic container with a tight-fitting cover.

Dark Chocolate Hazelnut Biscotti

THE DIFFERENCE BETWEEN THESE AND the Chocolate Chunk Biscotti on page 226 is that these use two different sugars and a lot of hazelnuts.

Makes about 60 biscotti

1¾ cups all-purpose flour

¾ cup unsweetened cocoa powder, sifted after measuring

2 teaspoons baking powder

¼ teaspoon ground cloves

Pinch salt

8 ounces (about 2 cups) hazelnuts, toasted, skins rubbed off, and coarsely chopped

4 large eggs

1 tablespoon dark rum

1 teaspoon vanilla extract

½ cup firmly packed dark brown sugar

⅔ cup granulated sugar

2 cookie sheets or jelly roll pans covered with parchment or foil

1 Set a rack at the middle level of the oven and preheat to 325 degrees. 2 In a bowl, combine the flour, cocoa, baking powder, cloves, and salt; stir well to mix. Stir in the hazelnuts. 3 In another bowl, whisk together the eggs, rum, and vanilla. Whisk in first the brown then the white sugar, one at a time. Stir in the flour mixture to form a dough. 4 On a lightly floured surface, press the dough together—it will be sticky. Flour your hands and the surface lightly, but do not add any more flour to the dough. Divide the dough in half and roll each half into a log the length of your pan (14 to 18 inches). Place the logs on a pan and flatten slightly. (Use a dry brush to remove excess flour, if necessary.) Bake for about 25 to 30 minutes, until well risen and firm. Cool the logs on the pan. 5 Using a sharp serrated knife, slice the baked logs diagonally about every ¼ to ½ inch. Return the biscotti to the pans, cut side down, and bake up to 20 minutes longer, or until the biscotti are dry and crisp. 6 Store the cooled biscotti between sheets of parchment or wax paper in a tin or plastic container with a tight-fitting cover.

Gingery Macadamia Biscotti (LEFT) *and Dark Chocolate Hazelnut Biscotti*

GINGERY MACADAMIA BISCOTTI

THESE ARE INSPIRED BY BUT NOT BASED on a recipe called Gingerful Biscotti by my friend and mentor Maida Heatter. Please note the two different macadamia nuts in the ingredients: 4 ounces are ground and 6 ounces are chopped.

Makes about 70 biscotti

2 cups all-purpose flour

¾ cup sugar

4 ounces (about 1 cup) unsalted raw macadamia nuts, finely ground in the food processor, plus 6 ounces (about 1½ cups), coarsely chopped

1 teaspoon baking powder

½ teaspoon baking soda

4 teaspoons ground ginger

1 teaspoon ground cinnamon

½ teaspoon freshly ground white pepper

¼ teaspoon ground cloves

2 large eggs

⅓ cup honey

2 cookie sheets or jelly roll pans covered with parchment or foil

1 Set a rack in the middle level of the oven and preheat to 350 degrees. **2** In a large bowl, combine the flour, sugar, ground macadamia nuts, baking powder, baking soda, and spices; stir well to mix. Stir in the chopped nuts. **3** In another bowl, whisk the eggs; whisk in the honey and add the mixture to the dry ingredients. **4** Use a rubber spatula to stir the ingredients together until they form a stiff dough. At first it will seem too dry, but keep mixing and it will eventually hold together. **5** Scrape the dough onto a lightly floured work surface and divide it in half. Roll each half under the palms of your hands into a cylinder a little shorter than your baking sheet. Place the logs of dough on the baking sheet, making sure they are not too close to each other or to the sides of the pan. Press down gently with the palm of your hand to flatten the logs. **6** Bake the logs of dough for about 30 minutes, or until they are well risen and have also spread to about double in size. The logs are done when, pressed with a fingertip, they feel firm. Place the pan on a rack to cool the logs completely. **7** Reset the racks in the upper and lower thirds of the oven but leave the temperature at 350 degrees. Place each of the cooled logs on a cutting board and slice it diagonally every ⅓ inch. Arrange the biscotti on the prepared pans, cut side down. It isn't necessary to allow any space between them. Bake the biscotti for about 15 or 20 minutes or until they are well toasted. Cool on the pan on a rack. **8** Store the cooled biscotti between sheets of parchment or wax paper in a tin or plastic container with a tight-fitting cover.

QUARESIMALI

THE NAME OF THESE BISCOTTI TRANS-
lates as Lentens—cookies meant to be con-
sumed during Lent, the traditional 40-day fast
that precedes Easter. Nowadays the rigors of
Lent are greatly relaxed; fasting is now
optional, so the fact that these cookies were
made without egg yolks or butter has less religious significance than it once did. This recipe
is loosely based on one by my late friend
Richard Sax.

Makes about 48 small biscotti

1½ cups all-purpose flour

1 cup sugar

¼ teaspoon salt

1 teaspoon baking powder

1 teaspoon ground cinnamon

**10 ounces (about 2½ cups) whole hazelnuts,
toasted and skins rubbed off**

2 large egg whites

2 tablespoons vegetable oil

**1 cookie sheet or jelly roll pan covered
with parchment or foil**

1 Set a rack in the middle level of the oven and preheat to 350 degrees. **2** In a medium bowl, combine the flour, sugar, salt, baking powder, and cinnamon; stir well to mix. Stir in the hazelnuts. **3** In a small bowl, whisk together the egg whites and the oil. Use a rubber spatula to scrape the egg white mixture into the dry ingredients, then continue to stir with the same spatula until the mixture forms a dough. The dough is some-what dry; if it doesn't come together after stirring with a rubber spatula, use your hands to squeeze and knead the dough into a coherent mass. **4** Divide the dough in half and roll each half into a log the length of your pan (14 to 18 inches). Place each log on the prepared pan and flatten slightly. Bake for about 30 minutes, until well risen and firm. Cool the logs on the pan on a rack. **5** Using a sharp serrated knife, slice the baked logs diagonally about ½ inch thick. Return the biscotti to the pan, cut side down, and bake up to 20 minutes longer, or until they are dry and crisp. **6** Store the cooled biscotti between sheets of parchment or wax paper in a tin or plastic container with a tight-fitting cover.

CAROLE WALTER'S ETHEREAL MANDELBROT

THESE ARE COOKIES I COULD MAKE (and eat) daily and never tire of them. They are fine and delicate and I think the best version of this cookie I have ever tried. Sometimes I cheat and substitute a stick of melted butter for the oil—they are even better. Carole told me that this recipe came from a friend in North Carolina and that she always uses pecans in them as a tribute to its Southern origin.

Makes about 60 biscotti,
depending on how thinly they are sliced

2½ cups all-purpose flour

1 tablespoon baking powder

1 teaspoon ground cinnamon, optional

4 ounces (about 1 cup) coarsely chopped pecan pieces

3 large eggs

Pinch salt

1 cup sugar

1 teaspoon vanilla extract

½ cup mild vegetable oil or 8 tablespoons (1 stick) unsalted butter, melted

2 cookie sheets or jelly roll pans covered with parchment or foil

1 Set a rack in the middle level of the oven and preheat to 350 degrees. **2** In a bowl, combine the flour, baking powder, optional cinnamon, and nuts; stir well to mix. **3** In a medium bowl, whisk the eggs and salt by hand until well mixed. Whisk in the sugar and vanilla and when the mixture is smooth whisk in the oil. **4** Fold the flour mixture into the egg mixture until all the flour is absorbed—the dough will be very soft. **5** Spoon the dough onto the prepared pan in two strips, each about 2 inches wide and the length of the pan, making sure they are not too close to each other or to the sides of the pan. Smooth and even off the sides, if necessary. **6** Bake the logs of dough about 25 to 30 minutes, or until they are well risen and have also spread to about double in size. The logs are done when, pressed with a fingertip, they feel firm. Cool on the pan on a rack to room temperature. **7** Using a sharp serrated knife, slice the baked logs diagonally about every ¼ to ½ inch. Return the biscotti to the pan, cut side down, and bake up to 20 minutes longer, or until the biscotti are a deep golden color. **8** Store the cooled biscotti between sheets of parchment or wax paper in a tin or plastic container with a tight-fitting cover.

TRADITIONAL
JEWISH MANDELBROT

MANDELBROT, THE MOST TRADITIONAL Jewish cookie, is really a type of biscotti. This recipe is a combination and variation of excellent recipes sent to me by Rhonda Kaplan of Toronto and Michele Lifshen-Reing, who was a student in my career baking course at Peter Kump's New York Cooking School.

Makes about 48 biscotti

2 cups all-purpose flour

1 teaspoon baking powder

¼ teaspoon salt

4 ounces (about 1 cup) whole blanched almonds, coarsely chopped

2 large eggs

½ cup sugar

1 teaspoon vanilla extract

1 teaspoon almond extract

½ cup mild vegetable oil

½ cup sugar mixed with 1 teaspoon cinnamon for finishing

2 cookie sheets or jelly roll pans covered with parchment or foil

1 Set a rack in the middle level of the oven and preheat to 350 degrees. **2** In a bowl, combine the flour, baking powder, and salt; stir well to mix. Stir in the almonds. **3** In another bowl, whisk the eggs by hand until well mixed. Add the sugar and whisk until smooth. Whisk in the extracts and oil. **4** Fold the flour mixture into the egg mixture until all the flour is absorbed. **5** On a lightly floured surface, press the dough together. Divide the dough in half and roll each half into a log the length of your pan (14 to 18 inches). Place each log on a pan and flatten slightly. Bake for about 25 to 30 minutes, until the are well risen and firm. Cool the logs on the pans and racks. **6** Reset the racks in the upper and lower thirds of the oven. Using a sharp serrated knife, slice the baked logs diagonally about every ½ inch. Place the cinnamon sugar in a shallow bowl and turn the cut biscotti in it. Return the biscotti to the pans, cut side down, and bake up to 20 minutes longer, or until the biscotti are dry and crisp. **7** Store the cooled biscotti between sheets of parchment or wax paper in a tin or plastic container with a tight-fitting cover.

ORANGE AND ALMOND BISCOTTI

THIS FOOLPROOF RECIPE FOR TENDER biscotti is from my friend and former student Andrea Tutunjian, who now teaches with me at Peter Kump's New York Cooking School.

Makes about 60 biscotti

1¾ cups all-purpose flour

¾ cup sugar

1 teaspoon baking powder

¼ teaspoon salt

8 tablespoons (1 stick) unsalted butter

4 ounces (about 1 cup) whole blanched almonds, coarsely chopped

⅔ cup candied orange peel, cut into ¼-inch dice

2 large eggs

2 teaspoons vanilla extract

Finely grated zest of 1 large orange

2 cookie sheets or jelly roll pans covered with parchment or foil

1 Set a rack in the middle level of the oven and preheat to 350 degrees. **2** In a bowl, combine the flour, sugar, baking powder, and salt; stir well to mix. **3** Cut the butter into six or eight pieces and add to the bowl. Rub the butter into the dry ingredients. Reach down to the bottom of the bowl and make sure no dry ingredients escape the butter. Rub and distribute the butter evenly until there are no longer any large pieces of butter and the mixture is cool and powdery. **4** Add the almonds and orange peel to the flour and butter mixture and toss to combine. **5** In another bowl, whisk together the eggs, vanilla, and orange zest and add the dry ingredients. Use a large rubber spatula to stir the ingredients together until they form a dough. **6** Scrape the dough onto a floured surface and press it together. Shape the dough into a 12-inch cylinder and divide it in half. Roll each half under your hands to re-form it as a thinner 12-inch cylinder. Place the logs on the prepared pan, not too close to each other or to the sides of the pan. Use the palm of your hand to flatten the logs gently. **7** Bake the logs for 25 to 30 minutes, or until they are well risen, well colored, and firm when pressed with a fingertip. Place the pan on a rack to cool. **8** Reset the racks in the upper and lower thirds of the oven but leave the temperature at 350 degrees. Place each of the cooled logs on a cutting board and slice it diagonally every ⅓ inch. Arrange the biscotti on the prepared pans, cut side down. It isn't necessary to leave space between them. Bake the biscotti for 15 to 20 minutes or until they are well toasted. Cool on the pan on a rack. **9** Store the cooled biscotti between sheets of parchment or wax paper in a tin or plastic container with a tight-fitting cover.

Buttery Anisette Biscotti

THIS RECIPE FOR FRAGILE, DELICATE biscotti comes from Chef Frank Garofolo, who teaches at Peter Kump's New York Cooking School. It is an adaptation of a recipe of his mother, Lucy Garofolo. If you are searching for the ideal biscotti, this is the recipe.

Makes about 50 biscotti,
depending on how thinly they are sliced

3 cups all-purpose flour

1 tablespoon baking powder

3 ounces (about ¾ cup) whole blanched almonds, coarsely chopped

8 tablespoons (1 stick) unsalted butter, softened

1 cup sugar

1½ teaspoons vanilla extract

1 tablespoon anisette or 1 teaspoon anise extract

3 large eggs

2 cookie sheets or jelly roll pans covered with parchment or foil

1 Set a rack in the middle level of the oven and preheat to 350 degrees. **2** In a bowl, combine the flour and baking powder; stir well to mix. Stir in the almonds. **3** In the bowl of a standing electric mixer fitted with the paddle attachment, beat together on medium speed the butter and sugar until soft and smooth, about 2 or 3 minutes. Beat in the vanilla and anisette or extract. **4** Add the eggs, one at a time, beating smooth after each addition. **5** Remove the bowl from the mixer and, with a large rubber spatula, stir in the flour and almond mixture. **6** On a lightly floured surface, press the dough together—it will be sticky. Flour your hands and the surface lightly, but do not add any more flour to the dough. Divide the dough in half and roll each piece into a log the length of your pan (14 to 18 inches). Place each log on a pan and flatten slightly. (Use a dry brush to remove excess flour, if necessary.) Bake for about 30 minutes, until well risen and firm. Cool the logs on the pans. **7** Using a sharp serrated knife, slice the baked logs diagonally every ½ inch. Return the biscotti to the pan, cut side down, and bake up to 20 minutes longer, or until the biscotti are dry and crisp. Cool on the pans on racks. **8** Store the cooled biscotti between sheets of parchment or wax paper in a tin or plastic container with a tight-fitting cover.

CORNMEAL BISCOTTI

THESE ARE A VERSION OF A DELICIOUS
Venetian cookie known as zaleti. (See page 88
for a version of zaleti from Bologna.) Crisp
and slightly grainy, these are perfect with tea
or coffee.

Makes about 50 biscotti,
depending on how thinly they are sliced

1⅓ cups all-purpose flour

1⅓ cups stone-ground yellow cornmeal

½ cup sugar

¼ teaspoon salt

1 teaspoon baking powder

10 tablespoons (1¼ sticks) unsalted butter

1 cup currants, rinsed under hot water,
cooled and drained on paper towels

2 large eggs

1 teaspoon vanilla extract

Finely grated zest of 1 medium lemon

1 cookie sheet or jelly roll pan covered
with parchment or foil

1 In a bowl, combine the flour, cornmeal, sugar, salt, and baking powder; stir well to mix. **2** Cut the butter into six or eight pieces and add it to the bowl. Rub the butter into the dry ingredients. Reach down to the bottom of the bowl and make sure no dry ingredients escape the butter. Rub in the butter until it is distributed evenly and there are no longer any large pieces. The mixture should be cool and powdery. Stir in the currants. **3** In another bowl, whisk together the eggs with the vanilla and lemon zest, then with a rubber spatula stir the eggs into the cornmeal mixture. Continue stirring until the mixture forms a soft dough. **4** On a lightly floured surface, press the dough together—it will be sticky. Flour your hands and the surface lightly, but do not add any more flour to the dough. Divide the dough in half and roll each half into a log the length of your pan (14 to 18 inches). Place each log on a pan and flatten it slightly. (Use a dry brush to remove excess flour, if necessary.) Bake for about 30 minutes, until well risen and firm. Cool the logs on the pans. **5** Using a sharp serrated knife, slice the baked logs diagonally every ½ inch. Return the biscotti to the pan, cut side down, and bake up to 20 minutes longer, or until the biscotti are dry and crisp. **6** Store the cooled biscotti between sheets of parchment or wax paper in a tin or plastic container with a tight-fitting cover.

ALL-CORN BISCOTTI

THESE DELICATE, CRUNCHY BISCOTTI
are wheat- and gluten-free. Be careful to let the
baked cake cool after the first baking or it will
be difficult to slice.

Makes about 70 biscotti

**8 ounces (about 2 cups) whole
unblanched almonds**

1 cup yellow cornmeal

1 cup cornstarch

½ teaspoon baking soda

½ teaspoon ground cinnamon

1 egg

⅔ cup sugar

¼ cup honey

2 tablespoons melted butter or vegetable oil

1 teaspoon vanilla extract

**One 9 × 13 × 2-inch pan, buttered and
the bottom lined with parchment or foil**

**2 cookie sheets or jelly roll pans covered
with parchment or foil**

1 Set a rack in the middle level of the oven and
preheat to 350 degrees. **2** In the work bowl of a
food processor fitted with the steel blade, place
1 cup of the almonds and pulse repeatedly until
finely ground. Transfer to a bowl with the
remaining whole almonds, cornmeal, cornstarch,
baking soda, and cinnamon. Stir well to mix.
3 In a separate bowl, whisk the egg, add the
sugar, honey, butter or oil, and vanilla, whisking
as you add each one. Stir in the dry ingredients
with a rubber spatula until a stiff dough forms.
4 Scrape the dough onto the 9 × 13-inch pan
and press with palm of your hand until the
dough is an even layer completely covering the
bottom of the pan, about ½ inch thick. **5** Bake
for about 30 minutes, until firm. Cool in the pan
for 5 minutes, then invert onto a cutting board
and cool completely. Reset the racks in the upper
and lower thirds of the oven. Leave the oven on.
6 Cut into three 3 × 13-inch strips, then slice
each strip every ½ inch. Arrange the biscotti on
the prepared cookie sheets or jelly roll pans and
bake again for about 15 minutes. **7** Store the
cooled biscotti between sheets of parchment or
wax paper in a tin or plastic container with a
tight-fitting cover.

TOTEBEINLI

THE NAME OF THESE ESPECIALLY CRISP and fragile biscotti means "dead men's bones" in Swiss German dialect. Thanks to Thea Cvijanovich from Berne for sharing this interesting variation on standard biscotti.

Makes about 90 biscotti

2⅓ cups all-purpose flour

1 teaspoon baking powder

4 ounces (about 1 cup) whole unblanched almonds, cut in half

4 ounces (about 1 cup) whole unblanched hazelnuts, cut in half

2 tablespoons (¼ stick) unsalted butter, softened

1¼ cups sugar

3 large eggs

Pinch salt

Finely grated zest of 1 medium lemon

1 teaspoon ground cinnamon

One 10 × 15 × 1-inch baking pan buttered and lined with parchment or foil

2 cookie sheets or jelly roll pans covered with parchment or foil

1 Set a rack in the middle level of the oven and preheat to 350 degrees. 2 In a bowl, combine the flour and baking powder; stir well to mix, then stir in the nuts. 3 In a medium bowl, beat the butter by hand with a rubber spatula, then beat in one third of the sugar. Add one egg and continue beating until smooth. Add another third of the sugar, then another egg, and beat again until smooth. Finally, add the remaining sugar and the last egg, and beat until smooth. Beat in the salt, lemon zest, and cinnamon. 4 Stir in the flour mixture to form a smooth dough. 5 Scrape the dough out onto the prepared 10 × 15-inch pan and press it into an even layer using a rubber spatula or the floured palm of your hand. Make sure the dough reaches into all the corners of the pan and that the top is flat and even. 6 Bake the dough for about 30 minutes, or until it is firm and well colored. Place the pan on a rack to cool for about 15 minutes. 7 Set the racks in the upper and lower thirds of the oven and adjust the temperature to 300 degrees. Turn the warm baked slab out onto a cutting board and with a large, sharp knife cut down the length of the slab to make three 3- to 3½-inch-wide lengthwise strips. Then slice each strip across into ½-inch-wide biscotti. Place the biscotti, cut side down, on the prepared pans and bake them for another 20 minutes, or until they are dry and crisp and golden in color. 8 Cool the biscotti on the pans on racks. 9 Store the cooled biscotti between sheets of parchment or wax paper in a tin or plastic container with a tight-fitting cover.

AUSTRALIAN ALMOND TOASTS

THIS IS A RECIPE THAT MY FRIEND
Kyra Effren brought back from a visit to
Australia. Kyra says they are everywhere Down
Under, made with all different types of nuts.
To be successful, these must be very thin, so
get out your sharpest serrated knife. And like
the Australians, use any type of nut you like.

Makes about 60 very thin biscotti

1 cup all-purpose flour

1 teaspoon baking powder

½ teaspoon salt

**6 ounces (about 1½ cups) whole blanched almonds,
coarsely chopped**

3 large egg whites (a little less than ½ cup)

½ cup sugar

1 teaspoon vanilla extract

**One 8 ½ × 4 ½ × 2¾-inch loaf pan, buttered
and the bottom lined with parchment or foil**

**2 or 3 cookie sheets or jelly roll pans covered
with parchment or foil**

1 Set a rack in the middle level of the oven and
preheat to 350 degrees. **2** In a bowl combine
the flour, baking powder, and salt; stir well to
mix, then stir in the almonds. **3** Pour the egg
whites into the bowl of an electric mixer fitted
with the whip attachment and whip on medium
speed until they become white, opaque, and
begin to hold their shape, about 2 or 3 minutes.
One tablespoon at a time, beat in the sugar, then
continue beating until the egg whites hold a firm
peak. Beat in the vanilla. **4** Remove the bowl
from the mixer and fold in the flour mixture.
Continue to fold until the mixture forms a soft
dough. **5** Scrape the dough into the prepared
loaf pan and smooth the top. **6** Bake the loaf

for about 35 to 40 minutes, or until it is well risen and a knife or toothpick inserted in the center emerges clean. Turn off the oven and unmold the loaf onto a rack, roll it onto its side, cover it with a piece of aluminum foil (to conserve moisture and make it easier to cut later), and allow it to cool to room temperature. **7** When you are ready to slice and rebake the biscotti, set the racks in the upper and lower thirds of the oven and preheat to 275 degrees. **8** Using your sharpest serrated knife, slice the loaf about every $\frac{1}{8}$ inch. Arrange the slices on the prepared pans and bake them for about 15 minutes or until they are light golden and dry. Be careful—these burn easily. If they are not all the exact same thickness some may color faster than others and you may have to remove them from the pans one at a time as they are done. **9** Cool the biscotti on racks. **10** Store the cooled biscotti between sheets of parchment or wax paper in a tin or plastic container with a tight-fitting cover. These keep indefinitely.

FRIED COOKIES

Bugnes Arlesiennes
(Fried Cookies from Arles)

Galani (Venetian Carnival Fritters)

Sour Cream Doughnut Holes

Sfingi
(Cream Puff Pastry Fritters)

Shenkeli
(Little Thighs)

Zeppole
(Italian Bread-Dough Fritters)

Olliebollen
(Dutch Currant Fritters)

DEEP-FRYING IS NOT WHAT YOU THINK OF WHEN YOU THINK OF MAKING COOKIES, though it produces some delicate and interesting ones. Fried pastries and cookies were originally the only type made at home, because until well into the twentieth century, most homes in Europe and many in America did not have ovens. Ovens were at the local bakery or belonged to a business. When you needed baking done, you brought the food to be baked to the oven and paid a fee to use it.

When I first visited my cousins in southern Italy in the early seventies, there was still a communal oven down the street from their house. I had a chance to visit once or twice, then unfortunately it was destroyed in a disastrous 1980 earthquake.

Carnival, the season of feasting that precedes the beginning of Lent, was traditionally a time for fried cookies and pastries. Many of the ones we eat today were originally prepared only for Carnival. Meat and meat products had to be avoided during the Lenten fasting, so fried pastries would also have been forbidden. They were usually fried in lard or beef suet—two animal fats with a high smoking point still widely used in Europe for deep-frying.

Fried cookies and pastries are not necessarily heavy or greasy. When foods are properly fried, they absorb only a minute amount of fat. So don't resist trying fried cookies—their textures vary from rich and creamy to shatteringly crisp, and are fun to make and eat on a cold winter night.

HINTS FOR FRIED COOKIES

1 Fry in a large pan, such as a Dutch oven, and don't fill it more than half full of oil: If the oil breaks down and begins to foam, there will still be room so it doesn't overflow. A pan with a cover is best. The cover isn't used during frying but it helps after the frying is finished. You can move the pan off the burner and cover it, thereby stopping the hot fat fumes from continuing to saturate the air. Leave the covered pan off the heat but on the stove until the oil is cold. Never pick up and move a pan filled with hot oil—it is too dangerous. An electric frying pan, especially one of the deeper models, is ideal for deep-frying. **2** Before you start to fry always have everything ready. Have all the cookies lined up on pans, then have other pans covered with paper towels to receive and drain the fried cookies. Also get out a skimmer or slotted spoon for removing the cookies from the oil. Trying to roll dough, cut out cookies, and fry at the same time will only result in burned cookies, and the temperature of the unmonitored oil can become dangerously high. When you are frying, don't do anything else. **3** Use a good deep-frying thermometer so you know the exact temperature of the oil. Then you can adjust the heat under the frying kettle according to any changes in temperature you read on the thermometer. A deep-frying thermometer is also known as a candy thermometer. Use the kind that looks like a ruler, not the less accurate stem with a round dial at the top. **4** The oil is ready when a bit of dough dropped in rises to the surface and begins to color almost immediately. Before you add large amounts of dough to the frying oil, test a few to see how quickly they will cook through. **5** Don't crowd the pan—too many cookies in the pan at once will bring down the temperature of the oil and make the cookies absorb fat. **6** If the cookies have been rolled out in flour, brush off any excess or it will accumulate in the oil and burn. **7** Remember, hot oil can be extremely dangerous. Banish the curious from the kitchen and keep distractions to a minimum so you can concentrate on the frying.

BUGNES ARLESIENNES
Fried Cookies from Arles

BUGNES ARE SO POPULAR ALL OVER central and southern France that most of the regions there claim them as their own. This version is loosely adapted from a recipe in *La Veritable Cuisine Provençal et Niçoise ("The Real Cooking of Provence and Nice")* by Jean Noel Escudier (Editions Provencia, Toulon, 1964). This excellent book was published in translation as *Wonderful Food of Provence,* translated by Peta Fuller (Harper & Row, 1988), and is long out-of-print—but it turns up occasionally in used book stores and is worth looking for.

Bugnes are crisp, rich little cookies that make a good accompaniment for a lean dessert such as a fruit salad or sherbet. Of course, they are also excellent on their own.

Makes about 36 bugnes

2 large egg yolks

Pinch salt

¼ cup granulated sugar

¼ cup white rum

1½ cups all-purpose flour

4 cups vegetable oil for frying

Confectioners' sugar for sprinkling

2 cookie sheets or jelly roll pans covered with parchment or other paper to hold the *bugnes* before they are fried, and 2 more covered with paper towels or brown paper on which to drain the fried *bugnes*

1 In a medium bowl, whisk the egg yolks and the salt. Whisk in the granulated sugar and continue whisking for a minute or two until the mixture is light-colored and fluffy. Whisk in the rum. **2** Use a medium rubber spatula to stir in the flour. When a soft dough forms, scrape it onto a floured work surface, and using a bench scraper or spatula, fold it over on itself several times. Keep folding the dough over on itself and pushing it away, then turning and repeating the operation. Continue to knead for a minute or two, or until the dough is smooth. **3** Coat the outside of the dough generously with flour, then place it on a piece of plastic wrap. Form it into a rectangle about ½ inch thick and wrap it up. Let the wrapped dough rest at room temperature for about an hour before you continue. **4** After the dough has rested, divide it into four equal parts. Generously flour half the work surface and the dough; roll it out into a 9-inch square. With a serrated pizza wheel cut the dough into 3-inch squares. As each is cut, place it on one of the prepared pans. Be careful they don't overlap. Repeat with the remaining dough. **5** To fry the *bugnes*, in a large kettle heat the oil to 375 degrees. Fry the *bugnes* a few at a time, moving them around constantly in the hot fat so they color evenly. When they are a light golden color, remove the *bugnes* from the oil and drain them on the prepared pans. **6** Cool to room temperature and sprinkle generously with confectioners' sugar before serving. **7** As with all fried pastries, these are best the day they are made, but leftovers may be kept for a while at room temperature, loosely covered with plastic wrap.

GALANI
Venetian Carnival Fritters

THESE LITTLE KNOTS OF DELICATE fried dough are similar to *bugnes* (page 244), but more elaborate both in flavor and in presentation.

Makes about 50 small galani

3 tablespoons unsalted butter, softened

3 tablespoons granulated sugar

½ teaspoon salt

2 large eggs

2 cups all-purpose flour

4 cups vegetable oil for frying

Confectioners' sugar for sprinkling

2 cookie sheets or jelly roll pans covered with parchment or other paper to hold the *galani* before they are fried, and 2 more pans covered with paper towels or brown paper on which to drain the fried *galani*

1 In a large bowl, beat together the butter, sugar, and salt with a medium rubber spatula. Whisk in one egg, then the other; the mixture may appear separated—that's all right. Use the rubber spatula to stir in the flour and form a soft dough. **2** Scrape the dough onto a floured work surface, and using a bench scraper or spatula, fold it over on itself several times. Keep folding the dough over on itself and pushing it away, then turning and repeating the operation. Continue to knead for a minute or two, or until the dough is smooth. **3** Coat the outside of the dough generously with flour and place it on a piece of plastic wrap. Form it into a rectangle about ½ inch thick and wrap it up. Let the wrapped dough rest at room temperature for about an hour before you continue. **4** After the dough has rested, divide it into three equal parts. Generously flour both the work surface and the dough. Roll one piece of the dough out into a 9-inch square and with a pizza wheel cut it into 1½ × 3-inch rectangles. As each piece is cut, place it on one of the prepared pans. Be careful not to let them overlap. Make a slash in the center of each rectangle of dough and thread one end back through it, as in the illustration. Repeat with the remaining dough. **5** Heat the oil in a large kettle to 375 degrees. Fry the *galani* a few at a time, moving them constantly in the hot fat so they color evenly. Fry to a light golden color and drain on the prepared pans. **6** Cool the *galani* to room temperature and sprinkle them generously with confectioners' sugar before serving. **7** As with all fried pastries, these are best the day they are made, but leftovers may be kept for a while at room temperature, loosely covered with plastic wrap.

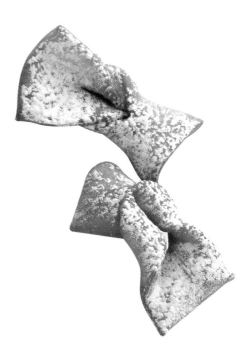

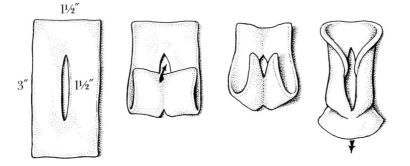

Step 4

SOUR CREAM DOUGHNUT HOLES

NOWADAYS WE AMERICANS NO LONGER eat doughnuts as regularly as our ancestors did. But once in a while indulge. Doughnut holes are a great way to enjoy doughnuts on a small scale. If you're a doughnut aficionado try to find a copy of Sally Levitt Steinberg's *Donut Book* (Knopf, 1987). You can't miss it—it has a hole in the cover! Seriously, it is filled with amusing doughnut lore and even a few recipes.

Makes about twenty-four 1½-inch doughnut holes

2 cups all-purpose flour

2 teaspoons baking powder

½ teaspoon baking soda

½ teaspoon salt

½ teaspoon ground cinnamon

½ teaspoon freshly grated nutmeg

1 egg

½ cup granulated sugar

3 tablespoons melted butter

⅔ cup sour cream

4 cups oil for frying

Confectioners' sugar for sprinkling

1 cookie sheet or jelly roll pan covered with parchment or other paper to hold the doughnut holes before they are fried, and 2 more covered with paper towels or brown paper on which to drain the fried doughnut holes

1 In a large mixing bowl, combine the flour, baking powder, baking soda, salt, and spices; stir well to mix. In another bowl, whisk the egg, then whisk in the granulated sugar. Whisk in the melted butter and sour cream. **2** Pour the liquid ingredients into the flour mixture and with a large rubber spatula mix gently until just combined. Do not overwork. The dough will be sticky. Turn the dough onto a lightly floured work surface and knead gently. Add pinches of flour, if necessary, until the dough just holds together. Cover the dough with plastic wrap and chill for about 1 hour. **3** On a floured surface, roll the dough out to ½-inch thickness. With a 1¼-inch round cutter, cut out the doughnut holes. **4** Heat the oil to 365 degrees, then fry the doughnut holes, a few at a time, turning them once. Try to keep the temperature of the oil between 360 and 375 degrees. It should take about 3 minutes for the doughnut holes to become nicely browned on both sides. Transfer them to one of the prepared pans to cool. Dust lightly with confectioners' sugar just before serving. **5** As with all fried pastries, these are best the day they are made, but leftovers may be kept for a while at room temperature, loosely covered with plastic wrap.

CHOCOLATE SOUR CREAM DOUGHNUT HOLES: Substitute 1½ cups flour and ⅓ cup unsweetened cocoa powder, sifted after measuring, for the flour in the recipe. If you wish, use Sugar-Based Chocolate Glaze for Cookies, page 319, to streak the doughnut holes or half-dip them.

SFINGI
Cream Puff Pastry Fritters

THESE ARE THE EASIEST AND MOST impressive of all fried specialties. They are as sweet and creamy as a small cream puff filled with sweetened pastry cream, even though they are made from a completely unsweetened dough and just rolled in cinnamon sugar.

Sfingi were one of the pastries my maternal grandmother, Clotilda Lo Conte, was famous for. She never gave out recipes, so everyone thought these were so much harder to make than they are. You'll see what I mean when you try them.

Makes about 30 sfingi

1 cup water

Pinch salt

6 tablespoons (¾ stick) unsalted butter, cut into 8 pieces

1 cup all-purpose flour

4 large eggs

4 cups vegetable oil for frying

1 teaspoon ground cinnamon

½ cup sugar

2 cookie sheets or jelly roll pans covered with paper towels or brown paper for draining the *sfingi*

1 In a medium saucepan, bring the water, salt, and butter to a boil over low heat. Remove from the heat and sift in the flour all at once. Use a wooden spoon to stir the flour in smoothly.
2 Return the pan to low heat and stir the paste vigorously until it holds together in one piece and the bottom of the pan is lightly filmed. Scrape the paste into a bowl and let it cool for 5 minutes.
3 Beat in the eggs one at a time, beating smooth after each addition. **4** To fry the *sfingi*, in a

4-quart saucepan, heat the oil to 350 degrees. To form the *sfingi,* use two teaspoons. Dip one teaspoon into the oil, then spoon up some of the dough with it. Use the other spoon to scrape the dough off the first one into the oil. Work quickly and fry six or eight *sfingi* at a time. Fry until the *sfingi* crack open and are a deep golden color.

Drain on the prepared pans. Just before serving, mix the cinnamon and sugar together in a shallow bowl and roll each of the *sfingi* in it. Arrange the *sfingi* on a platter. 5 As with all fried pastries, these are best the day they are made, but leftovers may be kept for a while at room temperature, loosely covered with plastic wrap

SHENKELI
Little Thighs

I FIRST ENCOUNTERED THESE WHEN I worked at a hotel in Zurich in the early seventies. The Christmas season had arrived and the hotel's pastry chef, Armand, and his assistants (I was working in the garde-manger department at the time), set about preparing all sorts of *Guetzli* (see page x for a full explanation of Swiss Christmas cookies). Because Armand was from Fribourg and came from a French-speaking family, his culinary practices were more those of western Switzerland—not a land of *Guetzli* traditions. So no one was sur-

prised when Armand made a big pan of *Shenkeli,* heretofore exclusively Carnival cookies, for the Christmas holidays.

By the way *Shenkeli* means "thighs" and are sometimes called *Dameshenkeli,* or "ladies' thighs." This makes making and eating *Shenkeli* seem vaguely naughty to the conservative Swiss Germans.

This recipe is adapted from *Guetzli* (Manus Verlag, 1987) by Marianne Kaltenbach, a popular Swiss German food writer and TV personality.

Makes about 48 Shenkeli

4 tablespoons (½ stick) unsalted butter, softened

½ cup sugar

2 large eggs

Pinch salt

1 tablespoon kirsch

Finely grated zest of 1 small lemon

2¼ cups all-purpose flour

4 cups vegetable oil for frying

2 cookie sheets or jelly roll pans covered with parchment or other paper to hold the *Shenkeli* before they are fried, and 2 more covered with paper towels or brown paper on which to drain the *Shenkeli*

1 In a medium bowl, beat the butter until it is soft and smooth with a large rubber spatula. Beat in the sugar. Switch to a whisk and beat in the eggs, one at a time. Then beat in the salt, kirsch, and lemon zest. **2** Use the rubber spatula to stir in the flour and make a soft dough. Scrape the dough onto a floured work surface, and using a bench scraper or spatula, fold it over on itself several times. Keep folding the dough over on itself and pushing it away, then turning and repeating the operation. Continue to knead for a minute or two, or until the dough is smooth. **3** Coat the outside of the dough generously with flour, then place it on a piece of plastic wrap. Form it into a rectangle about ½ inch thick and wrap it up. Let the wrapped dough rest in the refrigerator for about an hour before you continue. **4** After the dough has rested, divide it into four equal parts. Roll each part into a 12-inch length and cut into twelve equal pieces. Roll over each piece again with the palm of the hand to make it a cylinder about 2 inches long. Repeat with the remaining dough. Place the *Shenkeli* on the prepared pans. **5** Heat the oil to 350 degrees in a large kettle. Fry a few *Shenkeli* at a time, moving them constantly in the hot fat so they color evenly. Fry to a light golden color, then drain on the prepared pans. **6** Cool the *Shenkeli* to room temperature before serving; they are traditionally not covered with sugar since the dough itself is sweet. **7** As with all fried pastries, these are best the day they are made, but leftovers may be kept for a while at room temperature, loosely covered with plastic wrap.

Fried Cookies

ZEPPOLE
Italian Bread-Dough Fritters

THOUGH *ZEPPOLE* IS THE GENERIC Italian name for fritters of all kinds, it specifically refers to those chewy fritters of fried unseasoned bread dough covered with sugar and eaten outdoors during Italian street festivals.

When I was a child on Fourteenth Avenue in Newark there was a "feast" every weekend from July Fourth to Labor Day in our all-Italian neighborhood. Each feast involved processions of members of a saint's society bearing his or her statue through the streets. After the processions there were enormous street fairs that went on into the night with food stalls, games of chance, and several bandstands playing corny music. To this day if my mother hears loud, bad music or just a lot of noise she says: "It sounds like the feast on Fourteenth Avenue."

These *zeppole* are a delicate version of the greasy wads of fried dough you get at a feast. The taste of them never fails to bring back a flood of memories of my childhood and the closed little world of our immigrant neighborhood.

Makes about 24 zeppole

1 cup warm tap water, about 105 degrees

1 envelope (2½ teaspoons) active dry yeast

1¾ cups all-purpose flour

½ teaspoon salt

4 cups vegetable oil for frying

Confectioners' sugar for sprinkling

2 cookie sheets or jelly roll pans covered with paper towels or brown paper on which to drain the *zeppole*

1 Pour the water into a medium bowl. Whisk in the yeast. Use a rubber spatula to stir in the flour, but add the salt before the flour is completely absorbed. Continue stirring until the ingredients form a very wet dough. **2** Cover the bowl with plastic wrap. Let the dough rise at room temperature for about an hour, or until it is about double in bulk and very puffy. **3** To fry the *zeppole*, heat the oil to 375 degrees in a 4-quart saucepan. Use two soup spoons to form them (at the feast the *zeppole* makers snatched off pieces of dough with one hand): Dip one spoon into the hot oil, then spoon up some of the risen dough with it. Use the other spoon to scrape the dough off the first and drop it into the oil. Work quickly and fry six or eight of the *zeppole* at a time. Fry until the *zeppole* are a deep golden color. Drain on the prepared pans. When the *zeppole* are cool, dust generously with the confectioners' sugar. **4** As with all fried pastries, these are best the day they are made, but leftovers may be kept for a while at room temperature, loosely covered with plastic wrap.

OLLIEBOLLEN
Dutch Currant Fritters

THESE ARE LIKE LITTLE CLOUDS OF brioche dough, scented with lemon zest and cinnamon and studded with currants. Like so many Dutch specialties, they really deserve to be better known. Many thanks to my Dutch connections: Bonnie Slotnick, who supplied me with a couple of excellent Dutch baking books, from which this recipe is adapted, and Hans Polleman, who, with Bonnie, helped with translation while I struggled through those all but unintelligible recipes.

Makes about 30 small olliebollen

SPONGE

⅔ **cup milk**

1 envelope (2½ teaspoons) active dry yeast

1 cup all-purpose flour

DOUGH

3 tablespoons unsalted butter, softened

2 tablespoons firmly packed dark brown sugar

¼ **teaspoon salt**

½ **teaspoon ground cinnamon**

Finely grated zest of 1 small lemon

1 large egg

Risen sponge (see above)

1 cup all-purpose flour

⅔ **cup currants (or** ⅓ **cup each currants and golden raisins)**

4 cups vegetable oil for frying

Confectioners' sugar for sprinkling

2 cookie sheets or jelly roll pans covered with paper towels or brown paper on which to drain the *olliebollen*

(continued)

1 To make the sponge, heat the milk in a small saucepan over low heat until just lukewarm—about 105 degrees at the most. Pour the milk into a small bowl. Whisk in the yeast, then stir in the flour. This will still be very liquid. Cover the sponge with plastic wrap and let it ferment at room temperature for about 30 minutes, or until it is very well risen and foamy. 2 After the sponge has risen, make the dough: In the bowl of a standing electric mixer fitted with the paddle attachment, beat together on medium speed the butter, brown sugar, salt, cinnamon, and lemon zest until smooth. Beat in the egg (the mixture will appear separated—that's okay). Beat in the risen sponge. Stop the mixer and add the 1 cup flour, then beat on low speed until the dough is smooth, about 3 minutes. Beat in the currants.

3 Remove the bowl from the mixer, cover it with plastic wrap, and let the dough rise at room temperature for about an hour, or until it has almost doubled in bulk and is very puffy. 4 To fry the *olliebollen*, in a 4-quart saucepan, heat the oil to 350 degrees. Use two soup spoons to form the fritters: Dip one spoon into the hot oil, then spoon up some of the risen dough with it. Use the other spoon to scrape the dough off the first and drop it into the oil. Work quickly and fry six or eight of the fritters at a time. Fry until the *olliebollen* are a deep golden color. Drain on the prepared pans. When the *olliebollen* are cool, dust generously with the confectioners' sugar. 5 As with all fried pastries, these are best the day they are made, but leftovers may be kept for a while at room temperature, loosely covered with plastic wrap.

FILLED AND
SANDWICH COOKIES

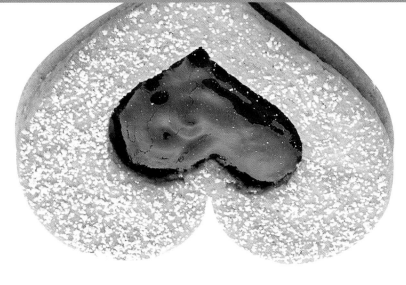

FILLED COOKIES

Cucidati
(Sicilian Fig-Filled Cookies)

Infasciadedde
(Sicilian Twisted Cookies)

Portland Fig Cookies

Mamoul (Syrian and
Lebanese Date-Filled Cookies)

Appenzeller Biberli (Filled
"Beavers" from Appenzell)

Railroad Tracks

SANDWICH COOKIES

Yoyos

Spitzbuebe ("Bad Boys")

Suvaroffs

Linzer Hearts

Lacy Chocolate
Oatmeal Cookie Sandwiches

Chocolate Chocolate
Sandwich Cookies

FILLED COOKIES

FILLED COOKIES, THE ARISTOCRATS OF THE COOKIE WORLD, INVOLVE A LITTLE extra effort. They are usually composed of a dough enclosing a rich filling. Like sandwich cookies, later on in this chapter, they provide an interesting contrast between their tender or crisp cookie component and creamy fillings.

HINTS FOR FILLED COOKIES

1 Make sure the dough is firm but malleable before trying to shape filled cookies. Success depends on having the dough and filling approximately the same consistency so they do not oppose each other as you are trying to shape the cookies. **2** Be accurate about dimensions. Use a ruler for best results. **3** Prepare both dough and filling in advance—then you can concentrate on shaping the cookies on the following day, or whenever you plan to do it. **4** Apply egg wash sparingly to the outsides of cookies. I dip a brush into the beaten egg, then wipe several times against the rim of the bowl or cup containing the egg. This is to make the excess egg drip off so that when you paint the wash onto the cookies it will not dribble down and puddle underneath them.

CUCIDATI
Sicilian Fig-Filled Cookies

No one seems to agree about exactly what—besides figs—goes into the filling for these classic Sicilian cookies. There are two distinct versions: One is for a small cookie, made from a filled cylinder of dough, as here, or formed as "ravioli" with the filling enclosed between two layers of the dough and shaped with a decorative cutter. The other is for a large ring-shaped cake about 6 inches in diameter referred to as a *bucellato*, or bracelet. I have read about them in Sicilian cookbooks but have never seen one, either in an Italian pastry shop in the United States or anywhere in Sicily. The following recipe makes a lot of cookies, but they keep indefinitely—so they are a good choice for holiday giving.

Makes about 60 cookies

PASTA FROLLA

4 cups all-purpose flour

⅔ cup sugar

1 teaspoon baking powder

1 teaspoon salt

16 tablespoons (2 sticks) cold unsalted butter, cut into 16 pieces

4 large eggs

FIG FILLING

12 ounces (about 2 cups) dried Calimyrna figs

½ cup raisins

⅓ cup candied orange peel, diced

⅓ cup whole almonds, chopped and lightly toasted

3 ounces semisweet chocolate, cut into ¼-inch pieces

⅓ cup apricot preserves

3 tablespoons dark rum

1 teaspoon instant espresso coffee granules

½ teaspoon ground cinnamon

¼ teaspoon ground cloves

EGG WASH

1 large egg, well beaten with 1 pinch salt

Multicolored nonpareils for finishing before baking

2 or 3 cookie sheets or jelly roll pans covered with parchment or foil

1 To make the dough, in the work bowl of a food processor fitted with the steel blade, combine the flour, sugar, baking powder, and salt. Pulse two or three times to mix. Add the butter and pulse repeatedly until it is finely incorporated and the mixture is cool and powdery. Add the eggs, all at once, and continue to pulse until the dough forms a ball. Scrape the dough onto a floured surface, then place it on a piece of plastic wrap. Press the dough into a square about an inch thick and wrap it. Chill the dough while preparing the filling. **2** For the filling, in a large bowl, stem and dice the figs. If they are hard, place them in a saucepan, cover them with water, and bring them to a boil over medium heat. Drain the figs in a strainer and allow them to cool before proceeding. **3** In a bowl, combine the diced figs with the rest of the filling ingredients and stir them together. In the work bowl of a food processor fitted with the steel blade, pulse to grind the filling mixture finely. Scrape the filling back into the bowl used to mix it. **4** When you are ready to bake the *cucidati*, set the racks in the upper and lower thirds of the oven and preheat to 350 degrees. **5** Take the dough out of the refrigerator, unwrap it, and place it on a floured surface. Knead the dough lightly to make it malleable again and roll it up into a cylinder. Cut the cylinder into twelve equal pieces. One at a time, on a floured surface, flatten each and make it into a rectangle 3 inches wide and 12 inches long. Paint the wash on the dough and evenly distribute ⅓ cup filling down its length. Bring the edges of dough up around the filling to enclose it, then press the edges of the dough together firmly to seal in the filling. Use your palms to roll over the filled cylinder of dough until it extends to 15 inches, then cut it

into 3-inch lengths. Set the filled cylinders aside while filling, rolling, and cutting the other pieces of dough. **6** To finish shaping the *cucidati*, use the point of a sharp paring knife to slash six or eight diagonal cuts in the top of each filled cylinder of dough. Place each slashed cookie on one of the prepared pans, and curve it into a horseshoe shape. Leave about an inch all around between the cookies. **7** After all the *cucidati* are on pans, paint the outsides lightly with the egg wash and sprinkle them sparingly with the nonpareils. **8** Bake the cookies for about 20 minutes, or until they are a light golden color. Slide the papers from the pans to racks. **9** Store the cooled cookies between sheets of parchment or wax paper in a tin or plastic container with a tight-fitting cover.

(continued)

Filled and Sandwich Cookies

FIG X'S: These are an amusing alternative way to shape the *cucidati*. After you cut the filled cylinders of dough into 3-inch lengths, make a 1-inch-long cut in the middle of each end and pull the cut sides apart to make the cookie an X, as in the illustration. Do not slash the tops of these cookies. Arrange them on the pans and brush them with egg wash, but do not sprinkle them with the nonpareils. If you wish, dust them with a little confectioners' sugar right before serving.

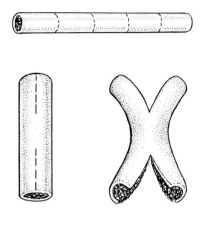

INFASCIADEDDE
Sicilian Twisted Cookies

THESE COOKIES ARE PART OF MY childhood memories. My great aunt Elvira Pescatore Basile, who married my maternal grandmother's brother Michele, always made them at the holidays. Although Zi' Elvira was not Sicilian herself, she had learned to make them from an unidentified Sicilian woman. Back then, in the days before food processors, the almonds were crushed to a paste with a rolling pin!

Makes about 96 narrow 4-inch cookies

1 batch Pasta Frolla, page 258

ALMOND FILLING

12 ounces (about 3 cups) whole unblanched almonds

1 cup honey

½ teaspoon ground cinnamon

FINISHING

Honey

About 2 ounces (½ cup) toasted sliced almonds

3 or 4 cookie sheets or jelly roll pans covered with parchment or foil

1 Wrap the Pasta Frolla in plastic and chill the dough in the refrigerator while you prepare the filling. **2** For the filling, place the almonds in a food processor fitted with the steel blade and pulse until finely ground. Add the honey and the cinnamon and pulse to make a smooth paste. Scrape the filling into a shallow bowl. **3** When you are ready to bake the cookies, set the racks in the upper and lower thirds of the oven and pre-heat to 350 degrees. **4** Take the dough out of the refrigerator, unwrap it, and place it on a floured surface. Knead the dough lightly to make it malleable again and roll it up into a cylinder. Cut the cylinder into four equal pieces. **5** Place one piece of the dough on a floured surface and roll it out to a 12-inch square. Cut the dough into eight strips, each 1½ × 12 inches. Spread about 1½ table-spoons of the filling in a narrow line down the middle of each strip of dough, then fold the strip

of dough so the two long ends meet, but do not press them together. Cut the folded strip into 4-inch lengths and twist each once or twice. Arrange the cookies on the prepared pans about an inch apart in all directions. Repeat with the other pieces of dough and the remaining filling. **6** Bake the cookies for about 15 minutes, or until they are golden. Slide the papers onto racks to cool the cookies. **7** Right before serving, driz-zle the cookies with the honey and sprinkle with the toasted sliced almonds. (Put the honey and the almonds only on the cookies that will be eaten then—the cookies are awkward to store once the honey is on them.) The honey and almonds make the cookies a little sloppy to eat, but they add an extra dimension to the flavor—the cookies would be bland without them. **8** Store the cooled cook-ies between sheets of parchment or wax paper in a tin or plastic container with a tight-fitting cover.

Filled and Sandwich Cookies

PORTLAND FIG COOKIES

In April 1998 I was in Portland, Oregon, along with about a thousand other cookbook authors, chefs, and cooking teachers at a convention of the International Association of Culinary Professionals. I went to visit Greg Mistell's Pearl Bakery with my friend Jeffrey Steingarten, the bread maven, and as soon as we got there several friends rushed over and exclaimed: "Try the fig cookies—they're out of this world."

Jeffrey and I were fortunate enough to get a tour of the production area from the owner and while we were in the back, I met the creator of the cookies, Lee Posey, then the pastry chef in charge of all the sweets made in the bakery. I brazenly asked for her recipe without even having tasted one of the cookies and to my surprise she gave it to me. Here it is—one of the best cookies I have ever tasted.

By the way, this recipe differs from the *Cucidati* on page 258 in that the dough here is much thinner and the filling more plentiful.

Makes about 30 cookies

FLAKY BROWN SUGAR DOUGH

2¼ cups all-purpose flour

⅔ cup firmly packed light brown sugar

Pinch salt

1 teaspoon baking powder

10 tablespoons (1¼ sticks) cold unsalted butter, cut into 12 pieces

1 large egg

1 teaspoon vanilla extract

FIG FILLING

12 ounces (about 2 cups) Calimyrna figs, stemmed and diced

⅔ cup currants

5 ounces (about 1¼ cups) walnut pieces, toasted

Finely grated zest of 1 large orange

¼ cup firmly packed light brown sugar

3 tablespoons unsweetened cocoa powder, sifted after measuring

1 teaspoon freshly grated nutmeg

1 teaspoon ground coriander

½ teaspoon ground cloves

⅔ cup honey

EGG WASH

1 large egg, well beaten with 1 pinch salt

2 cookie sheets or jelly roll pans covered with parchment or foil

1 To make the dough, in the work bowl of a food processor fitted with the steel blade, combine the flour, brown sugar, salt, and baking powder. Pulse half a dozen times to mix. Add the butter and pulse about a dozen times, or until the butter is in ¼-inch pieces. In a small bowl, whisk the egg and vanilla together and add to the processor. Continue to pulse just until the dough holds together. Scrape the dough onto a piece of plastic wrap, form it into a square, and wrap well. Chill the dough while preparing the filling.

2 For the filling, place the figs in a saucepan and cover them with water. Bring to a boil over medium heat. Drain and cool the figs. Combine them with the currants, walnuts, and orange zest and pulse in the food processor until finely minced. Add the remaining filling ingredients and pulse to combine. Scrape the filling into a bowl. 3 Unwrap the dough on a floured work surface. Flour the dough and roll it to a 12 × 16 ¼-inch rectangle. Use a ruler to measure, then cut the dough into five strips, each a little less than 3¼ inches wide by 12 inches long. Use a pastry bag with no tube in it to pipe the filling down the middle of each rectangle of dough. Pull the dough up around the filling to enclose it, then pinch it together firmly. Roll the filled cylinders of dough around so that the seam is on the bottom and roll over them with the palms of both hands to make sure the dough sticks to the filling. Arrange them on the same pans you will later use to bake them and refrigerate the filled cylinders for an hour. 4 When you are ready to bake the cookies, set the racks in the upper and lower thirds of the oven and preheat to 400 degrees.

5 Remove the filled dough cylinders to a cutting board and use a sharp paring knife to cut them into 2-inch lengths. Arrange them on the prepared pans leaving about an inch in all directions, and brush them with the egg wash. 6 Bake the cookies for about 12 to 15 minutes, or until they are a deep golden brown. Slide the papers from the pans onto racks. 7 Store the cooled cookies between sheets of parchment or wax paper in a tin or plastic container with a tight-fitting cover.

Filled and Sandwich Cookies

MAMOUL
Syrian and Lebanese Date-Filled Cookies

THIS IS A CLASSIC MIDDLE EASTERN pastry of a light dough wrapped around a rich filling. I first learned about *mamoul* from my friend Dahlia Bilger, who kept pressing me to make some with her when she was a student at the New York Restaurant School in the early eighties. Alas, in the intervening years I lost the recipe Dahlia and I concocted. This one is loosely based on a recipe in Claudia Roden's *A Book of Middle Eastern Food* (Knopf, 1972).

When you buy *mamoul* in Middle Eastern markets, they have usually been decorated with a kind of pastry pincer to make an attractive pattern of raised ridges on the surface of the dough. Presumably this is in order to hold the confectioners' sugar with which they are sprinkled. I find that pricking the tops with a fork in a regular pattern accomplishes the same thing.

Makes about 30 cookies

DATE FILLING

½ **pound pitted dates, finely chopped**

3 tablespoons water

DOUGH

1¾ **cups all-purpose flour**

12 tablespoons (1½ sticks) cold unsalted butter, cut into 20 pieces

2 teaspoons rose or orange flower water

2 tablespoons milk

Confectioners' sugar for finishing

2 cookie sheets or jelly roll pans covered with parchment or foil

1 For the filling, put the dates and water in a medium saucepan over low heat. Bring to a simmer, stirring occasionally, and reduce, stirring often, until the consistency is thick and jam-like. Spread the filling out on a plate or shallow bowl to cool. **2** When you are ready to make the cookies, set the racks in the upper and lower thirds of the oven and preheat to 350 degrees. **3** To make the dough, in the work bowl of a food processor fitted with the steel blade, place the flour. Add the butter and pulse about a dozen times, or until it is finely mixed in. Take the cover off the machine and sprinkle the flour and butter mixture with the rose water and milk. Replace the cover and pulse until the dough just forms a ball. Scrape the dough onto a floured work surface, then press it together and roll it into a cylinder 15 inches long. Slice the dough every ½ inch to make 30 pieces of dough. **4** To form a *mamoul*, roll a piece of dough into a sphere, then insert an index finger into the sphere to make a hole. Use your thumbs to enlarge the hole so that the dough becomes a little cup. Fill with a spoonful of the filling, then close the dough around the filling. Place each cookie seam side down on one of the pans. Leave about 1½ inches around in all directions. **5** Repeat with the remaining dough and filling. After all the *mamoul* have been formed, press each gently to flatten it, and use a fork to pierce the surface in a decorative design. **6** Bake the *mamoul* for about 20 to 25 minutes, making sure they remain very white. They should take on no color at all. Cool on the pans on racks. Dust heavily with confectioners' sugar just before serving. **7** Store the cooled cookies between sheets of parchment or wax paper in a tin or plastic container with a tight-fitting cover.

APPENZELLER BIBERLI
Filled "Beavers" from Appenzell

THESE SPICY COOKIES ARE FILLED
with a sweet almond paste filling. Though
they are available in a variety of different
shapes in Switzerland—some are filled disks,
or large rectangles—these are probably their
most common form, a filled cylinder cut into
fat trapezoid shapes. *Biberli* means "little
beavers" and Appenzell is the little canton
in northeastern Switzerland that is the butt
of hundreds of Swiss German jokes.

Makes about 50 cookies

BIBERLI DOUGH

2½ cups all-purpose flour

1 teaspoon baking powder

½ teaspoon baking soda

1 teaspoon ground cinnamon

1 teaspoon ground coriander

½ teaspoon ground cloves

¼ teaspoon freshly grated nutmeg

¼ teaspoon ground ginger

½ cup honey

¼ cup molasses

⅓ cup sugar

2 tablespoons water

Finely grated zest of 1 small lemon

FILLING

4 ounces (about 1 cup) whole blanched almonds

½ cup sugar, plus more if needed for rolling

Finely grated zest of 1 small lemon

2 tablespoons kirsch

2 cookie sheets or jelly roll pans covered
with parchment or foil

1 Set the racks in the upper and lower thirds of
the oven and preheat to 325 degrees. **2** In a
bowl, combine the flour, baking powder, baking
soda, and spices; stir well to mix. **3** In a large
saucepan, combine the honey, molasses, and
sugar with a wooden spoon. Place over low heat
and bring to a simmer, stirring occasionally.
Remove from the heat and stir in the water and
lemon zest. Stir in the flour mixture with a large
rubber spatula. Scrape the dough onto a lightly
floured work surface and cover it loosely with
plastic wrap. Let the dough cool while you prepare the filling. **4** For the filling, in the work
bowl of a food processor fitted with the steel
blade, combine the almonds and sugar. Pulse
repeatedly until the almonds are finely ground.
Add the lemon zest and kirsch and pulse until the
filling forms a ball. If it resists forming a ball add
a teaspoon of water and pulse again until it does.

5 Remove the filling from the food processor and roll it into a cylinder. Divide into three equal pieces. Roll out each piece into a cylinder 12 inches long. Use some sugar to help you roll if the filling is very sticky. Place the filling on a pan and cover with plastic wrap. **6** Divide the dough into three equal pieces and roll out each to a 12-inch cylinder. One at a time, on a floured surface, flatten a cylinder of dough to make it about 2½ inches wide. Paint the surface of the dough with water and place one of the cylinders of filling on it. Pull the dough up around the filling to enclose it completely. Turn the filled dough seam side down and roll it under the palms of your hands to make a cylinder 18 inches long. Repeat with the remaining dough and filling. **7** To cut the cookies, make alternating diagonal cuts that are an inch apart on one side and ½ inch apart on the other, as in the illustration. **8** Place the *biberli* on the prepared pans, leaving about an inch around each cookie in all directions. **9** Bake the *biberli* for about 20 to 25 minutes, until well risen and firm. Do not overbake or the filling might bubble out. **10** Slide the papers from the pans to racks. **11** Store the cooled cookies between sheets of parchment or wax paper in a tin or plastic container with a tight-fitting cover.

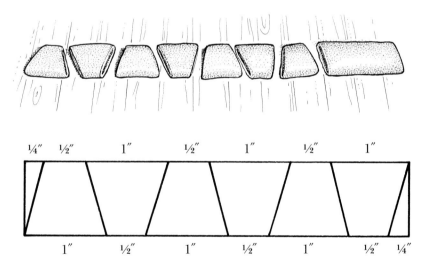

Sample cutting diagram

RAILROAD TRACKS

I DON'T KNOW IF THESE COOKIES—composed of a roll of dough flattened and filled with jam—are called this in the United States, but it is the standard European name for them. This is the special occasion for which you've been saving that jar of homemade or fine-quality jam or jelly. This delicate dough is a perfect foil for a subtly flavored filling. Thanks to Paul Kinberg for this recipe.

Makes about 40 cookies

2 cups all-purpose flour

½ teaspoon baking powder

Pinch salt

12 tablespoons (1½ sticks) unsalted butter, softened

⅔ cup granulated sugar

2 teaspoons vanilla extract

1 large egg

½ cup seedless raspberry jam or other jam or jelly of your choice

Confectioners' sugar for finishing, optional

2 cookie sheets or jelly roll pans covered with parchment or foil

1 In a bowl, combine the flour, baking powder, and salt; stir well to mix. **2** In the bowl of a standing electric mixer fitted with the paddle attachment, beat together on medium speed the butter and granulated sugar until well mixed, about 1 minute. Beat in the vanilla, then the egg, and continue beating until the mixture is smooth. **3** Remove the bowl from the mixer and stir in the flour mixture with a large rubber spatula. Scrape the dough onto a floured work surface. **4** Press the dough together and roll it into a cylinder. Divide the dough into six equal pieces and roll each to a narrow cylinder the length of your baking pan. **5** Transfer the dough to the pans (to move it easily you can coil it up, then uncoil it on the pan). Arrange three pieces of dough on each pan, equidistant from one another and from the sides of the pan. Use the side of your hand to press a ½-inch-wide trough down the middle of each piece of dough. **6** Set the racks in the upper and lower thirds of the oven and preheat to 350 degrees. **7** Beat the jam or jelly with a fork to liquefy it, then use a small spoon, a paper cone, or the snipped corner of a nonpleated plastic bag to fill the trough in each piece of dough with about 2 tablespoons of the jam. Only fill it about two-thirds full or the jam will overflow while the cookies are baking. **8** Bake the cookies for about 20 minutes, or until they are a light golden color. Transfer the pans to racks to cool. **9** Cut each of the cooled cookie logs into about six or eight diagonal slices. Right before serving, dust the cookies very lightly with confectioners' sugar, if you wish. **10** Store the finished cookies between sheets of parchment or wax paper in a tin or plastic container with a tight-fitting cover.

SANDWICH COOKIES

THE TRICK TO SATISFYING SANDWICH COOKIES IS TO MAKE THEM DELICATE.
Slathering melted chocolate between two already-rich-enough chocolate chip cookies is
not my idea of a successful sandwich cookie.

First of all, the cookies need to be light—thin, flaky, crisp, or lacy. Such bases can support any kind of filling. Generally, rich cookies are sandwiched easily and successfully with
reduced jam—who can resist a little round window of raspberry glaze peeking out between
two buttery cookies? Sometimes if the cookies are both rich and buttery they may be sandwiched with chocolate—a little excessive, but that's part of the thrill.

HINTS FOR SANDWICH COOKIES

1 Try to make all the cookies the same size—this is easy if you use a cutter. If you are
sandwiching drop cookies it's a little more difficult. In that case, scrupulously measure the
amount of batter you drop for each cookie. That way they'll have a better chance of being
uniform in size. **2** Cool cookies completely before attempting to sandwich them—especially if the filling is chocolate or butter cream. **3** Use a small amount of filling in each
cookie. Usually between ¼ and ½ teaspoon is enough. If you use more, it will squish out
when you bite into the cookie. **4** Finish sandwich cookies simply. If the instructions call for
sprinkling the cookie with confectioners' sugar, use a little—or else it will be all over your
clothes, not on the cookie. **5** Keep sandwich cookies in a cool place—or wait until the day
you intend to serve them to sandwich them. Thin fillings can't stand heat or moisture.

Yoyos, page 272

Yoyos

THE RECIPE FOR THIS AUSTRALIAN sandwich cookie was sent to me simultaneously by two different friends from Down Under— food stylists Janet Lillie and Maureen McKeon. The following is a combination/distillation of the two recipes.

Makes about 30 cookies

COOKIE DOUGH

1⅓ cups all-purpose flour

⅓ cup cornstarch

½ teaspoon baking powder

12 tablespoons (1½ sticks) unsalted butter, softened

⅔ cup confectioners' sugar

1 teaspoon vanilla extract

LEMON FILLING

6 tablespoons (¾ stick) unsalted butter, softened

1 cup confectioners' sugar

1 tablespoon lemon juice

2 cookie sheets or jelly roll pans covered with parchment or foil

1 Set the racks in the upper and lower thirds of the oven and preheat to 350 degrees. **2** Combine the flour, cornstarch, and baking powder in a bowl; stir well to mix. **3** In the bowl of a standing electric mixer fitted with the paddle attachment, beat together the butter and confectioners' sugar on medium speed until soft and light, about 3 or 4 minutes. Beat in the vanilla. Lower the speed and beat in the flour mixture. **4** Remove the bowl from the mixer and finish mixing the dough with a large rubber spatula. **5** Use a teaspoon measuring spoon or a small ice cream scoop to scoop up a piece of the dough. Roll each piece into a ball between the palms of your hands and place on the prepared pans, leaving about 2 inches around each cookie in all directions. Press each cookie with the back of a fork dipped in flour to flatten the cookies slightly, and make a crisscross pattern. **6** Bake the cookies for about 15 minutes, or until they are a uniform light golden color. Cool the cookies on the pans on racks. **7** While the cookies are cooling, prepare the filling. In the bowl of an electric mixer fitted with the paddle attachment, beat together the butter and confectioners' sugar on medium speed until very light, about 5 minutes. Beat in the lemon juice a little at a time, then continue beating until very light and smooth. **8** Turn half the cookies upside down so that the flat bottom side is uppermost. Pipe or spoon about ½ teaspoon of the filling on each. Cover with another cookie, bottom to bottom. **9** Store the finished cookies between sheets of parchment or wax paper in a tin or plastic container with a tight-fitting cover.

SPITZBUEBE
"Bad Boys"

WHY THIS FRAGILE COOKIE SHOULD bear this name is a mystery. It is one of the cookies that the Swiss always include in their Christmas assortments. But it is also popular, with good reason, all year long. Thanks again to Thea Cvijanovich for the dough recipe.

Makes about 18 cookies

12 tablespoons (1½ sticks) unsalted butter, softened

¾ cup confectioners' sugar

Pinch salt

1 teaspoon vanilla extract

2 cups all-purpose flour

¾ cup seedless raspberry jam for finishing

Confectioners' sugar for sprinkling

2 cookie sheets or jelly roll pans covered with parchment or foil

1 To make the dough, in the bowl of a standing electric mixer fitted with the paddle attachment, beat together the butter and the ¾ cup sugar on medium speed until soft and smooth, about 3 or 4 minutes. Beat in the salt and the vanilla. **2** Remove the bowl from the mixer and use a rubber spatula to incorporate the flour. Scrape the dough onto a piece of plastic wrap and form into a square about ½ inch thick. Wrap and chill the dough until firm—several hours to several days.

3 Cut the dough in half and refrigerate one part. Place the other on a floured surface and flour it lightly. Press and pound the dough gently with a rolling pin to soften it, then roll the dough out to about ³⁄₁₆ inch thick. Use a plain or fluted 2-inch round cutter to cut out the cookies. Place them on the prepared pans, leaving about an inch all around each. **4** Use a small round cutter or the small end of a #6 or #806 piping tube about ½ to ¾ inch in diameter to cut the center out of half the cookies, to make a "window" when they are sandwiched (traditional Swiss cookies have three tiny holes cut into the top cookie, made with a tiny pastry tube). Repeat with the remaining dough, then mass the scraps together and roll them once again to cut more cookies. Chill the cookies for an hour before baking, so that they will hold their shape well. **5** When you are ready to bake the cookies, set the racks in the upper and lower thirds of the oven and preheat to 350 degrees. Bake the cookies for about 15 minutes, or until they are a very pale golden color. Cool them on the pans on racks. **6** While the cookies are baking, prepare the jam for the filling. Bring the jam to a simmer in a small saucepan over low heat, stirring occasionally. Let the jam reduce until it thickens slightly, about 5 minutes. **7** After the cookies have cooled, dust the ones with the holes in them lightly with the confectioners' sugar. Invert the nonpierced cookies and spread each with about ½ teaspoon of the reduced jam. Top with the pierced cookies, sugar side up. Use a small paper cone or a tiny spoon to fill the hole(s) in the top cookies with more reduced jam. **8** Store the finished cookies between sheets of parchment or wax paper in a tin or plastic container with a tight-fitting cover.

SUVAROFFS

THIS IS A FANCY NAME THE SWISS HAVE given to a fairly simple cookie. It is composed of two diamond shapes sandwiched with a kirsch-flavored almond paste filling—definitely an adult cookie.

To cut these cookies into the traditional size and shape, you'll need a 2- to 2½-inch diamond-shaped cutter, either plain or fluted. If you can't find one, make a pattern from a piece of stiff cardboard; then you can use a knife to cut out the cookies, and they'll be all the same size. Of course, you can also use another 2- to 2½-inch shape for these.

Makes about 20 sandwiched cookies

COOKIE DOUGH

14 tablespoons (1¾ sticks) unsalted butter, softened

¼ cup granulated sugar

½ teaspoon lemon extract

Finely grated zest of 1 small lemon

2¼ cups all-purpose flour

FILLING

4 ounces almond paste

4 tablespoons (½ stick) unsalted butter, softened

½ cup confectioners' sugar

1 tablespoon kirsch

Green food coloring

2 cookie sheets or jelly roll pans covered with parchment or foil

1 To make the dough, in the bowl of an electric mixer fitted with the paddle attachment, beat together the butter, sugar, lemon extract, and lemon zest on medium speed until soft and light, about 5 minutes. **2** Remove the bowl from the mixer and use a rubber spatula to incorporate the flour. Scrape the dough onto a piece of plastic wrap and form it into a square about ½ inch thick. Wrap and chill the dough until firm—several hours to several days. **3** Cut the dough in half and refrigerate one piece. Place the other on a floured surface and flour it lightly. Press and pound the dough gently with a rolling pin to soften it, then roll the dough about 3/16 inch thick. Use a plain or fluted 2- to 2½-inch diamond-shaped cutter to cut the dough. Place the cookies on the prepared pans leaving about 1 inch around each in all directions. **4** When you are ready to bake the cookies, set the racks in the upper and lower thirds of the oven and preheat to 350 degrees. Bake the cookies for about 15 minutes, or until they are a very pale golden color. Cool them on the pans on racks. **5** While the cookies are baking, prepare the filling. In the bowl of a standing electric mixer fitted with the paddle attachment, beat together on medium speed the almond paste and butter until soft and very light, about 5 minutes. Lower the mixer speed and add the confectioners' sugar. Beat for another 2 or 3 minutes on medium speed. Beat in the kirsch, then stop the mixer and scrape down the bowl and beater. Beat in just enough food coloring to tint the filling a light, tender green. **6** After the cookies have cooled, invert half of them, so that the bottoms are facing up. Pipe or spoon about 1 teaspoon of the almond filling on each. Top with another cookie, bottom to bottom. Gently press them together. **7** Store the finished cookies between sheets of parchment or wax paper in a tin or plastic container with a tight-fitting cover.

Filled and Sandwich Cookies

Linzer Hearts

Though this recipe calls for ground hazelnuts, almonds or pecans will work just as well. And the raspberry jam that sandwiches the rich nut dough can be changed to apricot, which would be just as good.

Makes about 18 cookies

2⅔ cups all-purpose flour

½ teaspoon ground cinnamon

¼ teaspoon ground cloves

16 tablespoons (2 sticks) unsalted butter, softened

⅔ cup granulated sugar

4 ounces (about 1 cup) whole blanched almonds, finely ground in the food processor

1 cup seedless raspberry jam

Confectioners' sugar for sprinkling

2 or 3 cookie sheets or jelly roll pans covered with parchment or foil

1 In a bowl, combine the flour and spices; stir well to mix. **2** In the bowl of a standing electric mixer fitted with the paddle attachment, beat together on medium speed the butter and sugar until soft and light, about 5 minutes. Lower the mixer speed and beat in the almonds and the flour and spice mixture, one at a time. **3** Remove the bowl from the mixer and use a large rubber spatula to finish mixing the dough. Scrape the dough onto a piece of plastic wrap and shape it into a rectangle about ½ inch thick. Wrap and chill the dough until it is firm, about an hour, or up to several days. **4** When you are ready to bake the cookies, set the racks in the upper and lower thirds of the oven and preheat to 350 degrees. **5** Cut the dough into three parts and refrigerate two of them. Place one third on a floured surface and flour it lightly. Press and pound the dough gently with a rolling pin to soften it, then roll the dough about ¼ inch thick. Use a 2½- to 3-inch heart-shaped cutter (or any round one) to cut the dough. Place the cookies on the prepared pans, leaving about an inch around each in all directions. If you have a tiny heart-shaped cutter, use it to cut the center out of half the cookies, to make a "window" when they are sandwiched. Or use a small round cutter, or a pastry tube, or leave the cookies unpierced. Repeat with the remaining dough. Mass the scraps together and roll them once again to cut more cookies.

6 Bake the cookies for about 15 minutes, or until they are a very pale golden color. Cool them on the pans on racks. 7 While the cookies are baking, prepare the jam for the filling. Bring the jam to a simmer in a small saucepan over low heat, stirring occasionally. Let the jam reduce until it has thickened slightly, about 5 minutes. 8 After the cookies have cooled, dust the pierced cookies lightly with the confectioners' sugar. Invert the nonpierced cookies and spread each with about ½ teaspoon of the reduced jam. Top with the pierced cookies, sugar side up. Use a small paper cone, a tiny spoon, or the snipped corner of a nonpleated plastic bag to fill in the window of the cookies with more reduced jam. 9 Store the finished cookies between sheets of parchment or wax paper in a tin or plastic container with a tight-fitting cover.

LACY CHOCOLATE OATMEAL COOKIE SANDWICHES

THESE ARE SIMILAR TO THE ALMOND Lace Cookies on page 70, except that these are made with oatmeal instead of ground nuts. And sandwiching two of these crisp, candy-like cookies with chocolate makes them even more luscious.

Makes about 30 sandwich cookies

8 tablespoons (1 stick) unsalted butter, melted

1 cup rolled oats (regular oatmeal) finely chopped, but not ground to a powder, in the food processor

1 cup sugar

½ teaspoon salt

1 large egg

1 teaspoon vanilla extract

1 teaspoon orange juice, strained

6 ounces semisweet or bittersweet chocolate, melted and cooled, for sandwiching the cookies

3 or 4 cookie sheets or jelly roll pans covered with buttered foil

1 Set the racks in the upper and lower thirds of the oven and preheat to 350 degrees. **2** Pour the melted butter into a bowl; one at a time, stir in the remaining ingredients, except the chocolate, stirring smooth after each addition. **3** Use a ½-teaspoon measure to drop the batter on the prepared pans. Space the cookies about 3 inches apart in all directions, to allow room for them to spread. **4** Bake the cookies for about 8 to 10 minutes, or until they have spread and are brown around the edges and lighter toward the center. Slide the paper or foil onto racks to cool the cookies. **5** When the cookies are completely cool, peel them off the foil and arrange half of them bottom side up on a pan. Use a small offset spatula to spread about ½ teaspoon of chocolate on each inverted cookie. Top with another cookie, bottom to bottom. **6** Store the finished cookies between sheets of parchment or wax paper in a tin or plastic container with a tight-fitting cover.

Chocolate Chocolate Sandwich Cookies

This is a variation on a favorite cookie of mine—a dough that's made from just flour, chocolate, and butter (plus a pinch of spice) enhanced by a suave milk chocolate filling. It is particularly easy to make and has all the delicacy and sophistication of recipes that require ten times the trouble.

Makes about 24 sandwich cookies

COOKIE DOUGH

2⅓ cups all-purpose flour

¼ teaspoon salt

¼ teaspoon ground cloves

16 tablespoons (2 sticks) unsalted butter, softened

6 ounces semisweet chocolate, melted and cooled

FILLING

⅓ cup heavy cream

1 tablespoon butter

1 tablespoon light corn syrup

6 ounces milk chocolate, cut into ¼-inch pieces

2 cookie sheets or jelly roll pans covered with parchment or foil

1 To make the dough, combine the flour, salt, and cloves in a bowl; stir well to mix. **2** In another bowl, beat the butter with a rubber spatula until it is soft and creamy. Beat in the cooled chocolate, stirring until the mixture is smooth. Gently fold in the flour mixture, creating a smooth dough. Scrape the dough onto a piece of plastic wrap and shape it into a rectangle about ½ inch thick. Wrap and chill the dough until it is firm, about an hour. **3** For the filling, combine the cream, butter, and corn syrup in a small saucepan. Bring to a simmer over medium heat. Remove from heat and add the chocolate all at once. Shake the pan to make sure all the chocolate is submerged, then let the chocolate melt for about 2 or 3 minutes. Whisk smooth, then scrape into a bowl and cool to room temperature. **4** When you are ready to bake the cookies, set the racks in the upper and lower thirds of the oven and preheat to 350 degrees. Divide the dough into thirds and return two to the refrigerator. Place one third on a floured work surface. If the dough is hard, pound it gently with the rolling pin to soften it slightly, then flour the surface of the dough and roll it out about ¾₁₆ inch thick. Cut out the cookies with a fluted 2- to 3-inch cutter. Place them on the prepared pans, leaving about an inch around each in all directions. Repeat with the remaining dough. Save all the scraps, then reroll them and cut more cookies. **5** Bake the cookies for about 15 minutes, or until they are firm and dull in appearance. Cool the cookies on the pans on racks. **6** To sandwich the cooled cookies, turn half the cookies over, flat bottom side up. Spoon or pipe about ½ teaspoon of the chocolate filling on each. Top with other cookies, right side up so they are bottom to bottom. **7** Store the finished cookies between sheets of parchment or wax paper in a tin or plastic container with a tight-fitting cover.

WAFERS

Pizzelle

Krumkake
(Norwegian Wafer Cones)

Wafers, as Done at Newark

Gaufres des Tuileries
(Tuileries Wafers)

Oublies de Naples
(Naples Wafers)

WAFERS ARE AMONG THE OLDEST TYPES OF COOKIES STILL MADE. IN FACT, THE predecessors of *pâtissiers* or pastry cooks in France were known as *oublayeurs*, the makers of a type of ancient wafer. And delicate wafers of this type survive to this day in France and especially in Scandinavia.

These pleasantly old-fashioned cookies are made in an iron, like waffles. Some, like pizzelle, are probably familiar. Though these used to be made in stove-top irons, electric pizzelle makers are fairly common nowadays (some of them actually have reversible plates that allow then to double as standard breakfast-waffle irons).

Other types of wafers require a special iron that makes cookies thinner than the pizzelle iron does. Fortunately, there is a thriving Scandinavian tradition of wafer making in the Midwest, so it's easy to get both electric and stove-top versions of a *Krumkake* iron (see Sources). *Krumkake* are typical Norwegian and Swedish wafer cookies that are usually curved into a cone shape as soon as they come off the iron. You may also use a *Krumkake* iron to make versions of the French *gaufres* (recipes are in this chapter).

And finally, if you want to try some wafers first, before you decide if you want to invest in an iron, you may spread the batter very thin on a nonstick cookie sheet or jelly roll pan and bake it in a moderately hot oven (you'll have the advantage of being able to make several at the same time). This works well for all the recipes except the pizzelle, but doesn't make wafers as thin as an iron does.

HINTS FOR WAFERS

1 Make sure the iron is perfectly clean before you start heating it. Bits of batter stuck to the iron will make subsequent wafers stick. **2** Don't overheat the iron—wafers will stick if the iron is too hot. **3** Use a little vegetable oil, rather than butter, to grease the iron—it will be easier to apply and will not smoke as much as butter when it is hot. **4** If you are using a stove-top iron, make sure that it reheats slightly between wafers. **5** If you wish to roll the wafers into cones or cylinders, make sure they don't get too dark. The darker the wafers, the more quickly they become brittle. **6** Storage can be a problem. Most wafers, except pizzelle, are so fragile that it isn't practical to store them for a long time. Lay them on a baking pan in one layer and cover them loosely with aluminum foil if you make them a day or two in advance.

Wafers

PIZZELLE

THESE CRISP COOKIES ARE THICKER
than many other types of wafers. They are
made in a special iron (see Sources) and are
easy to shape into cones or cylinders after they
are baked. My favorite way to use these is to
remove the cookie from the iron, place it on a
cutting board, and quickly cut it into quarters.
These smaller pizzelle are more manageable
and easier to eat.

By the way, the correct pronunciation is
"peet-sellay."

Makes about 24 pizzelle

1¾ cups all-purpose flour

Pinch salt

2 teaspoons baking powder

2 large eggs

1 large egg yolk

¾ cup sugar

2 tablespoons anisette

8 tablespoons (1 stick) unsalted butter, melted

Vegetable oil for greasing the iron

An electric pizzelle iron

1 In a bowl, combine the flour, salt, and baking
powder; stir well to mix. **2** In another bowl,
whisk the eggs and yolk, just enough to mix them
together. Whisk in the sugar in a stream, then the
anisette and melted butter. Use a rubber spatula
to fold in the flour mixture. **3** Set the batter
aside while you heat the pizzelle iron. After the
iron has been heating for a few minutes, open the
cover and grease the top and bottom of the
imprints with an oiled paper towel. Close the iron
and finish heating. **4** Drop a rounded teaspoon
of the batter in the center of each imprint, close
the cover, and bake the pizzelle. They are usually
ready when the steam stops coming out from
between the plates of the iron. (You can peek
without ruining them—if they are too pale, close
the iron and bake longer.) **5** Use the point of a
paring knife to lift one of the pizzelle out of the
iron, then with a wide spatula transfer it to a rack
to cool. You may also cut it into quarters or roll it
into a cone or cylinder shape over a form. Repeat
with the other pizzelle in the iron. There is no
need to grease the iron again, unless the pizzelle
start to stick. Use the remaining batter to make
more pizzelle. **6** Store the cooled wafers
between sheets of parchment or wax paper in a
tin or plastic container with a tight-fitting cover.

VARIATIONS

VANILLA PIZZELLE: Omit the egg yolk and anisette. Substitute another whole egg (for a total of three) and 1 teaspoon vanilla.

ALMOND (OR HAZELNUT) PIZZELLE: Add ½ cup finely ground blanched almonds or unblanched hazelnuts to Vanilla Pizzelle.

CHOCOLATE PIZZELLE: In the Vanilla, Almond, or Hazelnut Pizzelle, reduce the flour to 1⅓ cups and add ¼ cup unsweetened cocoa powder (sifted after measuring).

KRUMKAKE
Norwegian Wafer Cones

ALTHOUGH THESE FRAGILE COOKIES ARE traditionally rolled into a cone shape, they may also be left flat. They are often served with sweetened whipped cream or ice cream.

To make these you need a *krumkake* iron (see Sources)—or other type of wafer iron. Unfortunately, the wafers made by pizzelle irons are too thick.

This recipe is adapted from one in *The Norwegian Kitchen*, edited by Kjell E. Innli (KOM Forlag, Kristiansund, Norway, 1993).

Makes about 24 wafers, depending on the size of the iron used

⅔ cup all-purpose flour

½ cup cornstarch

2 large eggs

⅔ cup sugar

½ teaspoon almond extract

8 tablespoons (1 stick) unsalted butter, melted

¼ cup milk

Vegetable oil for greasing the iron

A *krumkake* iron or other wafer iron

1 In a small bowl, combine the flour and cornstarch; stir well to mix. 2 In another bowl, whisk the eggs; whisk in the sugar, almond extract, and the melted butter. Finally fold in half the flour and starch mixture. Fold in the milk, then the remaining flour mixture. Cover the bowl and refrigerate the batter for 30 minutes. 3 When the batter has chilled, remove it from

the refrigerator and use a rubber spatula to mix it again before baking the wafers. Begin heating the iron, whether it is an electric or stove-top model. After the iron has been heating for a few minutes, use a paper towel dipped into a small amount of vegetable oil to grease both plates of the iron. Close the iron and finish heating.

4 To bake the wafers, open the iron and place a rounded teaspoon or so of the batter (the amount you use will depend entirely on the size of the iron) on the bottom plate. Close the iron and bake the wafer until it is a light golden color. It is usually ready when the steam stops coming out from between the plates of the iron. (You can peek without ruining it—if it is too pale, close the iron and bake longer.) **5** Open the iron to check the color of the wafer—if it is too light, close the iron and continue baking. Or, place the wafer on a parchment- or foil-lined cookie sheet in a 325 degree oven to finish baking. Use a wide spatula to lift the wafer from the iron. Leave the wafer flat or immediately roll it around the handle of a wooden spoon to make a cylinder or wrap it around a cone-shaped object to make a cone (most *krumkake* irons come with a wooden cone form). Cool the wafers on a rack. Use the remaining batter to make more *krumkake*. There is no need to grease the iron again, unless the *krumkake* start to stick.

6 Store flat wafers between sheets of parchment or wax paper in a tin or plastic container with a tight-fitting cover. Store cylindrical or cone-shaped wafers in a single layer. See "Hints for Wafers," page 283.

Wafers, as Done at Newark

THE ECCENTRIC TITLE OF THIS RECIPE is taken verbatim from *A New System of Domestic Cookery* by Maria Eliza Rundell, published in New York in 1817. The book was a gift from two dear friends from Southfield, Michigan, Shirley Nachman and Ann Malzberg, and of course the recipe fascinated mc because Newark is my hometown. The variation following the recipe is in honor of their hometown.

Makes about twenty 5-inch wafers

1½ cups all-purpose flour

⅓ cup sugar

½ teaspoon ground mace or freshly grated nutmeg

¾ cup heavy whipping cream

½ cup milk

Vegetable oil for greasing the iron

Confectioners' sugar for sprinkling

A *krumkake* iron (see page 285), or other wafer iron

1 In a large bowl, combine the flour, sugar, and mace; stir well to mix. **2** Make a well in the center of the dry ingredients and pour in the cream and milk. With a small whisk, gradually draw the dry ingredients into the liquid, slowly whisking the batter smooth. Cover the bowl and set it aside while heating the iron. **3** Begin heating the iron, whether it is an electric or stove-top model. After the iron has been heating for a few minutes, use a paper towel dipped into a small amount of vegetable oil to grease both plates of the iron. Close the iron and finish heating. **4** To bake the wafers, open the iron and place a teaspoon or so of the batter (the amount you use will depend entirely on the size of the iron) on the bottom plate. Close the iron and bake the wafer until it is a light golden color. It is usually ready when the steam stops coming out from between the plates of the iron. (You can peek without ruining it—if it is too pale, close the iron and bake longer.) **5** Open the iron to check the color of the wafer—if it is too light, close the iron and continue baking. Or place the wafer on a parchment- or foil-lined cookie sheet in a 325 degree oven to finish baking. Use a wide spatula to lift the wafer from the iron. Leave the wafer flat or immediately roll it around the han-

dle of a wooden spoon to make a cylinder. Use the remaining batter to make more wafers. There is no need to grease the iron again, unless the wafers start to stick. Cool the wafers on a rack. **6** Pack the cooled wafers between sheets of parchment or wax paper in a tin or plastic container with a tight-fitting cover. If the wafers are rolled, lay them on a baking pan in one layer and cover them loosely with aluminum foil if you make them a day or two in advance. Lightly dust with confectioners' sugar before serving.

VARIATION

SOUTHFIELD WAFERS: Replace the mace in the above recipe with cinnamon.

GAUFRES DES TUILERIES
Tuileries Wafers

This wafer is named after the for-mer French royal palace in Paris. It was on the site of what is now the Tuileries Garden, adja-cent to the Louvre, and also the former site of a roofing tile factory (see Tuiles, page 62), hence the name. Perhaps they were invented or prepared in the kitchens of that palace—or some enterprising pastry chef wanted to dig-nify his recipe with a noble name—no explana-tion was given with the recipe. It was adapted from the *Traité de Pâtisserie Moderne* ("*Treatise on Modern Pastry Making*") by Émile Darenne and Émile Duval (Flammarion, reissued 1974, origi-nally published in the early 1900s).

Makes about 24 wafers

1 cup confectioners' sugar

2 cups all-purpose flour

2 large eggs

2 tablespoons (¼ stick) unsalted butter, melted

1 cup milk

1 teaspoon orange flower water or
½ teaspoon orange extract

Vegetable oil for greasing the iron

A *krumkake* iron (see page 285) or other wafer iron

1 Sift the confectioners' sugar into a bowl and stir in the flour. Make a well in the center of the dry ingredients and add the eggs, melted butter, and half the milk. Whisk to a smooth batter. Whisk in the remaining milk, then the flavoring. **2** Begin heating the iron, whether it is an elec-tric or stove-top model. After the iron has been heating for a few minutes, use a paper towel dipped into a small amount of vegetable oil to grease both plates of the iron. Close the iron and finish heating. **3** To bake the wafers, open the iron and place a teaspoon or so of the batter (the amount you use will depend entirely on the size of the iron) in the middle of the bottom plate. Close the iron and bake the wafer until it is a light golden color. It is usually ready when the steam stops coming out from between the plates of the iron. (You can peek without ruining it—if it is too pale, close the iron and bake longer. Or place the wafer on a parchment- or foil-lined cookie sheet in a 325 degree oven to finish baking. **4** Use a wide spatula to lift the wafer from the iron. Leave the wafer flat and cool on a rack. Use the remain-ing batter to make more wafers. There is no need to grease the iron again, unless the wafers start to stick. **5** Store the cooled wafers between sheets of parchment or wax paper in a tin or plastic con-tainer with a tight-fitting cover.

OUBLIES DE NAPLES (NAPLES WAFERS):
This another recipe from Darenne and Duval, probably of ancient origin from the name *oublie,* much used in the Middle Ages. The literal meaning of *oublie* is "forget" or "forgotten" and may derive from the fact that these wafers were sold outside churches to penitents who hoped their sins would be forgiven and forgotten. The use of confectioners' sugar, however, dates it to no earlier than the beginning of the nineteenth century. It is an interesting and extremely light variation on the standard wafer recipe. Use the following ingredients, but mix the batter and bake as in the above recipe.

Makes about 30 wafers

2 cups confectioners' sugar

2 cups all-purpose flour

½ teaspoon salt

1 cup water

3 tablespoons melted butter

CRACKERS AND SAVORY COOKIES

Tillypronie Cream Biscuits

Herb Biscotti

Alumettes au Fromage
(Cheese Matchsticks)

Peppery Cheddar Coins

Gruyère and Almond Rosettes

Parmesan and
Paprika Palmiers

Salt and Pepper Sticks

Rye Caraway Crisps

Rosemary Bread Sticks

Viennese Caraway Pretzels

WHEN I FIRST STARTED READING COOKBOOKS THERE WAS AN IMPORTANT CHAPTER in every book on fancy hors d'oeuvres and all sorts of little canapés (tiny open-faced sandwiches). Nowadays, these fussy little morsels are limited to parties in elegant establishments and those elaborately catered.

When I entertain at home, it's usually a tea party in the afternoon so I can get away with serving mostly sweets, but I often include a savory pastry or two. On the rare occasions that I give dinner parties, I like to serve a couple of things to nibble with drinks before dinner. The recipes in this chapter are some of the things I make then. One really good cheese cookie or salty breadstick, a bowl of olives, and perhaps another bowl of thinly sliced fennel or celery stalks and I consider the hors d'oeuvre problem completely solved.

HINTS FOR CRACKERS AND SAVORY COOKIES

1 When the recipe says to roll the dough very thin, please do exactly that. Most crackers will taste quite dry and woolly if they are too thick. **2** Measure seasonings—especially if a hot or strong one—carefully. Many a recipe has been ruined by an overdose of cayenne pepper or dry mustard. Try the recipe first as written. Then if you think it could use more seasoning, add it. **3** As with all cookies, uniformity is important so they will bake evenly. Make sure you cut pieces of dough accurately so crackers will all be the same size. **4** Resting and chilling times are important with the doughs that need to be rolled very thin—don't rush the process. **5** Crackers and most savory cookies keep well—bake a lot when you know you'll be using them.

TILLYPRONIE CREAM BISCUITS

THESE PLAIN CRACKERS ARE EXCELLENT with cheese or any type of spread and are better and more delicate than any crackers you can buy. The recipe is adapted from *The Cookery Book of Lady Clark of Tillypronie* (Southover Press, 1994), a reprint of the manuscript cookbook kept by the chatelaine of Tillypronie Castle in Scotland, first printed at the beginning of the twentieth century.

Makes about thirty-six 2-inch-square crackers

1 cup all-purpose flour

½ teaspoon salt

⅓ cup heavy whipping cream

2 cookie sheets or jelly roll pans covered with parchment or foil

1 In a bowl, combine the flour and salt and stir well to mix. Stir in the cream with a rubber spatula and continue to stir until a dry dough forms. **2** Remove the dough from the bowl to a lightly floured work surface and knead for about 5 minutes, or until the dough is smooth and satiny. If the dough remains very dry, wet your hands occasionally to introduce a little more moisture while kneading, but the cream should be enough. **3** When the dough is smooth, wrap it tightly in plastic wrap and leave it to rest at room temperature for an hour. **4** When you are ready to bake the crackers, set the racks in the upper and lower thirds of the oven and preheat to 325 degrees. **5** Place the dough on a lightly floured work surface and lightly flour it. Roll the dough as thin as you can to make a 12-inch square. **6** Run a long knife or spatula under the dough to detach it from the surface if it is stuck, then trim the edges even, using a pizza wheel. Cut the dough into six 2-inch strips, then cut across the strips at 2-inch intervals to make 2-inch squares. **7** Arrange the crackers on the prepared pans and bake them for about 20 to 25 minutes, or until they are very dry, blistered, and golden. Cool on the pans on racks. **8** Store the cooled crackers between sheets of parchment or wax paper in a tin or plastic container with a tight-fitting cover.

HERB BISCOTTI

THESE UNUSUAL HORS D'OEUVRE COOKIES are the creation of Robert Bleifer, one of the backstage chefs at the Food Network. Try them with the blend of herbs here (for which 2 tablespoons *herbes de provence* can be substituted) or experiment with other combinations.

Makes about 80 thin cookies

2½ cups all-purpose flour

1 teaspoon salt

2 teaspoons baking powder

2 teaspoons dried thyme leaves

2 teaspoons dried oregano

2 teaspoons dried rosemary, finely chopped

4 large eggs

2 tablespoons mildly flavored honey

2 cookie sheets or jelly roll pans covered with parchment or foil (one for baking the logs, then a second later for baking the sliced biscotti)

1 Set a rack in the middle level of the oven and preheat to 350 degrees. **2** In a mixing bowl, combine all the ingredients except the eggs and honey; stir well to mix. **3** Make a well in the center of the dry ingredients and add the eggs and honey. Using a rubber spatula, gradually draw the dry ingredients into the eggs and honey to make a soft dough. Scrape the dough onto a generously floured work surface and shape into a fat cylinder. **4** Cut the dough in half, then roll each half into a cylinder about 12 inches long. Place the cylinders of dough on the prepared pan equidistant from each other and the edges of the pan and flatten them slightly with the palm of one hand. **5** Bake the logs of dough about 30 minutes, or until they are golden and firm. **6** Cool the logs on the pan on a rack. **7** Lower the oven temperature to 325 degrees and detach the logs of dough from the paper on which they baked. Place each of the cooled logs on a cutting board and with a sharp serrated knife slice every ¼ inch. Replace the cut biscotti on the prepared pans, cut side down, and bake them for about 20 minutes longer, or until they are dry and golden. Cool the biscotti on the pans on racks. **8** Store the cooled biscotti between sheets of parchment or wax paper in a tin or plastic container with a tight-fitting cover.

ALUMETTES AU FROMAGE
Cheese Matchsticks

THIS IS A TRADITIONAL AND TASTY French recipe adapted from that great source-book of French pastry, the *Traité de Pâtisserie Moderne ("Treatise on Modern Pastry Making")*, by Darenne and Duval.

Makes 48 cookies

2¼ cups all-purpose flour

1 teaspoon salt

10 tablespoons (1¼ sticks) unsalted butter, cut into 12 pieces

⅓ cup finely grated Parmigiano Reggiano (about 1½ ounces)

⅓ cup finely grated Swiss Gruyère (about 1½ ounces)

⅓ cup milk

2 cookie sheets or jelly roll pans covered with parchment or foil

1 In the work bowl of a food processor fitted with the steel blade, pulse the flour and salt together to mix. 2 Add the butter and pulse three or four times until it is reduced to pea-sized pieces. Add the cheeses and pulse twice more. 3 Add the milk and pulse repeatedly until the mixture forms a ball. 4 Scrape the dough out of the work bowl onto a piece of plastic wrap and shape it into a cylinder about an inch thick. Wrap the dough and chill for an hour. 5 When you are ready to bake the cookies, set the racks in the upper and lower thirds of the oven and preheat to 350 degrees. 6 Place the dough on a very lightly floured work surface and cut it in half. Cut each half in half again to make four pieces. Cut each of those four pieces in half again to make eight pieces of dough. Then cut each of those in half again to make sixteen pieces. 7 Roll out each piece of dough under the palms of your hands to a pencil-thin cylinder about 12 inches long. Carefully place them on the prepared pans, leaving about 1½ inches all around each piece of dough. 8 Bake the *alumettes* for about 12 to 15 minutes, or until they are a light golden color. 9 Immediately upon removing them from the oven, use the point of a sharp paring knife to cut them into 3-inch lengths. (The *alumettes* shrink while they are baking, so each length will yield only about 3 finished *alumettes*.) These have to be cut immediately once they are taken out of the oven. They will shatter if they cool. Cool the cut *alumettes* on a pan on a rack. 10 Store the cooled *alumettes* between sheets of parchment or wax paper in a tin or plastic container with a tight-fitting cover.

PEPPERY CHEDDAR COINS

THOUGH YOU MAY FLAVOR THESE WITH any type of hot pepper, including cayenne or hot paprika, I like black pepper best. For the best flavor use an extra-sharp Cheddar, though if you prefer the taste substitute Gruyère, Gouda, or even Emmenthal.

Makes about 40 cookies

1 cup all-purpose flour

½ teaspoon salt

1 teaspoon freshly ground black pepper

4 ounces (about 1 cup) sharp Cheddar cheese, coarsely grated (see Headnote)

8 tablespoons (1 stick) cold unsalted butter, cut into 10 pieces

2 cookie sheets or jelly roll pans covered with parchment or foil

1 Combine the flour, salt, and pepper in a bowl; stir well to mix. **2** In the work bowl of a food processor fitted with the steel blade, combine the cheese and butter and pulse five or six times to mix. Add the flour mixture and pulse about eight or ten more times, or until the mixture just forms a ball. **3** Scrape the dough onto a floured work surface and form it into a square about ½ inch thick. Cover the dough with plastic wrap and refrigerate it until it is firm enough to roll, 30 minutes to an hour. **4** When you are ready to bake the cookies, set the racks in the upper and lower thirds of the oven and preheat to 350 degrees. **5** Divide the dough in half and place one half on a lightly floured work surface, and the other half in the refrigerator until ready to use. Lightly flour the dough and roll it out to less than ¼ inch thick. Use a floured 2-inch plain or fluted round cutter to cut out the cookies. Place them on the prepared pans, leaving about an inch all around each. Repeat with the remaining dough. Press together and reroll the scraps as they are formed to make more cookies. **6** Bake the cookies for about 20 minutes, or until they are firm and a light golden color. **7** Slide the papers from the pans to racks to cool. **8** Store the cooled cookies between sheets of parchment or wax paper in a tin or plastic container with a tight-fitting cover.

Crackers and Savory Cookies

GRUYÈRE AND ALMOND ROSETTES

THIS EASY CHEESE COOKIE IS ELEGANTLY surmounted by a whole blanched almond for an extra bit of crunch. The recipe is loosely adapted from *Les heures et les jours Wittamer* (*"The Hours and Days at Wittamer"*) (Editions Lannoo, 1994) by Jean-Pierre Gabriel.

Makes about 40 cookies

1¼ cups all-purpose flour

½ teaspoon salt

8 tablespoons (1 stick) unsalted butter, softened

4 ounces (about 1 cup) finely grated Swiss Gruyère

EGG WASH

1 large egg, well beaten with 1 pinch salt

About 40 whole blanched almonds for finishing

2 cookie sheets or jelly roll pans covered with parchment or foil

1 To make the dough, in a bowl, combine the flour and salt and stir well to mix. 2 In the bowl of a standing electric mixer fitted with the paddle attachment, beat together on medium speed the butter and cheese for about 2 or 3 minutes, or until soft and well mixed. Scrape down the sides of the bowl and beater and add the flour mixture. Mix on low speed only until a dough forms. 3 Scrape the dough onto a piece of plastic wrap and form it into a square about ½ inch thick. Wrap the dough and refrigerate it until it is firm enough to roll, about 30 minutes to an hour. 4 When you are ready to bake the cookies, set the racks in the upper and lower thirds of the oven and preheat to 350 degrees. 5 Divide the dough in half, refrigerate one piece, and place the other piece on a lightly floured work surface. Lightly flour the dough and roll it out to just less than ¼ inch thick. Use a floured 1½-inch fluted round cutter to cut out the cookies. Place them on the prepared pans, leaving about an inch all around each in all directions. Repeat with the remaining dough, then press together and reroll the scraps to make more cookies. After all the cookies are on the pans, brush over one cookie with the egg wash,

then immediately place an almond on top of it. Repeat until all the cookies are egg washed and topped with almonds. **6** Bake the cookies for about 20 minutes, or until they are firm and a light golden color. **7** Slide the papers from the pans to racks. **8** Store the cooled cookies between sheets of parchment or wax paper in a tin or plastic container with a tight-fitting cover.

PARMESAN AND PAPRIKA PALMIERS

THESE ARE MADE FROM A QUICKLY PRE-pared imitation puff pastry. The layers of dough and butter are not quite as even as in the classic dough but it is just as flaky and fragile. Use this same dough for Salt and Pepper Sticks on page 301.

Makes about 30 cookies

FLAKY DOUGH

1 cup all-purpose flour

½ teaspoon salt

10 tablespoons (1¼ sticks) unsalted butter, cut into ¼-inch cubes

¼ cup cold water

CHEESE AND PAPRIKA

½ cup grated Parmigiano Reggiano Cheese (about 2 ounces)

½ teaspoon salt

2 teaspoons sweet Hungarian or Spanish paprika

EGG WASH

1 large egg, well beaten with 1 pinch salt

2 cookie sheets or jelly roll pans covered with parchment or foil

1 To make the dough, in the work bowl of a food processor fitted with the steel blade, combine the flour and salt. Add 2 tablespoons of the butter and pulse about six or eight times until the butter is finely incorporated. Add the remaining butter and pulse only twice. Add the water and pulse about six times, or until the dough almost forms a ball. **2** Use a rubber spatula to scrape the dough out of the work bowl onto a lightly floured work surface and lightly flour the dough. Shape it into a rectangle, then roll it out into a 9-inch square. Fold the top of the dough down over the middle, and the bottom upward, like a business letter, then roll the dough up from one side, as in the illustration on the following page. Wrap and chill the

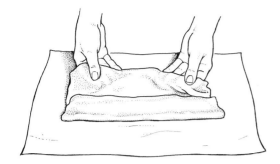

Step 2

prepared pans. **7** Bake the palmiers for about 15 to 20 minutes or until they have expanded and become crisp. Cool on the pans on racks. **8** These are best on the day they are baked; if you wish to bake them in advance, freeze them in a covered container, then reheat them at 350 degrees for about 5 minutes before serving.

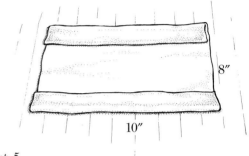

Step 5

dough for an hour, or up to a day. **3** When you are ready to make the palmiers, set the racks in the upper and lower thirds of the ovens and preheat to 375 degrees. **4** Place the dough on a floured surface. Lightly flour the dough and press it with a rolling pin to flatten and soften it slightly, then roll it out to an 8 × 10-inch rectangle. Mix together the cheese, salt, and paprika. Paint the dough with the egg wash, then strew it with the cheese mixture. Press the top well with the palms of your hands to make the cheese mixture adhere. **5** To form the palmiers, fold the bottom and top quarters of the dough in toward the center. Fold each over again, then fold over again, as in the illustration. **6** Slice the folded dough every ⅓ inch and place the cookies, cut side down, 2 inches apart on the

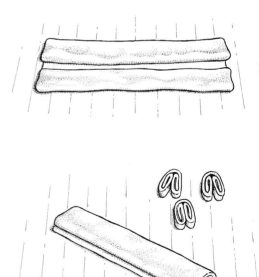

Step 6

SALT AND PEPPER STICKS

THIS FAMILIAR COMBINATION OF FLA-vors makes a tasty savory cookie in a buttery dough. Add some caraway seeds if you like that flavor, but they are really good with just the salt and pepper.

Makes 24 sticks

1 batch Flaky Dough (page 299)

EGG WASH

1 large egg, well beaten with 1 pinch salt

1 teaspoon kosher or other coarse salt

1 teaspoon freshly ground black pepper

1 cookie sheet or jelly roll pan covered with parchment or foil

1 Set a rack in the middle level of the oven and preheat to 375 degrees. **2** Place the dough on a lightly floured surface. Flour the dough and press it with a rolling pin to flatten and soften it slightly, then roll the dough out to a 9-inch square. Use a pizza wheel to trim the edges straight. **3** With the tines of a fork, pierce the dough all over at ½-inch intervals, then use the pizza wheel to cut the dough into three equal strips. Cut across the strips at 1-inch intervals—but don't separate them—to make twenty-four sticks in all. **4** Carefully paint the dough with the egg wash and sprinkle with the salt and pepper. **5** Transfer the sticks to the prepared pan, leaving about an inch around each in all directions. **6** Bake the sticks for about 20 to 25 minutes, or until they are well risen and dry. Cool them on the pan on a rack. **7** These are best on the day they are baked; if you wish to bake them in advance, freeze them in a covered container, then reheat them at 350 degrees for about 5 minutes before serving. Serve them warm or at room temperature.

RYE CARAWAY CRISPS

THIS IS DERIVED FROM A RECIPE I WAS working on several years ago, trying to make a rye-and-caraway-flavored focaccia that would be good with smoked salmon. Well, the focaccia wasn't light enough, but I discovered that the dough made a wonderful thin cracker.

You may shape these into neat squares as the recipe instructs, or divide the dough into small pieces and roll them into small, flat spears to use for dips.

Makes about 50 crackers

⅔ cup warm tap water

1 teaspoon active dry yeast

1 tablespoon olive or vegetable oil

1 cup all-purpose flour

⅔ cup whole grain or other rye flour

1 teaspoon salt

2 tablespoons caraway seeds, ground or crushed

2 cookie sheets or jelly roll pans covered with parchment or foil

1 Measure the water into a small bowl and whisk in the yeast. Whisk in the oil, then set aside while you prepare the remaining ingredients.
2 In a bowl, combine the flours, salt, and caraway seeds. Stir in the yeast mixture and continue stirring to form a soft dough. Scrape the dough onto a lightly floured work surface and fold it over on itself several times to make it smoother. Place the dough in an oiled bowl and cover it with plastic wrap. Let it rise at room temperature for about an hour—this dough will not puff very much. 3 After the dough has risen, press it to deflate, cover it again with plastic wrap, and refrigerate for about an hour, or until the dough is cold. 4 When you are ready to bake the crisps, set the racks in the upper and lower thirds of the oven and preheat to 350 degrees. 5 Place the dough on a lightly floured surface and roll it out into a thin 12 × 18-inch rectangle. Trim the edges even with a pizza wheel and pierce the dough all over with the tines of a fork. Cut the dough into 2-inch strips, then cut across to make the strips into 2-inch squares. 6 Arrange the crisps on the prepared pans leaving about an inch all around each. 7 Bake them for about 20 minutes, or until they are dry and crisp. 8 Cool on the pans on racks. 9 Store the cooled crackers between sheets of parchment or wax paper in a tin or plastic container with a tight-fitting cover.

ROSEMARY BREAD STICKS

THESE CRUNCHY BREAD STICKS ARE probably my favorite non-sweet cookie. They are excellent on their own, but sometimes I serve them alongside a platter of thinly sliced prosciutto. When I wrap the ham around them, it makes sort of a prosciutto lollipop.

Makes about 24 bread sticks

½ cup warm water, about 110 degrees

1½ teaspoons active dry yeast

1¼ cups all-purpose flour

⅓ cup stone-ground yellow cornmeal

2 tablespoons extra-virgin olive oil

1 teaspoon salt

2 tablespoons chopped fresh rosemary

2 jelly roll pans sprinkled with cornmeal

1 Pour the water into a small bowl and whisk in the yeast. Set aside while you prepare the other ingredients. **2** In the work bowl of a food processor fitted with the steel blade, combine the flour, cornmeal, oil, and salt and pulse five times to mix. Add the rosemary and the yeast mixture. Pulse repeatedly, ten or twelve times, until the dough forms a ball. **3** Scrape the dough into an oiled bowl, then turn it over so that the top is oiled. Cover the bowl tightly with plastic wrap and let the dough double in bulk at room temperature, about an hour. Press the dough to deflate it, then return it to the bowl. Re-cover the dough with plastic wrap and refrigerate it for an hour or two or up to 24 hours. **4** When you are ready to bake the bread sticks, scrape the dough onto a lightly floured surface and press it into a rough rectangle. Divide the dough into three equal pieces, then divide each in half to make six pieces. Finally, divide each piece into equal quarters, to make twenty-four. **5** One at a time, roll each of the pieces of dough under the palms of your hands to make a thin stick about 12 inches long. Place on one of the prepared pans. Repeat with the remaining pieces of dough.

(continued)

Crackers and Savory Cookies

Put twelve on each pan, spacing them about an inch or a little less apart. Set aside for half an hour or until the sticks puff a little. **6** About 20 minutes before you intend to bake the bread sticks, set the racks in the upper and lower thirds of the oven and preheat to 350 degrees. Bake the risen bread sticks about 15 to 20 minutes, or until they are golden and crisp. **7** Cool the bread sticks on the pans on racks. **8** Store the cooled bread sticks between sheets of parchment or wax paper in a tin or plastic container with a tight-fitting cover.

VIENNESE CARAWAY PRETZELS

THIS IS AN ADAPTATION OF A RECIPE in the revised edition of *Wiener Süss-speisen* (*"Viennese Sweets"*) (Trauner Verlag, Linz, Austria, 1990). The original work was written in the 1960s by Eduard Mayer; it was revised about twenty-five years later by Karl Schumacher.

Makes about 36 thin pretzels

⅓ cup water, at room temperature

1½ teaspoons active dry yeast

2 cups all-purpose flour

1 teaspoon salt

8 tablespoons (1 stick) cold unsalted butter, cut into 10 pieces

EGG WASH

1 large egg, well beaten with 1 pinch salt

Caraway seeds and kosher salt for finishing

2 cookie sheets or jelly roll pans covered with parchment or foil

1 Pour the water into a small bowl and whisk in the yeast. Set aside while preparing the other ingredients. **2** In the work bowl of a food processor fitted with the steel blade, combine the flour and salt. Pulse several times to mix. **3** Add the butter and pulse about twelve times at 1-second intervals until the butter is finely mixed into the flour. **4** Add the yeast mixture and pulse repeatedly until the dough forms a ball. Scrape the dough onto a floured surface and knead it gently, folding it over on itself, several times, to make it smooth. Place the dough in a small bowl and cover it tightly with plastic wrap. Let it rest at room temperature for about 30 minutes, or until it puffs slightly. Remove the dough from the bowl and flatten it into a rectangle. Wrap the dough in plastic wrap and chill it for at least one hour (or up to overnight). **5** When you are ready to form and bake the pretzels, set the racks in the upper and lower

thirds of the oven and preheat to 350 degrees.
6 Remove the dough from the refrigerator and place it on a lightly floured work surface. Mark the dough into 36 equal pieces, then use a pizza wheel or bench scraper to divide the dough. **7** To shape the pretzels, roll one of the pieces of dough under the palms of your hands into a rope about 8 inches long. Fold the rope in half and transfer it a prepared pan. Form the pretzel according to the illustrations on page 203. Leave about 2 inches all around each pretzel so it can puff while baking. Repeat with the remaining pieces of dough. **8** Brush each pretzel lightly with the egg wash and sprinkle with the caraway seeds and salt. **9** Bake the

pretzels for about 20 minutes, or until they are golden and firm. Slide the papers from the pans to racks. **10** Store the cooled pretzels between sheets of parchment or wax paper in a tin or plastic container with a tight-fitting cover.

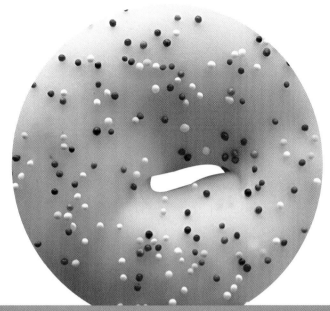

FILLINGS, ICINGS, AND GLAZES

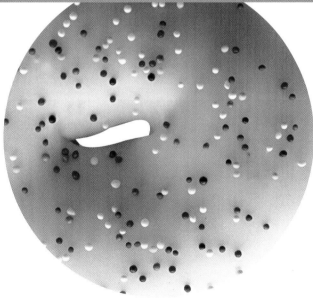

THESE COOKIE ACCESSORIES ARE GROUPED HERE SO THEY ARE ALL IN ONE PLACE, even though some are also included in many of the recipes that call for them. Create your own sandwich cookies by coupling drop or rolled cookies with one of the fillings here; dip cookies into one of the glazes, which will enhance the cookies' appearance and flavor.

MAKING A PAPER CONE

SINCE MANY OF THE FILLINGS AND GLAZES IN THIS CHAPTER MAY BE APPLIED TO cookies using a paper cone, here are the instructions for making one. Parchment paper works best because it is smooth and nonabsorbent, but I have used wax paper or even copier paper in a pinch.

Though it isn't necessary, it is usually better to make more than one cone at a time, so the second (and even third) one is near at hand if you need it.

Start with a right triangle of parchment paper that is approximately 12 x 18 x 21 inches, as in the first illustration. (You may make smaller cones if necessary, but a larger one is easier to roll and handle if you haven't tried the process before.) Using the area opposite the right angle as the point of the cone, curl the larger side angle around to start the cone, as in the second illustration.

To finish the cone, wind the other angle around the cone, as in the third illustration, then fold the edge in to secure the cone and prevent it from unraveling, as in the last illustration.

Note: If you have trouble rolling your first couple of cones and the paper becomes crumpled, start with a fresh, flat piece of paper—it is very difficult to make a cone with paper that is not perfectly flat, even if you have a lot of experience.

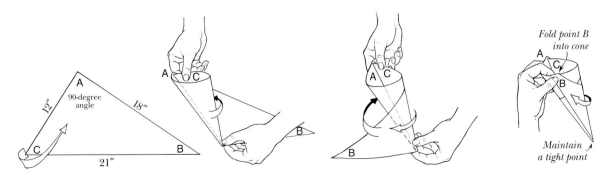

Fillings, Icings, and Glazes

EGG WASH

THIS SIMPLE PREPARATION HAS TWO purposes: to glue dough together and to help it take on a fine golden sheen while baking.

Makes enough for any batch of cookies in this book

1 large egg
Pinch salt

1 Combine the ingredients in a medium bowl. Use a small, flexible whisk to beat the mixture until it is very liquid. **2** Pour the egg wash through a fine strainer into a 1-cup glass measuring cup. (A brush will stand up better in a cup than in a small bowl.) **3** Use the egg wash immediately and discard any leftovers. **4** Follow this rule when using egg wash: Wipe the brush against the inside of the cup or bowl to let the excess egg drip back before brushing on the cookies. This way you can avoid applying egg wash too heavily or having puddles accumulate under the cookies.

NOTE To make a darker egg wash, add an extra egg yolk to the mixture.

COOKIE FILLING MADE FROM JAM OR PRESERVES

PRESERVES OR JAM STRAIGHT FROM the jar may be too thin to couple cookies together. They might become watery and soak into the cookies or ooze out. Heating and reducing the jam makes for a more reliable filling and glaze.

Makes about ¾ cup filling

1 cup jam

1 Place the jam in a saucepan and stir it off the heat with a small wooden spoon until it liquefies. Place over low heat and bring to a simmer. Let the jam simmer for about 3 or 4 minutes, or until it thickens slightly. **2** Use the jam while it is hot.

NOTE If the jam you plan on using has seeds or pulp in it, bring it to a simmer, then strain it into another small pan to reduce. If the pieces of pulp are very large, as in some types of apricot preserves, puree the jam in a blender or food processor before heating and straining.

MARZIPAN FILLING

THIS EASY ALMOND PASTE AND BUTTER filling goes well with any plain cookies. The kirsch helps to reinforce the almond perfume, but it is strictly optional. Marzipan used as a candy or cookie filling is traditionally colored a pale green—perhaps this is because it is the color of the outside of a freshly picked almond.

Makes about ¾ cup filling

4 ounces almond paste

4 tablespoons (½ stick) unsalted butter, softened

½ cup confectioners' sugar

1 tablespoon kirsch or white rum, optional

Green food coloring, optional

1 In the bowl of a standing electric mixer fitted with the paddle attachment, beat together on medium speed the almond paste and butter until soft and very light, about 5 minutes. Lower the mixer speed and beat in the confectioners' sugar. Then raise the speed again and beat for another 2 or 3 minutes on medium speed. Beat in the kirsch, then stop the mixer and scrape down the bowl and beater. Beat in the food coloring, just enough to tint the filling a light, tender green.

2 Use the filling immediately or scrape it into a container that has a tight-fitting cover. Refrigerate until needed and bring back to room temperature and spreadable texture before using. It will keep for about a week.

ROYAL ICING

THIS HARD, WHITE ICING IS PERFECT both for decorating gingerbread cookies and for finishing gingerbread houses. The base recipe calls for egg whites, but if you are concerned about using raw eggs you may substitute pasteurized egg whites or meringue powder (see Note).

Makes 2 generous cups icing

3 large egg whites

One 1-pound box confectioners' sugar (about 4 cups)

½ teaspoon lemon juice or distilled white vinegar

1 In the bowl of a standing electric mixer fitted with the paddle attachment, combine the egg whites and confectioners' sugar. Mix on the lowest speed until all the sugar is evenly moistened. Add the lemon juice, increase the speed to medium, and beat until the icing is light and fluffy, about 4 or 5 minutes. **2** If you are using the icing immediately leave it in the mixing bowl but press plastic wrap against the surface so a skin doesn't form. Cover the plastic wrap with a couple of wet paper towels to prevent the icing from drying. **3** If you are making the icing in advance, pack it into several plastic containers with tight-fitting covers. When a container is nearly full, cover the icing directly with the plastic wrap and paper towels, as above. Then cover tightly. Use it the same day you make it.

NOTE To use liquid pasteurized egg whites in the recipe, measure out 6 tablespoons egg white and proceed with the recipe. To use any brand of pasteurized powdered egg whites or meringue powder, follow the instructions on the package for reconstituting the product to make three egg whites.

To tint the icing, try to find paste colors (see Sources) because liquid colors will dilute it and alter its firm consistency.

CONFECTIONERS'
SUGAR ICING

USE THIS ICING FOR BRUSHING OR
streaking on cookies, or dip the top third of
cookies in, then let the excess icing drip back
into the pan before turning the cookies right
side up again. If the icing seems too thin after
it is heated, add a few tablespoons more confectioners' sugar; if it is too thick, a teaspoon
or so of water—it is easy to get the icing to the
right consistency.

Makes about 2 cups icing, enough for
several dozen cookies, depending on their size

3 cups confectioners' sugar

4 tablespoons water

1 tablespoon lemon juice

1 teaspoon vanilla extract

1 Combine all ingredients in a saucepan
and heat gently until lukewarm, stirring often.

2 Use the icing immediately.

NOTE The flavoring in the icing may be varied as
you wish. Feel free to substitute a liquor or
liqueur for the lemon juice, or even to add a
tablespoon or two of instant coffee.

FLUFFY EGG WHITE ICING

THIS VARIATION ON OLD-FASHIONED boiled frosting works well as a filling for cookies. The traditional method is simplified here: Instead of pouring a hot sugar syrup into beaten egg whites, all the ingredients are combined and heated over a pan of simmering water.

Makes about 2 cups icing or enough to fill several dozen cookies

3 large egg whites

Pinch salt

1 teaspoon vanilla extract

⅓ cup light corn syrup

1 cup sugar

1 Half-fill a 1½- to 2-quart saucepan with water and bring it to a boil over medium heat. 2 Meanwhile, in the bowl of a standing electric mixer fitted with the whisk attachment, combine all the ingredients. When the water in the pan boils, lower the heat so the water maintains a steady simmer and place the mixer bowl over the pan. Heat the mixture, stirring constantly and scraping it away from the inside of the bowl with a rubber spatula. Continue to heat the mixture until it is very warm, about 130 degrees, and the sugar is completely dissolved. 3 Place the bowl on the mixer and beat on medium speed until the icing is cooled and very white and fluffy, about 5 minutes. 4 Use the icing to fill or finish cookies as soon as it is ready.

CONFECTIONERS' SUGAR FILLING

THE BEST WAY TO DESCRIBE THIS FILLING is to say that it is an imitation of the white cream between such industrially made chocolate cookies as Oreos. This simple filling works best with not-too-sweet rolled or drop cookies.

Makes about ¾ cup filling

8 tablespoons (1 stick) unsalted butter, softened

1 cup confectioners' sugar

1 teaspoon vanilla extract

1 tablespoon lemon juice or water

1 In the bowl of an electric mixer fitted with the paddle attachment, beat the butter on medium speed until it is very soft and light. Gradually beat in the sugar and continue beating for another 3 or 4 minutes, or until the mixture is very light and fluffy. 2 Beat in the vanilla and lemon juice and continue beating until the filling is very smooth. 3 Use the filling immediately.

VARIATIONS

Substitute lime or orange juice, strong coffee, or even rum or brandy for the lemon juice.

BUTTER CREAM FILLING

THIS IS AN EASY, MERINGUE-BASED butter cream. If you make more butter cream than you need, pack the extra into a plastic container, press plastic wrap directly against the top, cover tightly, and freeze for up to several months.

Makes about 2 cups butter cream

2 large egg whites

Pinch salt

½ cup sugar

12 tablespoons (1½ sticks) unsalted butter, softened

Flavoring (see list at end of recipe)

1 Half-fill a 1½- to 2-quart saucepan with water and bring it to a boil over medium heat. **2** Meanwhile, in the bowl of a standing electric mixer fitted with the whisk attachment, combine the egg whites, salt, and sugar. When the water boils, lower the heat so the water maintains a steady simmer and place the mixer bowl over the pan. Whisk the contents gently until they are very warm, about 130 degrees, and the sugar has completely dissolved. **3** Put the bowl on the mixer and beat on medium speed until meringue has cooled and looks very white and fluffy, about 5 minutes. **4** Switch to the paddle attachment and beat in the butter, about a tablespoon at a time. Continue beating until the butter cream is thick and smooth, about 2 or 3 minutes. If the butter cream appears to separate while you are adding the butter, this is normal—just keep adding the butter and beat until smooth. **5** Add the flavoring, about a teaspoon at a time, if it is liquid, and continue to beat the butter cream until it is smooth. **6** Use immediately or refrigerate until needed. If refrigerated, soften to room temperature and beat again on the mixer with the paddle before using.

BUTTER CREAM FLAVORINGS

LEMON: 2 tablespoons lemon juice, strained

ORANGE: 2 tablespoons orange juice and 2 teaspoons finely grated orange zest

LIQUEUR: 2 tablespoons liqueur

CHOCOLATE: 6 ounces bittersweet chocolate melted with 3 tablespoons milk or water

LEMON CURD

This tangy cream is essential for French Coconut Macaroons (page 176) and may also be used for Shortbread Gems (page 208). But you can experiment and use it as a filling to sandwich any delicate rolled or drop cookies.

Makes about 1 cup filling

½ cup lemon juice, strained

6 tablespoons (¾ stick) unsalted butter, cut into 8 pieces

½ cup sugar

4 large egg yolks

1 In a small heavy enamel saucepan, combine the lemon juice, butter, and sugar. Bring to a simmer over low heat, stirring occasionally. **2** In a bowl, whisk together the egg yolks, then whisk in about ⅓ cup of the hot lemon mixture. Return the remaining lemon mixture to a simmer and whisk the yolk mixture into it. **3** Continue to whisk for about 3 or 4 more minutes, until the lemon curd thickens and begins to bubble slightly around the edge of the pan. Do not allow it to boil or it may curdle. **4** Pour the lemon curd into a small glass or nonreactive bowl and press plastic wrap against the surface. Refrigerate until cold and thick, at least 2 or 3 hours. **5** The lemon curd will keep almost indefinitely in a tightly covered container in the refrigerator.

VARIATIONS

LIME CURD: Substitute lime juice for the lemon juice.

ORANGE CURD: Substitute a combination of ⅓ cup orange juice and 2 tablespoons lemon juice for the ½ cup lemon juice.

TEMPERED CHOCOLATE
for Dipping or Streaking Cookies

TEMPERING CHOCOLATE ISN'T COMPLI-cated or difficult, but it takes time and attention to do it properly. The reward is a beautiful finish that will remain dry and shiny on the decorated cookies. The following method is what I call a "quick temper" and it will work very well for dipping or streaking cookies.

Make sure you use a couverture-grade chocolate for tempering—only this type of chocolate has a high enough cocoa butter content to make tempering and dipping possible. If you aren't sure whether the chocolate you have is couverture or not, melt a few ounces and check the consistency. If the melted chocolate is thin and fluid, go ahead and temper it. If the chocolate is very thick and heavy, use the method in the Untempered Chocolate recipe on page 318 to dilute the chocolate with oil.

Enough to dip or streak at least 4 dozen cookies

1 pound semisweet or bittersweet couverture chocolate

1 Cut off a 2-ounce piece of chocolate and reserve it. Cut the remaining chocolate into ¼-inch pieces. Place the cut chocolate in a heatproof bowl. **2** Half-fill a medium saucepan with water and bring it to a boil over medium heat. Remove the pan from the heat and place the bowl of chocolate over it. Stir the chocolate occasionally with a clean, dry metal spoon until it has melted and is very warm, between 115 and 120 degrees. **3** Remove the bowl from the pan of water, dry the bottom of the bowl, and set it aside for the chocolate to cool to about 90 degrees. Add the reserved 2-ounce chunk of chocolate and stir it in to lower the chocolate's temperature further into the low eighties. **4** While the chocolate is cooling, reheat the water in the pan. When the chocolate has cooled to the low eighties, remove the chunk of chocolate. Replace the bowl of melted chocolate over the hot water for only a second or two, then remove it. Continue heating briefly over the water until the chocolate temperature reaches between 88 and 91 degrees. Use the chocolate immediately. **5** Scrape any unused chocolate onto a piece of foil or wax paper and allow it to harden. It can be used again for any purpose.

VARIATIONS

MILK OR WHITE CHOCOLATE: Proceed as above, but reheat the chocolate to between 84 and 88 degrees for dipping.

Fillings, Icings, and Glazes

UNTEMPERED CHOCOLATE
for Dipping or Streaking Cookies

IF YOU WISH TO AVOID TEMPERING chocolate, I think it is easy to add a little oil to good quality chocolate. The oil helps to stabilize the cocoa butter crystals, which are what make untempered chocolate turn that unappealing gray color after it sets.

Makes enough for partially dipping or streaking several dozen cookies

2 teaspoons mild vegetable oil

4 ounces best quality bittersweet or semisweet chocolate, melted and cooled

1 Stir the oil into the chocolate. If the chocolate has cooled to the point of setting, reheat it over some hot water to soften again before using. **2** Keep any leftovers tightly covered at a cool room temperature. To reuse, reheat over warm water to liquefy.

CHOCOLATE BUTTER FILLING

THIS IS THE EASIEST COOKIE FILLING. It is also delicious. Feel free to substitute either milk or white chocolate if you wish.

Makes about ½ pound (¾ cup) filling

6 ounces semisweet or bittersweet chocolate, melted and cooled

4 tablespoons (½ stick) unsalted butter, softened

1 Make sure the chocolate is completely cool—to room temperature. Add the butter all at once, then stir and smash it in with a small rubber spatula. **2** Use the filling immediately.

SUGAR-BASED CHOCOLATE GLAZE FOR COOKIES

THIS EASY, BEAUTIFULLY SHINY GLAZE is for dipping cookies or biscotti. It works equally well as a decoration when streaked from a fork or spoon or from a paper cone, squeeze bottle, or the snipped edge of a non-pleated plastic bag.

Don't make this glaze until just before you intend to use it or it will harden and set.

Makes about 1½ cups glaze,
enough to finish several dozen cookies

⅓ **cup water**

⅓ **cup light corn syrup**

1 **cup sugar**

8 **ounces semisweet or bittersweet chocolate, cut into ¼-inch pieces**

1 Combine the water, corn syrup, and sugar in a medium saucepan over low heat and bring it to a boil, stirring often to dissolve all the sugar crystals. When the syrup has come to a boil, let it continue to boil for about 15 seconds. **2** Remove the pan from the heat and add the chocolate all at once. Shake the pan to make sure all the chocolate is submerged and let stand for 2 minutes. **3** Whisk the glaze smooth carefully. Overmixing will fill the glaze with bubbles. Pour the glaze into a shallow bowl to make dipping the cookies easy. **4** Dip the cookies in the glaze and set them on parchment or wax paper. Or arrange the cookies on the paper and streak them with the glaze. **5** If the glaze begins to get too thick, bring a pan of water to a boil and remove it from the heat. Set the bowl of glaze over the hot water and stir it occasionally until it comes back to the right consistency.

Ganache for Filling Cookies

Ganache, the classic chocolate and cream preparation, is perfect for filling cookies. This version, with a little butter and corn syrup added, is particularly smooth.

Makes about ¾ cup filling

⅓ **cup heavy whipping cream**

1 **tablespoon butter**

1 **tablespoon light corn syrup**

6 **ounces semisweet or bittersweet chocolate, cut into ¼-inch pieces (see Note)**

1 In a small saucepan, combine the cream, butter, and corn syrup. Bring to a simmer over medium heat. **2** Remove from the heat and add the chocolate all at once. Shake the pan to make sure all the chocolate is submerged; let the chocolate melt for about 2 or 3 minutes. Whisk smooth, then scrape into a bowl and cool to room temperature, when the ganache will set and thicken. **3** Use the cooled ganache immediately to sandwich any rolled or drop cookies.

NOTE You may substitute milk or white chocolate for the dark chocolate.

DECORATING PROJECTS: COOKIE EXTRAVAGANZAS

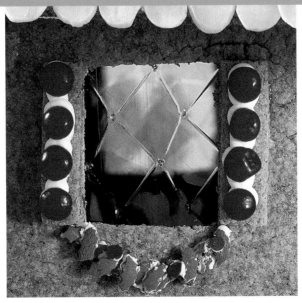

THE RECIPES IN THIS CHAPTER ARE FOR BAKING PROJECTS THAT REQUIRE A BIT more effort than whipping up a batch of chocolate chip cookies. They are recipes for cookie centerpieces and gingerbread houses of different types. These all make wonderful focal points for a holiday table or buffet, and best of all, they may all be made sufficiently in advance that you don't need to make any last-minute fuss. In fact, advance preparation is the key to preparing these well and easily—give yourself enough time and the work will be a pleasure rather than a nightmare.

EASY GRAHAM CRACKER HOLIDAY HOUSE

THIS IS A RECIPE YOU CAN MAKE almost entirely with ingredients found at the supermarket. The exception is the Royal Icing you'll need to glue the graham crackers together, attach the decorations, and create a little "snow." Many thanks to Barbara Bria Pugliese for spending countless hours decorating little houses.

Makes 1 small house

1 batch Royal Icing (page 312)

7 graham crackers, each about 2½ × 5 inches

1 corrugated cake cardboard, about 8 inches square or 10 inches in diameter

Decorations, such as Life Savers, Necco wafers, Hershey's Kisses, Chuckles, Smarties, gumdrops, nonpareils, marshmallows, pretzel sticks, nut meats; shredded sweetened coconut for finishing

1 Place a small dab of the icing on a whole graham cracker. Invert the cracker to the center of the base and press gently so that it adheres to the cake cardboard. **2** Pipe some of the icing onto the edges of the graham cracker on the base and stand a whole cracker next to one of the long edges. Repeat on the other side, as in the illustration on the next page. Carefully cut another

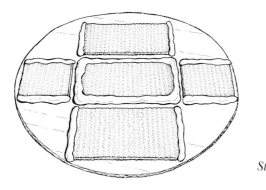

Step 2

cracker in half in the width and spread some icing on the side edges. Use it to close off one of the open ends on the house. Repeat with the other half cracker to form the fourth wall. **3** Spread some icing at the edges of another whole graham cracker and use it to cover the structure, so that it becomes a closed box. **4** Spread the long edges of two more crackers with some of the icing and use them to make a pointed roof, positioning them at the outside edges of the flat roof so the other end meets in the middle. Let the house dry for half an hour before adding the decorations. **5** Fill in the area under the peaked roof with marshmallows or gumdrops for stability, then spread some of the icing over the open ends to close them off. **6** Use some icing to stick the candies randomly all over the outside of the house. **7** For a more organized presentation, use the candies to represent roof tiles, doors, windows, and a chimney, as in the photographs. **8** To finish off the house, pipe or spoon more icing around the edges of the roof and decorations to simulate snow. Spread the base with some icing and cover it completely, then scatter coconut on the icing to cover it. **9** Let the house dry, uncovered, for a day, then cover it loosely with plastic wrap and keep it in a cool, dark place until needed. It will keep for up to a week or so.

NOTE The first house pictured here was decorated with Necco wafers, chocolate nonpareils, and Smarties.

The second house was completely covered with pretzel sticks, then decorated with nut meats and jelly mint leaves. It has a marshmallow chimney decorated with bits of red cinnamon candies.

HOLIDAY COOKIE TREE

THIS CONE-SHAPED TREE COVERED WITH cookies was inspired by a beautiful centerpiece I saw several years ago in the window of the great Parisian pastry shop Ladurée. In existence since the middle of the nineteenth century, Ladurée is one of the greatest pastry shops in Paris, well worth a visit either at its original location on the Rue Royale or in its newest on the Avenue des Champs Elysées. The Ladurée version of this tree was covered with different colors of Parisian macaroons (see pages 172–77.) Aside from that, I think you have two possibilities: Use one type of cookie to cover the entire cone, or use rows of different cookies spiraling around it.

This is meant to be more of a decoration than a way of serving cookies and would make a perfect centerpiece for a large platter of assorted cookies.

Makes one 18- to 20-inch-high decoration

One 18-inch Styrofoam cone, available in crafts stores

1 batch Royal Icing (page 312)

Chocolate Hazelnut Truffles, page 186

Virgules, page 158

Gingerbread Stars, page 117

Cinnamon Shells, page 150

Cherry Rosette Butter Cookies, page 146

Langues de Chat, **page 130, on a platter**

1 Spread about half the Royal Icing evenly all over the Styrofoam cone. Reserve the rest of the icing with plastic wrap and a damp paper towel pressed against the surface to keep the icing from crusting. 2 After the icing on the cone has dried, place the remaining icing in a pastry bag fitted with a small plain tube (Ateco #802) or a non-pleated plastic bag with a small hole snipped in one corner. Pipe a bulb of the icing on the bottom of each cookie, then press it against the cone. Repeat until the entire cone is evenly covered with the cookies.

3 Cover the cone loosely with plastic wrap and keep it in a cool dry place.

GINGERBREAD DOUGH FOR GINGERBREAD HOUSES

U SE THIS DOUGH FOR THE HOUSE IN this chapter. It is sturdy enough to make a house that doesn't warp or buckle, but it also has good eating qualities.

Makes a little less than 3 pounds dough

5 cups all-purpose flour

2 tablespoons ground cinnamon

2 tablespoons ground ginger

1 tablespoon ground cloves

1 tablespoon freshly grated nutmeg

1 tablespoon baking soda

1 teaspoon salt

16 tablespoons (2 sticks) unsalted butter, slightly softened

¾ cup firmly packed dark brown sugar

¾ cup granulated sugar

½ cup water

1 In a bowl, combine the flour, spices, baking soda, and salt; stir well to mix. **2** In the bowl of a standing electric mixer fitted with the paddle attachment, beat the butter, brown sugar, and granulated sugar until soft and light, about 3 or 4 minutes. **3** Scrape the bowl and beater and add a third of the dry ingredients. Beat in half the water, then another third of the dry ingredients. Finally, beat in the remaining water and the remaining dry ingredients. The dough will be somewhat dry and crumbly. **4** Scrape the dough onto a lightly floured work surface and knead it smooth, but don't overwork it to the point that the butter melts. **5** Cover the dough with plastic wrap and let it rest for a few minutes at room temperature. Use the dough immediately in any of the recipes that call for it.

GINGERBREAD HOLIDAY COTTAGE

THIS GREAT HOUSE IS BASED ON AN idea from my friend Kyra Effren: Rather than use random pieces to construct a house, Kyra developed a method for using two 10 × 15-inch pans of gingerbread dough and cutting the two resulting baked slabs of gingerbread into all the pieces necessary for constructing the cottage. Barbara Bria Pugliese took Kyra's pattern and designed the following beautiful Christmas cottage.

Makes 1 medium house

1 batch Gingerbread Dough for Gingerbread Houses (page 326)

1 batch Royal Icing (page 312)

Sheet gelatin or cellophane for the house windows

Candy canes; cinnamon red hots; red licorice All-Sorts; toasted sliced almonds; sweetened shredded coconut for finishing

Two 10 × 15-inch jelly roll pans buttered and lined with buttered parchment or foil

Stiff paper or cardboard

1 Photocopy the house patterns on pages 330–31 at 200 percent in order to double their size. Cut out the patterns and trace them onto stiff paper or cardboard. **2** Set the racks in the upper and lower thirds of the oven and preheat to 325 degrees. **3** Divide the dough into two pieces and roll each to the size of the pans. Transfer the dough to the pans and use the rolling pin or even the back of a spoon to smooth the dough evenly in the pans. **4** Bake the dough for 15 minutes, until it is firm, but not completely baked through. **5** Remove the pans of dough from the oven and place them on racks. Place one pattern on one pan of the dough, as in the illustrations on pages 330–31. Use a small, sharp knife to cut around the pattern. Repeat with the second pan of dough and the other pattern. **6** Return the pans of cut dough to the oven for another 15 minutes, or until the dough is firm and baked through. **7** Remove the pans of dough from the oven and place them on racks. Repeat the cutting around the patterns with a small, sharp knife. Remove the dough from the

window areas with the point of the knife.
8 Cool the cut pieces of dough in the pans on a rack. **9** To install the windows, place the four walls side by side with the sides that baked against the pan facing upward. Pipe or spread some of the icing around the window openings and press sheet gelatin or cellophane against the openings in the walls and the door to simulate windows. Let the icing dry for about 15 minutes. **10** After the icing has dried, invert the wall pieces and attach the shutter pieces on either side of all the windows, pasting them on with some of the icing. Let the icing dry for about 15 minutes. **11** Place the gingerbread base on a flat board or cutting board and arrange the walls around it, flat sides up, in the appropriate places, ready to put them in place. **12** Spread some icing on the bottom of one of the side walls and put it in place (use a small box to prop it up on the outside to support it until the icing dries). Spread some icing along the side of the side wall and on the bottom of the back wall and put the back wall in place at a right angle to the first wall. Prop it up also if necessary. Repeat the procedure to put the two remaining walls in place. Put some of the icing into a paper cone or a plastic bag with the corner snipped and pipe some icing to support the walls on the inside and outside of the base of each wall.
13 To attach the roof pieces, spread some icing on the tops of the walls and also on the tops of the roof pieces where they will meet. Arrange the roof pieces on top of the house and hold them in place for a few minutes, or until they are no longer in danger of sliding off. Pipe or spread some icing at the peak of the roof to reinforce it.
14 Starting at the bottom edge of one side of the roof, pipe or spread a line of the icing and adhere a row of toasted sliced almonds to it. Repeat with successive rows, higher on the roof, so that the almonds overlap. Repeat with the other side of the roof. **15** Decorate the areas over the windows with more almonds. adhering them with dabs of icing, as in the photograph at right. **16** Pipe a line of icing on each shutter and decorate with red cinnamon candies, as in the photograph on page 321. **17** Cut candy canes to fit, then use icing to adhere them, outlining the front edge of the roof, the doorway, and each corner of the house. **18** If you have a cookie with a cherry in the center, use it to decorate the front of the house over the door, or use more candies. **19** For the chimney, stack 3 or 4 red licorice All Sorts with icing, then use icing to adhere it to the roof. Edge the top of the roof with more cinnamon candies, adhering them with icing. **20** For the garlands under the windows, pipe an arc of the icing, then adhere some holly leaf and berry Jiggles to the icing. **21** Make a path of the red licorice All Sorts, piping some icing between them to simulate cement. **22** Scatter some coconut "snow" around the path and at the sides of the house. **23** Let the decorations dry, then loosely cover the house to prevent it from becoming dusty.

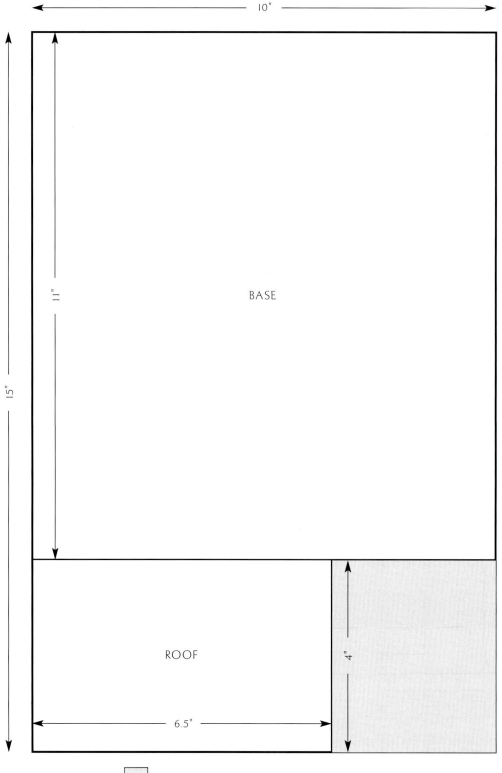

10"

15"

11"

BASE

ROOF

6.5"

4"

Extra dough   * Templates are 50 percent actual size

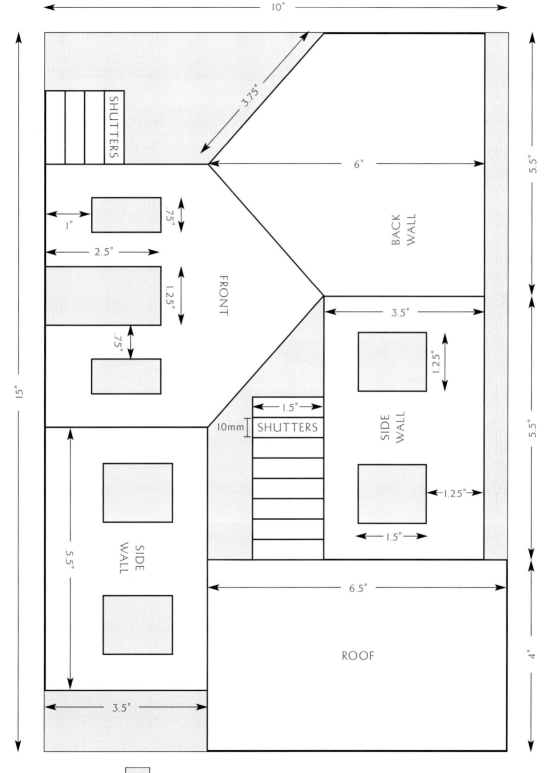

10"

15"

5.5"

5.5"

4"

3.75"

SHUTTERS

.75"

1"

2.5"

1.25"

.75"

FRONT

6"

BACK WALL

3.5"

1.25"

SIDE WALL

1.25"

1.5"

10mm

SHUTTERS

1.5"

SIDE WALL

5.5"

6.5"

ROOF

3.5"

*Extra dough   * Templates are 50 percent actual size*

SOURCES

KITCHEN GLAMOR

39049 Webb Court
Westland, MI 48302
Telephone: (800) 641-1252
Website: kitchenglamor.com

Free catalog available. Cookware, bakeware, chocolate. Also, sanding sugar, colored sugars and nonpareils, paste colors, crystallized ginger, Greater Zester, cookie cutters, cookie molds, cookie presses, madeleine pans, *krumkake* irons, pizzelle irons, conical and cylindrical metal forms for cream horns and cannoli to use for rolling cookies, offset serrated knives.

BRIDGE KITCHENWARE

214 East 52nd Street
New York, NY 10022
Telephone: (212) 688-4220; (800) 274-3435
Website: bridgekitchenware.com

Catalog available ($3.00, refundable with first order). Pans, molds, paste colors, cookie cutters, madeleine pans, *krumkake* irons, pizzelle irons, Silpat nonstick baking mats, offset serrated knives, conical and cylindrical metal forms for cream horns and cannoli to use for rolling cookies, and assorted baking equipment and cookware.

NEW YORK CAKE AND BAKING DISTRIBUTORS

56 West 22nd Street
New York, NY 10010
Telephone: (212) 675-2253; (800) 942-2539
Website: nycakesupplies.com

A full line of pans, decorating equipment, chocolate. Also, sanding sugar, colored sugar and nonpareils, crystallized ginger, Greater Zester, cookie cutters, cookie molds, Silpat nonstick baking mats, offset serrated knives, madeleine pans, paste colors.

SUR LA TABLE

Pike Place Farmers Market
84 Pine Street
Seattle, WA 98101
Telephone: (206) 448-2245; (800) 243-0852
Website: surlatable.com

Catalog available. Pans, cutters, cookie molds, and assorted baking equipment and cookware.

SWEET CELEBRATIONS
(formerly Maid of Scandinavia)

7009 Washington Avenue South
Edina, MN 55439
Telephone: (952) 943-1661; (800) 328-6722
Wesite: sweetc.com

Catalog available. Wide variety of decorating supplies. Also, sanding sugar, colored sugars and nonpareils, Greater Zester, cookie cutters, cookie molds, conical and cylindrical metal forms for cream horns and cannoli to use for rolling cookies, *krumkake* irons.

NORDICWARE

Highway 7 at Highway 100
Minneapolis, MN 55416
Telephone: (952) 920-2888; (800) 328-4310
Website: nordicware.com

Krumkake irons, plus a limited amount of discontinued electric ones.

DEMARLE, INC.

2666-B Route 130 North
Cranbury, NJ 08512
Telephone: (609) 395-0219
Website: demarleusa.com

Free catalog available. Silpat nonstick baking mats.

WILLIAMS-SONOMA

100 North Point Street
San Francisco, CA 94133
Telephone: (800) 541-2233
Website: williams-sonoma.com

Catalog available. Pans, cookie cutters, cookie presses, and assorted baking equipment and cookware.

BALDUCCI'S

424 Sixth Avenue
New York, NY 10011
Telephone: (212) 673-2600; (800) 225-3822
Website: balducci.com

Catalog available. Candied fruit, crystallized ginger, food products of all kinds.

THE HOUSE ON THE HILL

P.O. Box 7003
Villa Park, IL 60181
Telephone: (630) 969-2624
Website: houseonthehill.net

Catalog available ($3.00). Cookie molds, working replicas of speculaas and other historic cookie molds, cookie cutters.

THE BAKER'S CATALOGUE

P.O. Box 876
Norwich, VT 05055-0876
Telephone: (800) 827-6836
Website: kingarthurflour.com

General baking ingredients and equipment. Also, sanding sugar, colored sugar and nonpareils, crystallized ginger, ginger in syrup, candied fruit, Greater Zester, cookie cutters, Silpat nonstick baking mats, baker's ammonia.

PENZEY'S SPICES

P.O. Box 933
Muskego, WI 53150
Telephone: (262) 679-7207; (800) 741-7787
Website: penzeys.com

Catalog available. Herbs, spices, extracts, crystallized ginger.

APHRODISIA

264 Bleecker Street
New York, NY 10014
Telephone: (212) 989-6440
No website

Catalog available. Herbs, spices, essential oils, extracts.

ROYAL PACIFIC FOODS
(The Ginger People)

2700 Garden Road, Suite G
Monterey, CA 93940
Telephone: (831) 645-1090; (800) 551-5284
Website: gingerpeople.com

Information available. Ginger products of all kinds, including dried ginger, crystallized ginger, and ginger in syrup.

BIBLIOGRAPHY

All About Home Baking. New York: General Foods Corporation, 1937.

Ashbrook, Marguerite L., and Lois L. Sumption. *Cookies and More Cookies*. Peoria, Ill.: The Manual Arts Press, 1938.

Bachmann, Walter. *Continental Confectionery*. London: Maclaren and Sons Limited, 1950.

———. *Swiss Bakery and Confectionery*. London: Maclaren and Sons Limited, 1949.

Bau, Frederic. *Caprices de Chocolat*. Paris: Editions Albin Michel, 1998.

Book of American Baking. New York: American Trade Publishing Company, 1910.

The Book of Cookies: Recipes and Sales Ideas. Chicago: Baker's Helper Company, 1940.

Clem, Deloris K. *The Cookie Cookbook*. New York: Castle Books, 1966.

The Cookery Book of Lady Clark of Tillipronie. Lewes, England: Southover Press, 1994. This is a reprint of the original work published after Lady Clark's death in 1909.

Darenne, Émile, and Émile Duval. *Traité de Pâtisserie Moderne*. Paris: Flammarion, 1974.

Gabriel, Jean-Pierre. *Les heures et les jours Wittamer*. Tielt, Belgium: Editions Lannoo, 1994.

Heatter, Maida. *Maida Heatter's Brand-New Book of Great Cookies*. New York: Random House, 1995.

Hermé, Pierre, and Dorie Greenspan. *Desserts by Pierre Hermé*. New York: Little Brown and Company, 1998.

Innli, Kjell E., ed. *The Norwegian Kitchen*. Kristiansund, Norway: KOM Forlag, 1993.

Lanigan, Anne. *The Cookie and Cracker Cookbook*. New York: Quick Fox, 1980.

Mayer, Eduard. *Wiener Suss-speisen*. Linz, Austria: Trauner Verlag, 1968.

Mayer, Eduard, and Karl Schumacher. *Wiener Suss-speisen*. Linz, Austria: Trauner Verlag, 1990. This is an edition of the previous entry revised by Karl Schumacher.

Menkveld, H. *Banket-Bakkersvakboek voor het Gemengd Bedrijf*. Doetinchem, Holland: Uitg.-Maatschappij C. Misset N.V., 1955.

Pasley, Virginia. *The Christmas Cookie Book*. Boston: Little, Brown and Company, 1949.

Retail Bakers Reference Book. New York: American Trade Publishing Co., 1928.

Richemont Craft School. *Swiss Confectionery*. Lucerne: Bakers and Confectioners Craft School Richemont, 1985.

Robert, Jean-Louis. *Gâteaux Secs, Biscuits et Cookies*. Paris: Solar, 1987.

Roden, Claudia. *A Book of Middle Eastern Food*. New York: Alfred A. Knopf, 1972.

Rundell, Maria Eliza. *A New System of Domestic Cookery*. New York: Robert McDermut, 1817.

Sax, Richard. *Classic Home Desserts*. Shelburne, Vt: Chapters Publishing, Ltd., 1994.

Seranne, Ann. *Delectable Desserts*. Boston: Little, Brown and Company., 1952.

Scholte-Hoek, C. H. A. *Gastronomische Geneugten: Het Nagerecht*. The Hague: N.V. Uitgeverij Nijgh en Van Ditmar, no date.

Steinberg, Sally Levitt. *The Donut Book*. New York: Alfred A. Knopf, 1987.

Teubner, Christian. *Christmas Baking*. Woodbury, N.Y.: Barron's, 1985.

Zenker, John J., and Hazel G. Zenker. *Cookie Cookery*. M. Evans and Company, 1969.

ACKNOWLEDGMENTS

MANY THANKS ARE DUE TO ALL WHO MADE this book possible, especially Susan Friedland, my editor, Phyllis Wender, my agent, and Nancy Nicholas, who so ably translates my recipes into English.

At HarperCollins, Ellen Morrissey, then Vanessa Stich, Susan's assistants, have provided invaluable help, as well as Publicity Director Stephen Sorrentino and publicists Leonida Karpik, Carrie Weinberg and Corinne Alhadeff. Special thanks to production editor Chris Tanigawa for her astute eye.

Thanks to Joel Avirom and his crew, Jason and Meghan, for the wonderful design and to Tom Eckerle and Ceci Gallini for the truly beautiful photographs. As usual, Laura Hartman Maestro delivered accurate and artistic line drawings.

My friend and associate Andrea Tutunjian worked harder than anyone else on this project, and I give her my heartfelt thanks. She tested most of the recipes and also prepared most of the cookies for the photographs. After all that, she helped me go through the manuscript and galleys countless times to make sure all the corrections were entered. Barbara Bria Pugliese and Cara Tannenbaum also took time from their busy schedules of teaching and catering to test recipes and bake for photography. Special thanks go to gingerbread house architects Barbara Bria Pugliese, Kyra Effren, and Tony Burns.

Many friends contributed recipes, most notably Jayne Sutton, who shared so many delicious recipes from her vast collection, she should be listed as a coauthor. Other friends who shared recipes are: Mary Aimutis, Tammy Algood, Ellen Baumwoll, Nancy Berzinec, Robert Bleifer, Flo Braker, Marilynn Brass, Sheila Brass, Dennis Canciello, Marie Ciampi, Marion Cunningham, Thea Cvijanovich, Liza Davies, Bennie Sue Dupy, Kyra Effren, Julie Ellis-Clayton, Michel Ernest, Carrie Fisher, Claudia Fleming, Peter Fresulone, Frank and Lucy Garofolo, Toba Garrett, Gregg Golden, Dorie Greenspan, David Grice, Alexis Grossman, Patsye Hardin, Maida Heatter, Pierre Hermé, Sue and Lynn Hoffman, Rhonda Kaplan, Paul Kinberg, Tina Korting, Phil Krampetz, Sandy Leonard, Michele Lifshen-Reing, Janet Marsh Lillie, Karen Ludwig, Maureen McKeon, Jennifer Migliorelli, Marilyn Miller, Ann Nurse, Carol Pascarella, François Payard, Gary Peese, Peggy Pinckley, Hans Polleman, Sheri Portwood, Lee Posey, Irene Sax, Myrtle Singer, Bonnie Slotnick, Bonnie Stern, Amy Stevenson, Kyle Stewart, Amber Sunday, Peggy Tagliarino, Michelle Tampakis, Cara Tannenbaum, Andrea Tutunjian, Rose Valenti, Brenda van Horn, Carole Walter, Stephanie Weaver, and Jeff Yoskowitz.

And a last, special thank-you to Arthur Boehm and Dorie Greenspan, great authors and generous friends.

SELECTED RECIPE INDEX

GENERAL INDEX

accidental cookie dough, 107–8
all-American coconut macaroons, 170
all-corn biscotti, 236
all-purpose flour, xiii
almond(s):
    in all-corn biscotti, 236
    in *Appenzeller Biberli*, 266–67
    apricot ruglach, 123–24
    bars, chewy, 9
    bars, elegant, 8
    in *Basler Leckerli*, 13
    batons, 134
    in *biscotti di vino*, 203–4
    blanching of, xv
    butter fingers, 141
    in buttery anisette biscotti, 234
    in *cantuccini*, 124
    cookies, Chinese, 193
    cookies, Dutch, 84–85
    cream wafers, 78
    crescents, Little Viennese, 189
    in *cucidati*, 258–60
    in French coffee macaroons, 174–75
    in fruitcake bars, 18–19
    and Gruyère rosettes, 298–99
    and hazelnut biscotti, 227
    in Hungarian apricot bars, 26–27
    in *infasciadedde*, 260–61
    in *kourabiethes*, 187
    lace cookies, 70–71
    in linzer hearts, 276–77
    in Little Italy pine nut macaroons, 167
    in *mostaccioli baresi*, 196–97
    and orange biscotti, 233
    in *petits financiers*, 210–11

    pizzelle, 285
    in smooth French macaroons, 172–73
    in Swiss chocolate rings, 148–49
    in Tennessee icebox cookies, 80
    toasts, Australian, 238–39
    in totebeinli, 237
    in traditional French tuiles, 63
    in traditional Jewish mandelbrot, 232
    tuiles, orange-scented, 64–65
    in *Utziger Hasselnuss Leckerli*, 120–21
    in Viennese linzer squares, 23
    in *virgules*, 158–59
    in *Wiener Mandelgipferl*, 189
almond paste:
    in cherry macaroon rosettes, 165
    in elegant almond bars, 8
    in fruitcake bars, 18–19
    in *gommés*, 166–67
    in marzipan filling, 311
    in old-fashioned chewy macaroons, 164–65
    in suvaroffs, 274–75
alumettes au fromage, 296
Anisbroetli, 215–16
    in *Badener Chrabeli*, 217
anise:
    cookies, Swiss, 215–16
    disks, 133
    love knots, 200–201
anisette:
    biscotti, buttery, 234
    in pizzelle, 284–85
ANZAC biscuits, 47

Appenzeller Biberli, 266–67
apricot(s), apricot preserves:
    almond ruglach, 123–24
    in banana walnut squares, 15
    bars, Hungarian, 26–27
    bars, pecan-studded, 14
    in *cucidati*, 258–60
    in hazelnut fingers, 135
    in lemon fruit swirls, 97–98
    in Sicilian fig pinwheels, 94–95
Arnhem cookies, 122–23
Aunt Ida's poppy seed cookies, 50
Australian almond toasts, 238–39

"bad boys," 273–74
Badener Chrabeli, 217
baking powder, xiv
baking soda, xiv
baking techniques, xviii
banana walnut squares, 15
bar cookies, 1–36
bar mitzvah cookies, Philip Portwood's, 144
Basel "lickers," 13
Basler Leckerli, 13
"beavers," filled, from Appenzell, 264–65
benne wafers, 54
Berner Hasselnuss Staengeli, 119
bicarbonate of ammonia, xiv
    in crisp coconut cookies, 184–85
biscotti, 221–39
    all-corn, 236
    almond and hazelnut, 227
    Australian almond toasts, 238–39
    buttery anisette, 234
    cantuccini, 224

biscotti (cont.)
    chocolate chunk, 226
    cornmeal, 235
    dark chocolate hazelnut, 228
    gingery macadamia, 229
    herb, 295
    lemon pistachio, 225
    orange and almond, 233
    quaresimali, 230
    totebeinli, 237
    see also mandelbrot
biscotti di vino, 203–4
biscuits:
    ANZAC, 47
    Tillypronie cream, 294
bittersweet chocolate shortbread
        squares, 6
blanching, of nuts, xv
brandy:
    in *koulourakia,* 198–99
    in *kourabiethes,* 187
bread crumbs, xiii
bread sticks, rosemary, 303–4
Breton shortbreads, "truffled,"
        82–83
brownies, xii, 30–36
    cheese cake, 30–31
    espresso, 32
    pecan, 33
    West Tenth Street, 36
    white chocolate chunk, 34–35
brown sugar, xiv
    pecan macaroons, 169
    shortbread, 105
brushes, xvi
bugnes arlesiennes, 245–46
burned cookies, xviii
butter, xii
    almond fingers, 141
    balls, pecan, 183–84
    cookies, cherry rosette, 146
    cream filling, 315

buttermilk, xiii
    cookies, 111
    fudge gems, 207
buttery anisette biscotti, 234

cake flour, xiii
canary's tongues, 131
candied fruit, xv
    in fruitcake bars, 18–19
    in *Utziger Hasselnuss Leckerli,*
        120–21
    see also cherry(ies), candied;
        orange peel, candied
cantuccini, 224
caramel pecan cookies, 69–70
caraway:
    pretzels, Viennese, 304–5
    rye crisps, 302
Carole Walter's ethereal mandel-
        brot, 231
champagne fingers, 132–33
    in almond batons, 134
checkerboard cookies, 92–93
Cheddar coins, peppery, 297
cheese:
    in Gruyère and almond
        rosettes, 298–99
    matchsticks, 296
    in Parmesan and paprika
        palmiers, 299–300
    in peppery Cheddar coins, 297
    in ricotta drops, 41
    see also cream cheese
cheese cake brownies, 30–31
cheesecake squares, 22
cherry(ies), candied:
    in Doreen's ginger squares, 20
    macaroon rosettes, 165
    rosette butter cookies, 146
    rosette butter cookies, in holi-
        day cookie tree, 325
chewy almond bars, 9

chewy oatmeal raisin cookies, 49
Chinese almond cookies, 193
chocolate, xv–xvi
    in almond batons, 134
    butter cream filling, 315
    butter filling, 318
    buttermilk fudge gems, 207
    chocolate sandwich cookies,
        279–80
    chunk biscotti, 226
    chunk cookies, 55
    cookies, crackled, 192
    in *cucidati,* 258–60
    -filled stars, 145
    filling, in *virgules,* 158–59
    ganache, *see* ganache for filling
        cookies
    hazelnut biscotti, dark, 228
    hazelnut truffles, 186
    hazelnut truffles, in holiday
        cookie tree, 325
    -iced peanut squares, 12
    madeleines, 210
    meringue rocks, 59
    meringue wreaths, 157
    mint wafers, 90
    oatmeal cookie sandwiches,
        lacy, 278
    peanut S cookies, 147–48
    pizzelle, 285
    in Portland fig cookies, 262–63
    in Richard Sax's spumetti, 168
    rings, 114–15
    rings, Swiss, 148–49
    sablés, dark, 89
    sablés, dark, in checkerboard
        cookies, 92–93
    shortbread, 106
    shortbread squares, bittersweet,
        6
    in Sicilian fig pinwheels, 94–95
    sour cream doughnut holes, 249

sour cream fudge cookies, 57
squares, dark, 90
in "truffled" Breton short-
    breads, 82–83
tulipes, 213
in two-tone peanut butter
    thins, 98–99
walnut slices, 91
see also brownies
chocolate, tempered, for dipping
    or streaking of cookies, 317
in hazelnut sticks, 156
in spritz cookies, 142
chocolate, untempered, for dip-
    ping or streaking of cookies,
    318
in hazelnut sticks, 156
chocolate chip(s), xii
in chewy oatmeal raisin cook-
    ies, 49
in chocolate meringue rocks,
    59
in cinnamon pecan meringues,
    58
cookies, glazed chocolate, 56
cookies, loaded with chips, 55
refrigerator cookies, 83–85
in West Tenth Street brownies,
    36
chocolate glaze for cookies,
    sugar-based, 319
in almond batons, 134
in chocolate-filled stars, 145
in chocolate mint wafers, 90
in chocolate rings, 114–15
in glazed chocolate chocolate
    chip cookies, 56
in sour cream fudge cookies,
    57
in spritz cookies, 143
in Swiss chocolate rings,
    148–49

chunky peanut butter cookies,
    195
cigarettes, 136–37
cinnamon:
    diamonds, 7
    pecan meringues, 58
    shells, 150
    shells, in holiday cookie tree,
        325
    sour cream drops, 42
classic Tuscan biscotti, 224
coarse sugar, xiii
    in Arnhem cookies, 122–23
cocoa, xvi
coconut:
    in ANZAC biscuits, 47
    cookies, crisp, 184–85
    drops, easy, 53
    tuiles, 67
coconut macaroons:
    all-American, 170
    French, 176–77
    golden, 171
coffee:
    in confectioners' sugar icing,
        313
    in *cucidati,* 258–60
    in espresso brownies, 32
    in hermits, 45
    macaroons, French, 174–75
    pecan meringues, 155
commas, 158–59
confectioners' sugar, xiv
    filling, 314
    icing, 313
"cookie," origin of word, xii
cookie cup dessert shells, 212–13
cookie cutters, xvii
cookie dough, accidental, 107–8
cookie filling, made from jam or
    preserves, 310
cookie molds, xvii, 181–82

cookie presses, 127
cookies, history of, xii
cookie sheets, xvii, xix
cooling cookies, xviii, xix
cornmeal:
    in all-corn biscotti, 236
    biscotti, 235
    in *paste di meliga,* 151
    in rosemary bread sticks, 303–4
    in zaleti bolognesi, 88
cornstarch, xiii
corn syrup, xiv
crackers and savory cookies,
    291–305
crackled chocolate cookies, 192
cream, xiii
    biscuits, Tillypronie, 294
    cookies, orange, 110
    wafers, almond, 78
cream cheese:
    in apricot almond ruglach,
        123–24
    in cheese cake brownies, 30–31
    in cheesecake squares, 22
    in Philip Portwood's bar mitz-
        vah cookies, 144
cream puff pastry fritters, 249–50
crème de menthe, in chocolate
    mint wafers, 90
crescents, little Viennese almond,
    189
crisp, crispy:
    coconut cookies, 184–85
    St. Nicholas cookies, 113
crisps, rye caraway, 302
crystallized ginger, xv
cucidati, 258–60
currant(s):
    in cornmeal biscotti, 235
    in fancy jumbles, 44–45
    in fruitcake bars, 18–19
    in *olliebollen,* 253–54

holiday cottage, 327–31

people, 117–18

stars, in holiday cookie tree, 325

gingersnaps, the Good Cook's, 194

gingery macadamia biscotti, 229

glazed chocolate chocolate chip cookies, 56

golden coconut macaroons, 171

golden syrup, xiv

in ANZAC biscuits, 47

gommés, 166–67

Good Cook's gingersnaps, 194

graham cracker holiday house, easy, 323–24

graters, xvii

Greek:

almond cookies, 187

sesame ring cookies, 198–99

Gruyère:

and almond rosettes, 298–99

in *alumettes au fromage,* 296

"gummed" or glazed macaroons, 166–67

hazelnut(s):

and almond biscotti, 227

in *Berner Hasselnuss Staengeli,* 119

blanching of, xv

in chocolate meringue rocks, 59

chocolate truffles, 186

dark chocolate biscotti, 228

fingers, 135

macaroons, French, 175–76

in *petits financiers,* 210–11

pizzelle, 285

in quaresimali, 230

in Richard Sax's spumetti, 168

sticks, 156

in totebeinli, 237

tuiles, 66

in *Utziger Hasselnuss Leckerli,* 120–21

in Viennese linzer squares, 23

in *virgules,* 158–59

herb biscotti, 295

herbs and spices, xvi

hermits, 45

holiday cookie tree, 325

honey, xiv

in all-corn biscotti, 236

in almond and hazelnut biscotti, 227

in ANZAC biscuits, 47

in *Appenzeller Biberli,* 266–67

in *Basler Leckerli,* 13

in gingery macadamia biscotti, 229

in herb biscotti, 295

in *infasciadedde,* 260–61

pecan squares, 24–25

in Portland fig cookies, 262–63

Hungarian apricot bars, 26–27

icebox cookies, Tennessee, 80

ice cream scoops, xvii

icing:

confectioners' sugar, 313

see also fluffy egg white icing; royal icing

infasciadedde, 260–61

ingredients, xiii-xvi

Italian:

bread-dough fritters, 252–53

cornmeal butter cookies from Piemonte, 151

jam, cookie filling made from, 310

jelly roll pans, xvii, xix

jumbles, fancy, 44–45

kirsch:

in *Appenzeller Biberli,* 266–67

in *Basler Leckerli,* 13

in marzipan filling, 311

in *Shenkeli,* 250–51

in suvaroffs, 274–75

in *Utziger Hasselnuss Leckerli,* 120–21

knives, xviii

koulourakia, 198–99

kourabiethes, 187

krumkake, 285–86

lacy chocolate oatmeal cookie sandwiches, 278

ladyfingers, 140

langues de chat, 130

in holiday cookie tree, 325

leaveners, xiv

Lebanese and Syrian date-filled cookies, 264–65

lekvar squares, 28–29

lemon:

butter cream filling, 315

cookies, Palm Beach, 79

cream cookies, 110

filling, in yoyos, 272

fruit swirls, 97–98

glaze, in Doreen's ginger squares, 20

jumbles, 45

love knots, 200–201

madeleines, 210

in orange shortbread squares, 5

pistachio biscotti, 225

squares, ultimate, 21

lemonade cookies, 43

lemon curd, 316

in French coconut macaroons, 176–77

in shortbread gems, 208

lemon rind, candied, in *Utziger Hasselnuss Leckerli*, 120–21

"lickers," Basel, 13

lime:
   curd, 316
   macadamia cookies, 188

linzer:
   hearts, 276–77
   roll, 95–96
   squares, Viennese, 23

liqueur butter cream filling, 315

little claws from Baden, 217

little financier cookies, 210–11

Little Italy pine nut macaroons, 167

little thighs, 250–51

little Viennese almond crescents, 189

loaded with chips chocolate chip cookies, 55

love knots, 200–201

macadamia(s):
   biscotti, gingery, 229
   lime cookies, 188
   in pecan wafers, 52

macaroon(s), 161–77
   all-American coconut, 170
   brown sugar pecan, 169
   French coconut, 176–77
   French coffee, 174–75
   French hazelnut, 175–76
   golden coconut, 171
   gommés, 166–67
   Little Italy pine nut, 167
   old-fashioned chewy, 164–65
   Richard Sax's spumetti, 168
   rosettes, cherry, 165
   smooth French, 172–73

madeleines, 209–10

Maida Heatter's skinny peanut wafers, 51–52

mandelbrot:
   Carole Walter's ethereal, 231
   traditional Jewish, 232

marzipan:
   filling, 311
   topping, in fruitcake bars, 18–19

meringue(s), 153–59
   cinnamon pecan, 58
   coffee pecan, 155
   hazelnut sticks, 156
   nut topping, in Hungarian apricot bars, 26–27
   powder, in royal icing, 312
   rocks, chocolate, 59
   virgules, 158–59
   walnut boulders, 154
   wreaths, chocolate, 157

Metaxa:
   in *koulourakia*, 198–99
   in *kourabiethes*, 198

milk, xiii

mint chocolate wafers, 90

mixer, xvi

molasses, xiv
   in *Appenzeller Biberli*, 266–67
   cookies, old-fashioned, 115–16
   cookies, Pennsylvania Dutch soft, 46
   in gingerbread people, 117–18
   slices, old-fashioned, 86
   in spicy oatmeal walnut cookies, 48

molded cookies, 179–220

molds, cookie, xvii

mostaccioli baresi, 196–97

Mother B's, 4

Naples wafers, 289

nonpareils, xiv

Norwegian wafer cones, 285–86

nuts, xv

see also almond(s); hazelnut(s); macadamia(s); pecan(s); pistachio(s); walnut(s)

oatmeal:
   in ANZAC biscuits, 47
   chocolate cookie sandwiches, lacy, 278
   raisin cookies, chewy, 49
   walnut cookies, spicy, 48

oils, xiii
   flavoring, xvi
   olive, in *biscotti di vino*, 203–4

old-fashioned:
   chewy macaroons, 164–65
   molasses cookies, 115–16
   molasses slices, 86

olive oil, in *biscotti di vino*, 203–4

olliebollen, 253–54

orange:
   and almond biscotti, 233
   butter cream filling, 315
   cream cookies, 110
   curd, 316
   -scented almond tuiles, 64–65
   shortbread squares, 5
   spice refrigerator wafers, 87
   tuiles, Pierre Hermé's, 68

orange flower water:
   in *gaufres des Tuileries*, 288–89
   in *mamoul*, 264–65

orange peel, candied:
   in *Basler Leckerli*, 13
   in *cucidati*, 258–60
   in fruitcake bars, 18–19
   in orange and almond biscotti, 233
   in *Utziger Hasselnuss Leckerli*, 120–21

Osgood squares, 25–26

oublies de Naples, 289

Palm Beach lemon cookies, 79
palmiers, Parmesan and paprika, 299–300
pans, xvii, xix
paper cone, making of, 309
paprika and Parmesan palmiers, 299–300
parchment, lining pans with, xvii, xix
Parmesan:
    in *alumettes au fromage*, 296
    and paprika palmiers, 299–300
pasta frolla, 258–59
    in *cucidati*, 258–59
    in *infasciadedde*, 260–61
paste di meliga, 151
peanut:
    butter cookies, chunky, 195
    butter thins, two-tone, 98–99
    chocolate S cookies, 147–48
    squares, chocolate-iced, 12
    wafers, Maida Heatter's skinny, 51–52
pecan(s):
    brownies, 33
    brown sugar macaroons, 168
    butter balls, 183–84
    caramel cookies, 69–70
    in Carole Walter's ethereal mandelbrot, 231
    in chewy oatmeal raisin cookies, 49
    cinnamon meringues, 58
    coffee meringues, 155
    honey squares, 24–25
    in lemon fruit swirls, 97–98
    in loaded with chips chocolate chip cookies, 55
    in Osgood squares, 25–26
    sand tarts, 112
    in sour cream fudge cookies, 57

-studded apricot bars, 14
wafers, 52
in West Tenth Street brownies, 36
Pennsylvania Dutch:
    soft molasses cookies, 46
    soft sugar cookies, 40
pepper and salt sticks, 301
peppery Cheddar coins, 297
petit beurre cookies, 108–9
petits financiers, 210–11
petits fours, xii
Philip Portwood's bar mitzvah cookies, 144
Pierre Hermé's orange tuiles, 68
pineapple, candied, in fruitcake bars, 18–19
pine nut macaroons, Little Italy, 167
piped cookies, 125–59
pistachio(s):
    blanching of, xv
    lemon biscotti, 225
    thins, 81
pizzelle, 284–85
plain jumbles, 45
poppy seed cookies, Aunt Ida's, 50
Portland fig cookies, 262–63
preserves, cookie filling made from, 310
pretzels:
    vanilla, 202–3
    Viennese caraway, 304–5
prune butter, in lekvar squares, 28–29

quaresimali, 230

racks, xviii
railroad tracks, 268
raisin(s):
    in *cucidati*, 258–60

drops, Swiss, 152
golden, in fruitcake bars, 18–19
golden, in *olliebollen*, 253–54
in hermits, 45
oatmeal cookies, chewy, 49
in Osgood squares, 25–26
in walnut boulders, 154
raspberry jam:
    in linzer hearts, 276–77
    in linzer roll, 95–96
    in railroad tracks, 268
    in smooth French macaroons, 172–73
    in Sonja Henies, 190–91
    in *Spitzbuebe*, 273–74
    in Viennese linzer squares, 23
red wine cookies, 203–4
refrigerator cookies, 73–99
Richard Sax's spumetti, 168
ricotta drops, 41
rolled cookies, 101–24
rolling pin, xvi
rosemary bread sticks, 303–4
rose water, in *mamoul*, 264–65
royal icing, 312
    in easy graham cracker holiday house, 323–24
    in gingerbread holiday cottage, 327–31
    in gingerbread people, 117–18
    in holiday cookie tree, 325
ruglach, apricot almond, 123–24
rum, dark:
    in *cucidati*, 258–60
    in dark chocolate hazelnut biscotti, 228
    in hazelnut tuiles, 66
    in *petits financiers*, 210–11
rum, white:
    in *bugnes arlesiennes*, 245–46
    in marzipan filling, 311
rye caraway crisps, 302

sablés:
    in checkerboard cookies, 92–93
    dark chocolate, 89
    French vanilla, 77
St. Nicholas cookies, crispy, 113
salt, xv
    and pepper sticks, 301
sanding sugar, xiii
    in Arnhem cookies, 122–23
sand tarts, pecan, 112
sandwich cookies, 269–80
savory cookies and crackers,
    291–305
Scottish shortbread, 104–5
sesame seed(s):
    in koulourakia, 198–99
    wafers, 54
sfingi, 249–50
Shenkeli, 250–51
shipping cookies, xix
shortbread(s):
    chocolate, 106
    gems, 208
    Scottish, 104–5
    squares, bittersweet chocolate,
        6
    squares, orange, 5
    "truffled" Breton, 82–83
Sicilian:
    fig-filled cookies, 258–60
    fig pinwheels, 94–95
    twisted cookies, 260–61
"Sid and Sis" cat's tongues, 130
silicon mats, xviii
smooth French macaroons,
    172–73
Sonja Henies, 190–91
sources, 333–34
sour cream:
    cinnamon drops, 42
    diamonds, 111
    doughnut holes, 248–49

fudge cookies, 57
Southfield wafers, 287
spatulas, xviii
speculaas, 218–20
spice, spicy:
    cookies from Bari, 196–97
    oatmeal walnut cookies, 48
    orange refrigerator wafers, 87
spices and herbs, xvi
Spitzbuebe, 273–74
Springerle molds, xvii
spritz cookies, 142
spumetti, Richard Sax's, 168
squares:
    banana walnut, 15
    bittersweet chocolate short-
        bread, 6
    cheesecake, 22
    chocolate-iced peanut, 12
    currant, 16–17
    Doreen's ginger, 20
    honey pecan, 24–25
    lekvar, 28–29
    orange shortbread, 5
    Osgood, 25–26
    ultimate lemon, 21
    Viennese linzer, 23
storage, of cookies, xix
striped tulipes, 213
sugar, xiii-xiv
    decorative colored, xiv
    see also brown sugar; coarse
        sugar; confectioners' sugar;
        sanding sugar
sugar-based chocolate glaze, see
        chocolate glaze for cookies,
        sugar-based
sugar cookies, Pennsylvania
        Dutch soft, 40
suvaroffs, 274–75
Swiss:
    anise cookies, 215–16

chocolate rings, 148–49
hazelnut bars from Berne, 119
hazelnut cookies from the
        Château of Utzigen, 120–21
raisin drops, 152
Syrian and Lebanese date-filled
        cookies, 264–65
syrup:
    corn, xiv
    ginger in, xv
    golden, xiv
    golden, in ANZAC biscuits, 47

taralli dolci di Pasqua, 205–6
tarts, pecan sand, 112
techniques, xviii-xix
tempered chocolate, for dipping
        or streaking of cookies, 317
    in hazelnut sticks, 156
    in spritz cookies, 142
Tennessee icebox cookies, 80
Tillypronie cream biscuits, 294
toasts, Australian almond, 238–39
totebeinli, 237
traditional French tuiles, 63
traditional Jewish mandelbrot,
        232
"truffled" Breton shortbreads,
        82–83
truffles, chocolate hazelnut, 186
Tuileries wafers, 288–89
tuiles, 62–71
    almond lace cookies, 70–71
    caramel pecan cookies, 69–70
    coconut, 67
    hazelnut, 66
    orange-scented almond, 64–65
    Pierre Hermé's orange, 68
    traditional French, 63
tulipes, 212–13
two-tone peanut butter thins,
        98–99

General Index